The Americans and Germans in Bastogne

The Americans and Germans in Bastogne

First-Hand Accounts from the Commanders

Gary Sterne

Pen & Sword
MILITARY

First published in Great Britain in 2020 by
Pen & Sword Military
An imprint of
Pen & Sword Books Ltd
Yorkshire – Philadelphia

Typeset by Mac Style
Printed and bound in the UK by TJ International Ltd,
Padstow, Cornwall.

Pen & Sword Books Limited incorporates the imprints of Atlas,
Archaeology, Aviation, Discovery, Family History, Fiction, History,
Maritime, Military, Military Classics, Politics, Select, Transport,
True Crime, Air World, Frontline Publishing, Leo Cooper, Remember
When, Seaforth Publishing, The Praetorian Press, Wharncliffe
Local History, Wharncliffe Transport, Wharncliffe True Crime
and White Owl.

For a complete list of Pen & Sword titles please contact

PEN & SWORD BOOKS LIMITED
47 Church Street, Barnsley, South Yorkshire, S70 2AS, England
E-mail: enquiries@pen-and-sword.co.uk
Website: www.pen-and-sword.co.uk

Or

PEN AND SWORD BOOKS
1950 Lawrence Rd, Havertown, PA 19083, USA
E-mail: Uspen-and-sword@casematepublishers.com
Website: www.penandswordbooks.com

Contents

Introduction

By the end of 1944 the Third Reich was retreating. Russian forces were pushing in from the East and the Allies were advancing to the borders of Germany from the West. Given the losses that they had sustained, it was almost inconceivable that the German army had the capability to mount a counter offensive in either direction. It must have seemed to the Allies that the complete capitulation of the Third Reich was just around the corner.

However, the Allies were unaware that Adolf Hitler had been secretly amassing men and *matériel* for what can only be described as the last roll of the dice and it could be argued that he had nothing left to lose – yet everything to gain. The loss of vast numbers of their men made little or no dent in the Russian forces' ability to wage war and every month that went by the Russian armies were resupplied with new units and better equipment. The complete opposite was the case with the German forces.

The 'special weapons' that Adolf Hitler had been promising his generals were on the whole too little, too late. Deployment of the ME262 jet as a bomber interceptor could have changed the air-war if committed *en masse* against Allied bomber units; Tiger and Panther tanks could have been more widely deployed if produced with less of an eye on technical detail and more on mass production.

What the Allies lacked in quality, they made up for in sheer volume. They could field huge numbers of tanks and on paper could lose them at a greater rate than the German Army – and still win the war by attrition. The same was the case with the Luftwaffe and Kriegsmarine in both personnel and equipment. Germany had simply reached a point in the war where it was being crushed by combined Allied forces who had a seemingly endless supply of men and equipment. Something had to be done to break the cycle of losses before it was too late, and it was Adolf Hitler who decided to offer a glimmer of hope to the Nazi regime, as well as help to raise the much-weakened morale of the German people.

In theory the plan was quite simple. German forces were to gather in total secrecy, attack during a period of predictably bad weather, through an area of Belgium where it would be least expected, against an enemy who were also battle-worn, tired and at the very end of their supply lines. At worst it might prolong the war for another year and at best it may create a climate where it was possible to stop the Allies short of the total destruction of the Third Reich. It was an audacious plan and one which would not be expected by the Allies. For that one reason alone, it offered the German forces a slim chance of success.

The plan had some merit – a cut across the Allies' lines towards Antwerp through the densely wooded and hilly Ardennes region could cause chaos and, with luck, lead to the capture of many weapons, fuel and possibly large numbers of American prisoners; but would this be enough to create the political will in the US and UK for a negotiated peace in the West? It was unlikely given all that had gone before, but it was a last-ditch attempt to do something to alter the balance of power in the region.

The whole plan depended on secrecy and the swift movement of large numbers of troops into the area, some from quite long distances away. The terrain was difficult and the weather would be terrible, but that created an opportunity for the German forces. It imposed a natural 'no fly zone' upon the Allies for as long as the bad weather held. Would it be long enough for the offensive to reach its objectives? That was the gamble.

Standing in the way of the German advance were Allied occupied towns and villages, large and small, which were each to be taken by direct assault or surrounded and then left for follow-on units to capture. One such town was Bastogne.

Bastogne stood at a junction where seven main roads converged. Its capture by the German forces would allow the free flow of men and *matériel* through that area to continue the main advance. But the German Army had not taken account of the fact that the US 101st Airborne had been ordered to stop them.

As with any battle there are always After Action Reports, lists of casualties, company and battalion reports to research, as well as orders for activities on any given day and the battle for Bastogne was no different. It is fair to say that historically this battle is a well-covered subject with little detail left out of most modern books. However, whilst going through the US National Archives, I came across a post war intelligence interview with General Heinz Kokott by the US Historical Records Office.

Kokott had been the commanding officer of the 26th Volksgrenadier Division during their time at Bastogne and his description of the battles, casualties, losses and gains was interesting. This led to researching interviews with the other unit commanders who had taken part in the same battle, some only recorded in German. It soon became clear that these were a vitally important historical addition to the Battle of Bastogne story. It is a direction of research which I had not seen before – perhaps because for dozens of years these interviews were stored under the 'Top Secret' laws of their day.

Some months after the Bastogne battle in mid to late 1945 many of the German unit commanders had been captured and incarcerated in prisoner of war camps across Europe. When the US Army Historical Division – or more correctly the Office of the 'Chief of Military History Department of the Army, Washington DC' – approached them many were happy to discuss their memories of the Bastogne battle with their captors. The unique point of these interviews was that they were not made under duress or interrogation, but they took on more the air of general discussions about the actions and eventualities that took place through the eyes of the individuals concerned.

The US Army also interviewed its own commanding officers after the majority of the Bastogne battle had finished and their input is an invaluable record of events as they saw it. However, as a narrative it is one-sided and some rightly argue that it is too heavily focused on the success of the US forces. The list of officers interviewed for these records is shown at the end of this book and it was compiled in a work called *BASTOGNE – The First Eight Days by Colonel S.L.A. Marshall* which was commissioned by the US Army while the battle was still raging in the area.

The book is a comprehensive and detailed evaluation of the US Army in battle. But what of the German forces? Obviously, those units able to retreat from Bastogne could not be asked what had happened to them at the time, so these interviews had to wait at the very least until the end of the war.

My aim with this book was to put together both the US and German soldiers' history of this very specific battle and, by using the memories of the men from both sides in the conflict, tell the complete story in their own words. To my knowledge this has not been gathered together before in this way and I think that reading the events as they unfolded in both directions adds a dimension to this battle which has been missing.

Assumptions made by one side are counter-balanced by comments from the opposition and then by reading their orders and directives – certainly in the case of the German forces – it is possible to gauge just how much the US Airborne troops really delayed, harassed and foiled their advance.

Not only did this battle cost the German Army large numbers of men, but it is reasonably well agreed by the German officers themselves that in their eyes – the battle cost them the campaign. The historic behaviour of the 101st Airborne ultimately contributed significantly to the failure of the whole offensive. The courage of the Airborne forces to hold on until literally the last bullet, at a time when many of them thought that they would not last another day, shows their spirit and determination over a prolonged period in a way not recorded in many other battles. They had nowhere to go, so they stood their ground and fought for every inch of it – and many paid with their lives.

From the beginning of the German offensive on the morning of the 16 December to the 26 December 1944, it is safe to say that the actions of the Airborne forces in Bastogne caused so much disruption to the German advance as to be pivotal to the whole movement of German troops. The longer Bastogne held out, the more it had to be guarded on all sides and that in turn removed pressure on other areas of the German advance. Each tank, lorry or group of men engaged in or around Bastogne had been taken away from the main thrust into Belgium – to the point at which in late December the initiative was finally lost by the Germans and the balance had irrevocably swung back in favour of the defenders.

The German Army had simply failed to reach Antwerp as they had planned. They had also been unable to obtain significant amounts of fuel to keep their engines running and, as soon as the skies cleared of fog and cloud, they became easy prey during daylight hours to the Allied air force which was hungry to get into the fight. In a matter of ten days the battle was lost and the war was approaching its end – some could argue more quickly than before. It is quite possible that with the failure of this huge undertaking months had been taken off the duration of the war.

The natural geographic obstacles that surrounded Germany could have been supplemented with the troops that were used in the Ardennes Offensive and, if embedded in well prepared positions, they would have proved very difficult to overcome. Bastogne turned, as many battles do, into a last stand, as Stalingrad did for the Russians and as Arnhem did for the British. Bastogne became a position which was going to be held to the last man by the defending troops – no matter what.

In my view the Germans did not help themselves. Unlike the battles for other regions earlier in the war, they were not able to choose optimum weather conditions for their surprise attack. Their biggest worry was that the Allied air force was capable to destroying any troop or vehicle movements during daylight. The answer, which sounded very feasible at the time, was to instigate the Ardennes troop movements in the worst possible flying weather, but this also meant the worst possible ground conditions. The argument put forward was that the advance would stand every chance of success if the odds could be improved by the removal of the Allied air forces from the equation. It was a gamble that Hitler was convinced would work but, like the thrust towards Moscow in 1941/2 his plans were eventually beaten in no small part by changes in the weather.

This book is the story of those ten days in December 1944. To quote the official US Army report:

> *The Siege of Bastogne was written from interviews with nearly all the commanders and staff officers who participated in the defence of Bastogne. It does not attempt to tell the whole story of Bastogne or even of the siege itself, but it presents an intimate picture of command in an action that received world attention.*
>
> *The Siege of Bastogne is essentially the account of how a single strong defensive force was built from separate commands of armour, airborne infantry, and tank destroyers – a force convinced that it could not be beaten.*

The interviews were conducted by the US Army whilst they were still in Bastogne from 31 December 1944 to 25 January 1945 and undertaken by Colonel S.L.A. Marshall, Captain Hohn G. Westover and Lieutenant A. Joseph Webber.

They were not just with individual with individual officers but also by interviewing whole groups whenever possible. The information was checked by historians and then the final narrative was written by Colonel Marshall.

The German officers interviewed are all named at the start of their accounts and where possible I have married up the timelines for both the Allied and Axis groups. There were problems in particular with the US narrative when an officer would simply generalise and refer to all the events of the day, in a single paragraph. When possible, I tried to keep that to a minimum to create as clear a daily diary as I could. The translations from German to English of some interviews had to be done with a degree of latitude. As a German friend of mine who was translating some of the text said: '*The problem is, that this chap is talking in sentences that seem to be endless. Also the language used is "heroic" and "embellished" – nobody today would use such language.*'

Thus we have to accept that some of the German officers were speaking almost a year afterwards, with a degree of exaggeration and perhaps some glorification of their own roles in the action.

Now many years later, most of these men are dead and this may be all that we have left to give us a glimpse into the thinking of the men from both sides who fought one of the most iconic battles of the Second World War.

The background to Bastogne dates from the autumn of 1944. At that time three American armies, forming the 12th US Army Group, were in position on the central portion of the western front. The First and Third US Armies were located along the Siegfried Line while the Ninth US Army was facing the Roer River in Germany. All three armies were heading for the Rhine over difficult terrain, across swollen rivers, and against determined enemy resistance. Except in the Aachen sector, where an advance was made to the Roer, the line did not move during October and November. The Third Army fought near Metz, the First and Ninth Armies made the advance farther north, near Aachen. Between these two major efforts an extensive line of defence was maintained by the First Army; of this line the southern and major part was maintained by the VIII US Corps.

VIII Corps, which was under the command of Major General Troy H. Middleton, had its headquarters in Bastogne, Belgium and extended to Loshein, Germany, to a point where the Moselle River crosses the Franco-German border. Generally parallel to the German frontier along eastern Belgium and Luxembourg, it comprises a front of 88 miles. This section of the country, the Ardennes, has rugged hills, characterised by high plateaux, deeply incised valleys and a restricted road network. The mission which First Army gave VIII Corps was to defend this line in place. New divisions were brought into this part of the front for battle indoctrination and battle-worn divisions were sent to the corps for re-equipment and rest. As divisions were rotated into the sector, they took over existing wire networks and other facilities.

At the start of the German attack in December, the US Army VIII Corps front was held by two battle-weary divisions, a fresh infantry division, part of a green armoured division and a cavalry group. The battle-tested divisions were there in the form of the 4th Infantry Division, which in November had fought a costly action in the Hürtgen Forest below Düren, Germany, and the 28th Infantry Division, which had sustained heavy casualties in the First Army drive to the Roer. The 106th Infantry Division, newly arrived on the continent, had entered the Corps line four days before the German offensive began. The 14th Cavalry Group, consisting of the 18th and 32nd Cavalry Squadrons, held the north flank of VIII Corps, and the 9th Armoured Division, minus CCB (Combat Command B) was with V Corps, which had the majority of its units attached to the divisions.

The enemy facing VIII Corps was at that time estimated at four divisions. From north to south these were the German 18th, 26th, 352nd and 212th.

US Army intelligence had no idea that the Germans planned to advance right across their positions to Antwerp ...

Chapter 1

September–7 December 1944:
Setting the Scene

MAJOR HERBERT BÜCHS – Luftwaffe aide to Generalobst Alfred Jodl

During the period 23-30 September, the line had become stabilised so that we could see the organisation of Allied forces, where you had your troop concentrations and where the line was weakest. Later, the plan was to cut one of your main supply lines which ran from places in France, through Namur and Liège to the Aachen area. Antwerp, your main point for bringing in supplies, was not too far from the lines in the south.

Another idea was to attack to the south, but in the meantime, Army Group G suffered reverses. There was no bridgehead and there was no limiting point, such as Antwerp in the north. There was a great danger that Army Group G could not maintain a bridgehead until all the troops could arrive from the south. These troops were in such condition that they couldn't be used offensively immediately upon arrival. Two new divisions, 3rd and 15th Panzer Grenadier Divisions, were brought from Italy for this possible attack. It was a long trip by rail; both divisions took two or three weeks to come from the south to the Moselle area. Army Group G, coming from the south, had no divisions fit to make a strong counterattack. All its panzer-type divisions were in very poor condition. We needed so much time to prepare the attack that Army Group G was not able to maintain the necessary wide bridgehead.

The next idea after this was abandoned; it was to attack through the Ardennes and turn to the south or northwest. At that time, you were assembling American and British forces in the Aachen area and making preparations for a big offensive in the direction of the Rhine. Therefore, we abandoned the idea of turning to the south, since there would be no limiting point in that direction.

Turning north to the area of communications and supplies assembled for the Allied attack against the Rhine, we could attack in the direction of Antwerp and thereby force the Allies to change their plans. Later on this plan was accepted and we never considered at any time afterwards, turning south following the breakthrough.

We thought it would take until the first or second week in November to prepare the attack, because we needed a great deal of time for movements by railroad. At that time, supplies, fuel and ammunition could be transported by rail only as far as the Rhine. We needed a long time to collect fuel and ammunition and to bring panzer divisions up to strength. Six panzer divisions needed considerable time for re-organisation. It took nearly 900 trains to bring troops and supplies up to the assembly area.

Should the army capture the strongly defended areas of St Vith, Malmedy and Bastogne in the course of the push forward to the Meuse, or leave this task to the infantry divisions in the second and third waves? This was the question we asked ourselves. Hitler said success required a breakthrough and a push forward to the Meuse to capture bridges intact on the first and second days. In order to get a bridgehead across the Meuse, the divisions following should, for example, take Bastogne if necessary, because Hitler said the troops in Bastogne could not hold out long if we succeeded in getting across the Meuse in one, two, or three days.

GENERALFELDMARSCHALL GERD VON RUNDSTEDT

At the beginning of November 44, orders were given and plans and the date communicated by the German High Command to Genfldm Model and his three Army commanders – Manteuffel, Dietrich and Brandenberger, and 1 December 44 was chosen as a probable date of launching the offensive. It was already obvious at that time that the date could not be met. The date of 16 December 44 therefore, was proposed. The reason for this postponement was that the build-up of sufficient stocks of war matériel of all kinds, especially fuel, was yet incomplete. In addition, the Sixth Panzer

Army, which was spread out in the neighbourhood of Bad Salzuflen, had to be collected from both sides of the Rhine and reassembled.

The attack of the US Army on the line of the Roer was without influence on the situation, as was the expected attack of the Third US Army on the West Wall; furthermore, this plan of the Americans was unknown to us at the time. The situation on the Eastern Front played no role in our plan of offensive, nor was the offensive undertaken with view of improving the morale of the Army.

The Führer's wish was for a large-scale offensive beyond the Meuse above Liège and directed against Antwerp, with the purpose of cutting off the rear communications of the English and Americans and, by this means, perhaps changing the whole course of the war. Hitler stated that upon his own responsibility he had assumed a great risk on the Eastern Front and that he had called upon every man possible for this offensive.

In complete accord with Genfldm Model, Genfld von Rundstedt proposed the so-called 'Small Solution' for the offensive, which means that he wished for a pincer movement offensive. This was to have been made against an arc beginning east of Aix-la-Chapelle and south of Maastricht, with the Fifth and Sixth Panzer Armies moving from Monschau and Eifel across the Ardennes and east of Liège. This 'Small Solution' was rejected, for the end in view was impossible due to the insufficient forces, materiel and fuel at his disposal. Genfldm von Rundstedt considered success more likely only on the east of the Meuse River, and even then, only if a German attack were judged opportune, which he did not believe to be the case.

The solution of the Führer, 'a great offensive', required very large forces for adequate protection against an enemy counter-offensive directed against both sides of the wedge. This counter-offensive, furthermore, had to be expected to develop very shortly following our attack. In addition, it would be necessary to prepare very strong supporting panzer and infantry divisions to reinforce the offensives. These forces were entirely lacking.

It was a serious error to reinforce the right wing at the expense of the left wing, and to subordinate this right wing to Sixth Panzer Army; this mistake was paid for later at great cost. In this last effort, it was necessary to employ selected Army leaders and not inexperienced SS commanders.

A general radio silence was ordered and the military moves and concentrations of Fifth and Sixth Panzer Armies were kept extremely secret. The troops and civil population were informed that these divisions were being held in readiness for the expected great enemy offensive west of the Rhine, and that they would be placed as reserve units for Fifteenth and

Seventh Armies and under the control of the Western High Command. All of the artillery was re-employed for defence purposes, and only the artillery regiments of the assault division, on the last two nights, were used as direct reinforcement for the advance movement.

The movement of Sixth Panzer Army had already started at the beginning of November 1944. Additional forces were requested verbally and in writing by Genfld von Rundstedt, but the Führer and OKW paid no attention to these requests. In this way, OKW practically assumed the responsibility for carrying out the operation.

2 November

GENERAL HASSO von MANTEUFFEL – Commander of Fifth Panzer Army

The first discussion of the Ardennes Offensive took place in the presence of Genfldm von Rundstedt at Genfldm Model's Headquarters on 2 or 3 November 1944. Initially, Sixth Panzer Army was intended to push from the Losheim–Monschau area to Antwerp. Fifth Panzer Army was to thrust through the Eifel, past Namur to Brussels (exclusive), in order to protect the west flank of Sixth Panzer Army. Expected counterattacks from the area of Reims, Sedan, and Charleville were to be stopped by Seventh Army, which was to cover the south flank of Fifth Panzer Army between Dinant and Neufchateau. The main effort was to be made in the Sixth Panzer Army sector.

As soon as the British Army Group disengaged its forces in order to counterattack Sixth Panzer Army (and this would probably happen on the third or fourth day of the operation), a reinforced corps group of Fifteenth Army was to attack Maastricht from Maeseyck–Sittard area, east of the canal.

After missions were assigned, the allocation of troops was discussed. Genfldm Model and I were of the opinion that the distance to the objective was too great. Asked by Genfldm von Rundstedt, I told him that I believed my forces strong enough to reach the Meuse.

4 November

The next day, I discussed the operations plan with Genfldm Model and his Chief of Staff, Gen. Inf. Krebs. We agreed that:

a) In view of the allocation, a so-called 'small solution' had to be found. We planned to have Fifth Panzer Army drive to the Meuse, then veer to the north, and, in conjunction with Sixth Panzer and Fifteenth Armies, destroy the enemy forces located east of the Meuse.

b) If the ordered 'big solution' was to be carried out, the Fifteenth Army thrust would have to be cancelled, so that its forces could reinforce Fifth and Sixth Panzer Armies.

c) Under no circumstances must the promised allocation of personnel and *matériel* be reduced, nor must any forces be taken from Fifth Panzer and Seventh Armies. Furthermore, we insisted on the following conditions:

  1) A sufficient supply of fuel and ammunition would have to be in the hands of the troops before the attack started.

  2) The panzer divisions and Volksartillery Corps, exhausted from the defensive battles of Aachen, would have to be re-organised.

  3) Sufficient air support for the fighting forces on the ground and reconnaissance would have to be maintained.

  4) Auxiliary traffic control of Organisation Todt forces would have to be provided by the front-line regiments, because all available engineer forces had to be committed for important tasks and the roads would be congested.

  5) Re-organisation of troops' and staffs' signal units would have to be effected. Also, I wanted to have an influence on the entire distribution of appointments. This request was immediately granted by Hitler.

It was obvious that the attack had to be postponed. I remember exactly that I said on the day of the meeting, realising the conditions of the railroad system in Germany and how long it would take to reorganise personnel and *matériel*, that the attack could not start before 10 December 1944. Although Genfldm Model agreed with my reasoning, he had to insist on 1 December for the start of the attack. Based on our conversation, he submitted to OB WEST and OKW a detailed plan, the so called 'small solution'. This plan did not affect preparations for the 'big solution', which were made with regards to crossing the Meuse by Fifth Panzer Army. The strategic objective and the direction of the attack after the crossing of the river could not be fixed, because they would depend on the countermeasures taken by the enemy.

At that time, we knew that the enemy front line between Vianden and Hallschlag was occupied only by weak forces (two to three divisions) and that no reserves to speak of were situated behind the front line. The main enemy forces were to be expected from the direction of Reims, Sedan, and Charleville and from Brussels, Liège and Namur.

There was no doubt that the chief factor for the offensive's success would be surprise of the enemy. Therefore, the strictest secrecy had to be maintained, even if it delayed the concentration of troops. All orders were closely checked for security leaks. (The initial successes proved that the enemy was completely surprised.) The troops were informed that the new divisions (especially Volksgrenadier divisions), which had been recently organised in the rear, east of the Rhine, were being assembled in order to relieve the exhausted divisions in the vicinity of Aachen and to repulse an expected enemy offensive in and south of the Hürtgen Forest area. This explanation was generally accepted. Also, I spread the rumour that we wanted to attack in January or February 45 in order to win back the Saar area.

Genfldm von Rundstedt was appointed C-in-C of the operation, which was to be carried out by Army Group B (Genfldm Model). OKW attached general staff officers to the armies.

GENERALOBERST ALFRED JODL – Chief of Operations Staff

The plan was entirely Hitler's. All of us had been trying to decide on the location for an offensive, for example, in Italy, on the Eastern Front, or in the West. The first idea to counterattack in the West contemplated the zone of A Group Blaskowitz (A. Gp GP. Blaskowitz was ordered back from Italy on 17 August 44.) Then we considered a counterattack from the area of the German border. The first place was to strike the flank of the Allied forces moving northward from Metz by attacking toward Belgium. Blaskowitz was to advance and attack the Third US Army from the rear. The other German forces were to hold their ground.

This was early in September 44. The plan was never executed. The bridgehead was too weak and could have been reduced easily. Blaskowitz was driven back in the Nancy-Épinal area. We could not launch an operation easily from the Vosges. Gradually, on the basis of the picture presented in the regular operational reports, it appeared that although the Ardennes presented many terrain difficulties, the enemy troop dispositions there offered the best chances for a successful attack.

Hitler was closely involved in the details of the plan. There were various opinions. I wanted to avoid the danger of having Sixth Panzer Army attack against the strong Allied forces around Aachen and run into enemy pressure from the north and south. Model, on the other hand, wanted to try to pinch off the Aachen sector. Hitler was firmly opposed to Model's plan, especially concerning the commitment of Sixth Panzer Army in the Aachen area. Then Model suggested that Sixth Panzer Army attack between Monschau and Liège, but Hitler also rejected this area.

The idea of a counter-offensive of some kind was first stated in principle. It came up as soon as it was realised that the American army was advancing on a broad front and not in depth, soon after Avranches, when the Americans struck for the Loire and did not wheel around. We believed that the American advance would outrun its supplies. If we had had the strength, this would have been the moment with the greatest chance for success of a counter-offensive. But the moment found us too weak.

When Hitler conceived the first idea, he was sick in bed with an attack of jaundice. No very lengthy conferences were held. At 1200 hours daily, the headquarters staff met, some twenty to thirty people. Being relieved from attending to many details, on account of his illness, Hitler had all day in which to think. I saw him alone as he lay in bed (he usually disliked anyone seeing him in bed except his aides), and he spoke of the idea. I made a rough sketch on a map, showing the direction of the attack, its dimensions and the forces required for it. Hitler wanted to make the base of the penetration wider, with a direct attack on Luxembourg included in the plan. He feared that otherwise it would form a wedge and might be driven in from the sides by the first Allied counterattack. Hitler's ideas were very sound. It was my task simply to convert his ideas into practical form, bearing in mind the troops we had at our disposal.

A draft of the plan was the next step. There was a conference of Hitler, Genlt Westphal, Gen Inf Krebs and myself. Westphal and Krebs were informed of the plan and charged with notifying Von Rundstedt and Model, their commanders, and submitting detailed plans for the attack. Soon thereafter, Genfld Model, I believe, arrived with maps and a plan of the attack. There were slight differences between our ideas and those of the troop commanders. Model thought Antwerp was too far to reach and beyond our means. He thought the troops around Aachen would be a danger to our advance unless they were wiped out first.

Hitler and I believed that we could not wipe out these very strong and well-armed Allied forces, with their masses of tank and artillery. A frontal attack or even a flank attack would be against the enemy's strongpoint. We thought our only chance was a surprise operation which would cut off the line of the Allied forces at Aachen, and in that way alone neutralise them.

I fully agreed with Model that the Antwerp undertaking was an operation of the most extra daring – there was no question of that – but we were in a desperate situation, and the only way to save it was by a desperate decision. By remaining on the defensive, we could not hope to escape the evil fate hanging over us. By fighting, rather than waiting, we might save something. We realised that it would not be as simple as the 1940 campaign. It was an act of desperation, but we had to risk everything. A major battle at Aachen seemed inadvisable. The only chance of success was in a fluid advance over the Meuse.

MAJOR PERCY ERNST SCHRAMM – Wehrmacht Operations Staff

Only those officers of OKW, and especially of the Wehrmacht Operations Staff, were initiated – those who absolutely had to be informed. They were required to give an oath of secrecy in writing. The same applied to the few draughtsmen and secretaries whose assistance could not be dispensed with. At the conferences on the situation held by the Führer, only the officers working on the preparations stayed for the discussion of the plan for the offensive. Although the other members of the staff at the Führer's headquarters in the field sensed that something was going on, they were nevertheless surprised by the start of the attack in the Ardennes.

All orders and instructions, and also the corresponding messages, which were connected with the offensive were dispatched to the competent authorities by officers acting as couriers. Neither telephone nor teletype were to be used for this type of communication because the leaking of the secret plans was to be anticipated, in spite of the scrambling of telephone conversations and the use of cryptograms. This, of course, entailed loss of time, because the same delays occurred at OB WEST, Army Group B, the

Armies, and finally, also at corps level after the initiation of the participating Corps. But, these inconveniences had, of necessity, to be borne.

The subordinate command authorities maintained the secrecy along the same lines. Above all, care was taken that the exchange of radio messages should not exceed the usual average. As a special precaution, the Armies used a different code name for the offensive in their communications with the Corps to the one employed in their messages to their ranking commands, while the Corps chose another one in their communications with their subordinate units. These code names were being changed every two weeks. In addition, each command authority was only initiated to the extent absolutely essential for the preparations. The Armies, Corps, etc. barely knew which unit was to attack in the adjacent sector and were not aware of the missions which had been given to the units beyond their immediate neighbours.

In order to avoid transmitting by courier the attack date, which it was customary to designate X-Day, it was preferred to use code letters which were automatically changed. There was another special code for the clock time. The most important medium for maintaining secrecy was to delay the initiation to the latest possible moment. The initiation was echeloned in the following manner:

- On 11 Oct 44, some of the personnel of the Wehrmacht Operations Staff, and at the end of Oct 44, OB WEST and A Gp B were informed.
- The Army Commanders were subsequently informed. With the Army Staffs only the Commanding Officer, the C-of-S, the Ia, and one additional person were allowed to be initiated.
- The initiation of the Ic, the OQu (*Oberquartiermeister*), the Engineer, Signal and Senior Artillery Commanders only took place, when it had become unavoidable, and Army Group had given its authorisation.

JODL: The first discussions with Hitler were about the end of September or early in October 44. The conference with Krebs and Westphal was perhaps a week later (by this time Hitler was up again). The conference with Model was perhaps in the second half of October 44. Of course, there were some discussions on the plan every day. Besides those persons already mentioned, the plan had been disclosed to Genfldm Keitel and to my staff officers (Obstlt Waizenecker and Major Büchs). Then, as secrecy was relaxed a little at the end of October 44, Ogruf Fegelein, liaison officer of RF-SS Himmler, and Gen Inf Burgdorf, Hitler's aide and the Personnel Adjutant, from whom we could secure the best possible artillery officers and those of other branches, were informed of the plan. Everyone had to sign a pledge to the effect that if he let a word of the plan leak out, he would be shot. That is an exaggeration, of course. But the statement was worded that any discloser, whether intention or through negligence, would bring punishment by court-martial.

GENERAL SIEGFRIED WESTPHAL – General of Cavalry

On 24 or 25 October 1944 I was called to a conference at Hitler's Headquarters. Initially, it had been hoped that von Rundstedt would attend this conference also, but he was unable to come. The conference included Hitler, Keitel, Johann, and General Krebs, the Chief of Staff of Army Group B (Model). Krebs and I arrived at Rastenburg early in the morning. Genmaj Von Buttlar, Deputy Chief of the *Wehrmachtführungsstab*, gave us a secret study entitled *Wacht am Rhein*. It gave no indication of the Ardennes Offensive, but merely indicated that certain troops would be transferred to the West. I was happy at first, as I thought it would mean that our defences would be reinforced, and that the title of the operation indicated we might abandon the Netherlands front.

After dinner at 1300 hours, Krebs and I attended the regular situation orientation in the Führer's headquarters. Following the regular discussion of the situation on all fronts, certain individuals were asked to leave the conference room and only about fifteen remained.

Hitler opened the discussion by stating that the West had always asked for reinforcements for its front, and he felt this was justified during World War One. Hitler then said that although it may be justified to reinforce the Western Front, he had not been able to do so up until that time because he did not think it feasible to supply forces for the defence, and therefore the only solution was to launch an attack. Because of this, he said he had developed the plan to make a surprise attack towards Antwerp. He said he had decided to attack in the weakest area – south of Liège. He promised 2,000 planes in support and said he would hold off the planes for some time in order to do this. He said that because of the weather considerations he would prefer to launch the offensive at the beginning of November 1944, but that it would probably take almost all of that month to assemble the forces.

My immediate reaction was that in order to launch such an offensive it was first necessary to reinforce three critical areas with greater defensive forces to stem enemy attacks: around Aachen, in the Nineteenth Army area, and around Belfort. I had the impression that Hitler, Jodl, and Keitel did not want to discuss those things, and that they had their minds set on an offensive.

After the meeting had been completed, I wanted to talk to Jodl about additional details, but it was already late in the day and I was whisked away in order to catch my transportation back to OB West Headquarters in Ziegenberg. I wanted to tell Jodl that it was hardly possible to reach the Meuse below Liège with the forces he planned to use. I also wanted to discuss the possible use of these forces defensively instead of offensively: however, I realised the plan was only a paper one, and that if I had raised these objections, WFST probably would have accused me of defeatism.

JODL: By the middle of November 44, the small circle had to be increased still more. Bühle (Gen Inf, Chief of the Organisation Division, Army General Staff) had to be consulted on supply matters, and representatives of the Air Force and Navy had to be conferred with. The head of the Replacement Army had to be asked when he could have the divisions ready for action. Gen Inf Gercke (Director of Army Transport) had to be queried on the availability of transportation. Every day the plan was discussed and maps were made of the approach routes for our forces.

I went to OB West in Ziegenberg to discuss the details. Hitler discussed many details. In the case of the 1940 offensive in the West, he had gone into details even more minutely. Owing to his illness, he was not quite so painstaking now. I made this trip perhaps in the first half of November 44. There were thousands of things to discuss with Von Rundstedt and Model, details such as artillery preparations, disposition of divisions, within the various armies, choice of routes, etc. We were to avoid being drawn in towards Liège, therefore, the plan of attack was changed in favour of a more westerly route for the panzer armies, to avoid their being cut off by a lack of sufficient crossings.

Hitler went into all these matters intensely. The time allotted for preparatory artillery fire and the allocation of GHQ units, (artillery etc) among the various armies had to be settled. Supply shortages and ways of making them up were discussed. Naturally, we could not discuss any of these things on the telephone.

Some of the Operations Division of the Staff worked on the plan, but none of the staff who were concerned with other theatres of war knew about the plan for a counter-offensive in the Ardennes. No reflection on Von Rundstedt, but the plan was Hitler's. If any general should be identified with it, that man is Model, who particularly developed the plan. Von Rundstedt neither originated it nor was he specially concerned with it. His function was merely to execute the plan. He was concerned with the routing and allotment of troops; for example, other army groups farther south also needed more men. He was merely carrying out instructions of the High Command.

Important discussions were held in Berlin about 23 November 44. Hitler spoke to all the leaders, down to the rank of army commander. Von Rundstedt, Model, Westphal, Krebs, Von Manteuffel and Dietrich were present. Dietrich complained about non-receipt of supplies, and Bühle and Thomale (Genmaj, C of S to the Inspector General of Panzer Troops) proved to him that the supplies had been sent. He probably had not yet received notice of their receipt. Dietrich was present at the meeting on 23 November 1944. I remember it definitely. We had coffee together.

Everything was again explained to the generals, who all had their maps with them. We discussed what still remained to be done. Pressure was exerted to get all the equipment still needed. By this time, forms were no longer being signed. This practice had been dropped at the end of October 1944.

Hitler discussed these matters in a final conference with his commanders. It was 'now or never' and we had to risk everything. We were not getting any stronger, and a better opportunity was not likely to present itself later. Hitler had done all he could and had thrown in his last reserves for this attack although they were sorely needed in the East. A large number of tanks and assault guns had been provided. If the attack were successful, Hitler believed the entire situation on the Western Front could be changed radically. He emphasised this, since we had thought earlier that no attack could be made in the West at all, in view of the unprecedented Allied air superiority.

We had to attack in the West because the Russians had so many troops that even if we succeeded in destroying thirty divisions, it would not make any difference. On the other hand, if we destroyed thirty divisions in the West, it would account for more than one-third of the whole Invasion Army. We counted on surprise for our success.

Hitler discussed these matters in a final conference with his commanders. The fact that we were still in a position to launch an attack, after the defeat in France, should have raised morale, especially at Christmas time. Feeling became hopeful at home and on all fronts. This factor did play a part during the preparatory phase and the first stage of the counter-offensive. Hitler said that after all the reverses, the offensive would produce a positive impression on the Wehrmacht and the people.

Our object was to avoid enemy night air attacks, so that you could not observe our nightly troop movements. On the basis of past experience, the worst flying weather is always in November. From December on, conditions gradually improve for flying. But this exercised no decisive influence on the success or failure of the operation. The decisive factor was that we had expected hard, frosty ground, not deep mud. With solid enough ground, we would have expected to push through with our tanks in one day.

We simply were not ready (until the 16th), and our troops had not arrived. The entire Sixth Panzer Army, the Volksgrenadier Divisions and the transportation facilities were not ready. The original date set (end of November 44) was just a tentative or estimated date, which we had hoped to be ready for. We told Hitler that we figured we could be ready by that date, but when we began conferring with Replacement and Panzer officers, we found that preparations could not be completed rapidly enough. Formerly (1940-43), the Replacement Army was able to deliver divisions exactly at the times promised, but by this time supplies and equipment of many kinds were short, and delays resulted.

The Luftwaffe meteorologists played a big part in 1940 in the Campaign in the West. Obst. Diesing was later succeeded by Dr (Obstlt) Schuster (Director in the Luftwaffe Weather Service).

GENERALLEUT FRITZ BAYERLEIN – Panzer Lehr Division

I heard for the first time of the planned offensive and the role of the Panzer Lehr by means of a plan rehearsal at the staff headquarters of XLVII Panzer Corps in Kyllburg (Eifel). In the course of this, the first part of the attack, as far as the Meuse near Namur and Dinant was discussed. Present were: General von Manteuffel, General Krueger of the LVIII Panzer Corps, the commanders of the Panzer Lehr, 2nd Panzer and 26 Volksgrenadier Divisions.

We had already recognised earlier that something special was intended in the West, without knowing exactly what it was. In November the Panzer Lehr was recuperating in Westphalia, as part of the Sixth SS Panzer Army. On 9 November all the divisions of this Army were unexpectedly shifted to the West Bank of the Rhine and in the arrangement in which they later went into action. There were also rumours about offensive plans in the region of Aachen and further south. Sepp Dietrich's Army was to play the main part in this.

Panzer Lehr was separated from the Sixth SS Panzer Army and was assigned to LVIII Panzer Corps. It was to camp west of Castellaun in the Hunsrück. But from there the division was unexpectedly committed in the Saar region.

SCHRAMM: It was to be avoided that groups of officers suddenly appeared with maps etc, to reconnoitre the terrain, because the various commanders from division on down to battalion level might feel a natural urge to carry out very thorough reconnaissance. This information would have been of the greatest value to the newly arrived divisions as well as to those which had already previously been committed. Here again, disadvantages had to be taken into account in favour of the maintenance of secrecy. Those officers, who were authorised to visit up front, had to wear the uniforms of the units committed along the corresponding sector. The names of each person, who had been initiated, were listed; they were bound to secrecy and were informed that any offence was punishable by the death penalty.

Reconnaissance patrol activities were not to be increased. At the end of November 44, they were stopped altogether. The artillery forces, which were being assembled, and the newly arrived staffs were not permitted to cross certain lines in a western direction. They were therefore unable to sufficiently reconnoitre the terrain before the attack – a disadvantage which especially affected the solution of technical problems by the engineers. In order to check the danger presented by deserters, no troops hailing from Alsace, Lorraine or Luxembourg were committed along the front.

The greatest problem obviously was the maintenance of secrecy for the moving into the assembly areas. The wooded terrain of the Eifel greatly facilitated the concealment of the troops from air reconnaissance. The only difficulty was caused by the smoke from the fires, which had to be built for cooking and heating purposes, and which in clear weather, might have led to the discovery of the presence of troops. For this reason, charcoal was distributed to the units.

In the assembly areas, the camouflage was being carried out with utmost care. A *Tarnmeister* (camouflage commander) was appointed for each village, traffic was reduced to a minimum. Signs to indicate roads and to show the location of telephone and radio stations were not permitted. In order to avoid all noises, it was attempted to use horse-drawn vehicles. But this means of transportation was limited by the number of horses available. Also, it proved difficult to take back the horses along the crowded roads for their next haul. Anyhow, this expedient was out of the question for the transport of heavy guns. The element of surprise, which the German Supreme Command had considered as one of the most essential pre-requisites for the execution of its plans, had actually been attained.

GENERALLEUTNANT HERMANN PRIESS

On taking command of the 1 SS Panzer Corps, I was informed by my chief of staff, Lt. Col. of the SS Hehmann, that an offensive operation was planned, and that the Corps was to be prepared accordingly under conditions of the utmost secrecy. It was not supplied with further details.

MANTEUFFEL: Security measures for the Ardennes Offensive:

1. Some of the additional steps we took to ensure surprise related to the method by which we withdrew troops from the line during late November and early December 1944. We made very careful plans for this withdrawal of troops, and gradually we spread out the divisions which were to be left in the line, using them to replace the units which we intended to utilise in the attack. To put these troops off guard, we informed them that we were expecting further attacks by the Americans and it would be necessary to concentrate reserves to meet these attacks.

2. We brought the troops forward into the attack areas in three separate phases:

a) During the first phase we brought troops as far forward as the Krefeld–Kiel area; these were mainly troops which had been transferred from other areas, such as the centre of Germany and Hungary.

b) We relieved troops from the Western Front and pulled them back into the first assembly areas.

c) The SS troops of Sixth Panzer Army, which had been moved west of the Rhine as OKW reserves, were shifted south to the attack area.

3. In order to utilise concealment to a maximum, troops were billeted in various villages behind the proposed attack area and were cautioned to keep themselves and their equipment under cover whenever possible. They were to build no fires, and there were to be no daylight marches. In my area, I ordered no motor vehicles brought nearer than 8km from the front line. Between 1 and 10 December 44, all three of these groups mentioned above were in position west of the Rhine, and shortly before the 12 December meeting with Hitler, we began to move our troops into the final assembly areas, preparatory to the attack.

4. Further security measures were taken by prohibiting any advance reconnaissance lower than battalion level; and only those company commanders who were to lead assault companies were allowed to go forward to reconnoitre the terrain. I, myself, started a rumour in a restaurant early in December, to the effect that we were preparing to attack in the Saar area in January; I mentioned this in a loud voice to some of my commanders while we were having dinner one night.

I was unaware of any American troops movements into the Ardennes sector during the early part of December 1944.

1 December

BAYERLEIN: On 1 December after bitter fighting and considerable losses the division was unexpectedly pulled out in order to be swiftly refitted in the Cochem district on the Moselle. Something unusual must have been in mind for the division as the press for top speed was suspicious and yet no one could believe it would be re-committed so soon as it was hardly ready. This made all the more surprising the order for the division to participate in an offensive.

The intention to attack and the plans of attack could not be announced to the regimental commanders until three days before the attack began (i.e.

on 12 or 13 December). Up to that point all orders and actions had to be camouflaged, i.e as 'Study of a plan for a counterattack' or as an order in the event of an enemy attack or penetration. Nevertheless, one could recognise indications of an offensive as the numbers of railroad trains of troops and materiel in the Moselle Valley and the Eifel could not be concealed. Maps could be issued only just before the beginning of the attack.

The commanders of the artillery and of the divisional engineers were oriented at the same time since they had to prepare plans for the employment of artillery and for building bridges near Gemünden.

The Supply Officer had been oriented by the Supply authorities of Corps and Army, since considerable work was necessary in the supply field. The other staff officers of the division were oriented as the need arose (between 10 and 13 December). Regimental commanders and commanders of independent battalions were informed on 12 December. Battalion commanders were told on 12 and 14 December before moving into the jump-off positions.

2 December

MANTEUFFEL: In the conference with Hitler on 2 December 44, Von Rundstedt was represented by his Chief of Staff Genlt. Siegfried Westphal, who did not know anything about the conditions and situation of the front-line troops. Hitler was astonished by this, he told me so, personally. Model had requested the conference, because I had quite different suggestions to make concerning the width of the attack front, the time of the attack, the commitment of the panzer divisions, and the anti-aircraft searchlights, etc. Only a few members of the staffs were present at this meeting which lasted several hours.

Finally, Hitler approved my suggestions, which were now the basis for further preparations. Towards the end of the meeting, Model repeated his objections against the 'big solution', and Hitler said that the 'small solution' would always be possible. However, all preparations had to be made for the 'big solution'. Model also pointed out that movements to the front, even at that time, were often delayed, and that neither the allocation of personnel and materiel, nor the deployment of the units in depth would be sufficient.

In the beginning, it was planned that Sixth Panzer Army was to cross the Meuse between Liège and the Ardennes (inclusive) and Fifth Panzer Army between the Ardennes (exclusive) and Namur (inclusive).

Much of the gasoline which had been accumulated for our attack was east of the Rhine River and had to be hauled a great distance to the front lines, once the attack got under way. The gasoline was kept east of the Rhine for two reasons: first, because the railroad system west of the Rhine was almost completely smashed; and, second, because it was considered safer there, should (US) forces launch any attacks prior to 16 December.

I informed Hitler on 2 December that we would require 5 units of gasoline (a unit is one tankful), but actually we received only 1½ units. As a result, we could move forward only half of our artillery and *nebelwerfers*. All our attacks on Bastogne were made by small groups, because of this gasoline shortage. The location of the gasoline east of the Rhine led to some confusion at higher headquarters, because the supply and administrative group stated that the gasoline was available, but it was not received by the tanks doing the fighting. Thus, when I would say we were unable to move because of lack of gasoline, the higher commanders would always tell me their reports showed that we had a sufficient supply. It was difficult for them to understand that we could not supply the tanks immediately with gasoline.

PRIESS: About 2 December 1944, small staffs and billeting parties were seconded from various units to prepare the way in and about the area. The commitment of the 1st SS Panzer Corps was determined by type of terrain and by road and route conditions. The plan of attack for a penetration as far as Antwerp was ambitious, considering the forces at our disposal. It could only succeed if tactical surprise was complete, if the Allies only had small reserves at their immediate disposal, and if they did not take active countermeasures immediately. Nevertheless, in view of the promised support and the general buoyancy displayed by the troops, the Corps considered that there was every possibility of obtaining the Maas.

GENERALMAJOR HEINZ KOKOTT – Commander 26th Volksgrenadier Division

The period of re-organisation lasted five weeks. Delivery of weapons and equipment functioned smoothly. The personnel replacements were of good quality: they were fresh, healthy young men of great willingness – mostly former navy and air force personnel – but they lacked any combat experience and infantry type of training. The replacement NCOs were varied: the remaining NCOs with their combat experience in the East were now joined by some older ones from the air force, navy and army who had for some time been assigned to administrative positions in the interior, and also by a number of very youthful NCO trainees. Both categories had either very little or no experience at the front at all.

The officer material was good. The regimental and battalion commanders as well as the company commanders were those officers who had proven themselves time and again during the Russian Campaign and who knew their stuff. The young officers who were then joining the division – all of them experienced in battle – brought, in addition to their ability, the best of spirits and willingness. The bringing up and arrival of new units in the rearward area, together with the strict order for cessation of reconnaissance activities for the first time, gave rise to conjecture that some major operation was being planned.

During the first days of December 1944, the commander of the 26th Volksgrenadier Division was ordered to report to the Corps Commander (General Lucht). There, under maintenance of the greatest secrecy, he was for the first time and in rough outlines, informed about the intention for the Ardennes Offensive.

The attack was then planned for 10 November. The objective of the offensive was to tear open the enemy front north of Trier and a quick breakthrough over the Maas (Meuse) River towards Antwerp.

With rigid regulations for secrecy, preparations for the attack began immediately. All reconnaissance had to be carried out in an inconspicuous manner, but by our own troops and other participating units. By means of map exercise, whose true purpose was being camouflaged, and strenuous three-day manoeuvres, leaders and troops were once more trained for swift and mobile methods of attack.

Chains of military police sentries about 10km behind the front stopped the major east/west traffic during daylight hours. Roving patrols kept supervising the camouflaged assembly of vehicles and materiel in the forests and villages. No markings and guideposts whatsoever were put up for the reinforcement units which were brought up by sectors during the night only and without any light. Unknown officers appeared at our positions, made reconnaissance and familiarised themselves with the terrain. Mincfields beyond and along the front were cleared or shifted.

6 December

PRIESS: At first only the commanding generals and the chief of staff knew of the orders. All detailed orders and instruction had to be worked out by the chief himself. About ten days before the commencement of the attack the Ia (Intelligence Officer) of the Corps was initiated, as well as the divisional commanders and the divisional Ias.

7 December

COLONEL ALFRED ZERBEL – Staff Officer XXXXVII Panzer Corps

The Staff of the XXXVII Panzer Corps arrived on 7 December at Kyllburg/Eifel. At the beginning of the offensive operation the Corps had under its command the 2nd Panzer Division, the Panzer-Lehr Division, the 26 Volksgrenadier Division, the Army Engineer Battalion No 600, 1 Volkswerfer brigade, 1 Volksartillery Corps. The Corps had the order to cross on the Our 16 December at the left wing of the 5th Panzer Division in the sector Dahnen–Stolzembourg and to reach the Meuse at Namur.

KOKOTT: At the end of the first week in December, during a meeting held at the divisional command post by the Commander-in-Chief of the Fifth Panzer Army and Commander of the XXXXVII Panzer Corps – the division was subordinated to the latter – detailed information was given with regards to the planned offensive.

The Bastogne question was discussed a number of times during the conference and map exercises. The Commanding General kept emphasising that Bastogne was to be taken at all costs and with concentration of all the forces, before the continued drive to the northwest of the armoured units could be considered. A definite agreement or concise decision as to how to deal with the Bastogne road junction, however, could not be arrived at during these conferences.

All regiments and battalions were familiar with their missions, directions and targets of the neighbouring units. In order to keep the troops mobile in the difficult Eifel–Ardennes terrain, their equipment was reduced to a minimum; the number of supply vehicles was cut down to the extreme limits. The combat strength of the infantry companies was reduced to eighty men to facilitate leadership.

Chapter 2

10–15 December: The Plan of Attack

SCHRAMM: On 10 December 44, Fifth Panzer Army issued extensive instructions on the assembly and fighting. They were subdivided into a number of parts.

a) Sixth Panzer Army: After strong artillery preparation, Sixth Panzer Army will – on X-Day – break through the enemy front in the sector on both sides of Hollerath and will relentlessly thrust across the Maas (Meuse) toward Antwerp. For this purpose, Army will make full use of its motorised forces and will disregard the protection of its flanks. The following instructions are hereby issued for this purpose:

  • 1st SS Panzer Corps will start its attack at 0600 hours on X-Day and will break through the enemy positions in the Monschau–Uden–Breth–Losheim sector. Subsequently, 12th SS Panzer Division will thrust on the right wing of Corps, with 1st SS Panzer Division on the left wing. They will cross the Maas and continue their attack in the Liège–Huy sector. According to developments in the situation, it will thereafter be the mission of corps to relentlessly pierce towards Antwerp by making full use of its motorised elements, or to be available for the protection of the right flank along the Albert Canal.

  • Carefully selected advance detachments, led by particularly daring commanders, will advance rapidly and capture the bridges in the Maas sector before their demolition by the enemy.

  • The following units will be subordinated to Corps: the 277th and 12th Volksgrenadier Divisions and 3rd Fallschirmjäger (FS) Division.

  • After the breakthrough across the main defensive area of the enemy has been achieved, 3rd FS Division and 12th Volksgrenadier Division will again be subordinated to Army.

  • The II SS Panzer Corps will be held in readiness in the rear of 1st SS Panzer Corps and will immediately follow the latter during its advance. It is the mission of Corps to thrust – together with 1st SS Panzer Corps – toward the Maas, cross the river, then continue its advance on Antwerp, disregarding any enemy contact with its flanks.

- Liaison with 1st SS Panzer Corps will constantly be maintained. Armoured advance detachments will immediately follow the last combat elements of 1st SS Panzer Corps. The Corps is therefore responsible for keeping open the roads of advance behind 1st SS Panzer Corps.
- On X-Day LXVII Inf. Corps, with 326th and 246th Volksgrenadier Divisions, will break through the enemy positions on both sides of Monschau, will cross the road Mützenich–Elsenborn, then turn off to the north and west, and will build up a secure defensive front along the line Simmerath–Eupen–Limburg–Liège.
- The 12th Volksgrenadier Division and 3rd FS Division will be committed west of Limburg for the purpose of prolonging the defensive front. Army will be responsible for moving up these divisions. Roadblocks, supported by armoured detachments, will be established far to the north across the main roads and across the lines of communication leading from north to south. The hilly terrain around Elsenborn will be seized and firmly held.
- A special order was issued for the artillery; it regulated the preparation, the support to be given during the attack, the additional duties, and the subordination of the artillery while the attack was progressing. Apart from its organic artillery, Army was assigned three Volksartillery Corps, two Volks Werner brigades and three heavy artillery battalions. The artillery of the panzer corps was to take part in the preparation.

b) Fifth Panzer Army: The mission of Fifth Panzer Army is to break through the enemy positions in the Olzhein–Gemünd sector under cover of darkness, and to thrust across the Maas on both sides of Namur up to Brussels.

- The first objectives of the attack are the bridgeheads across the Maas. It is of vital importance to pierce any enemy resistance, to keep moving by day and by night, to relentlessly advance, disregarding prescribed routes of advance; if necessary, the advance will be continued dismounted and on foot. For this purpose, LXVI Infantry Corps, with 18th and 62nd Volksgrenadier Divisions, were to execute a double envelopment of the enemy forces in the Schnee Eifel, and to capture St Vith; then, Corps was to thrust on, echeloned in depth, reach the Maas, and cross the river in the Huy–Andennes sector, or else be moved to the left Army wing.
- The LVIII Panzer Corps, with 116th Panzer Division and 560th Volksgrenadier Division, were to force the crossing of the Our on a wide front on both sides of Ouren, move up to the Maas via Houffalize,

thrust across the Maas in the Ardennes–Namur sector, and establish bridgeheads.

- The XLVII Panzer Corps, with 2nd Panzer Division and 26th Volksgrenadier Division, were to force the crossing of the Our on a wide front in the Dasburg–Gemünd sector, by-pass the Clerf sector, capture Bastogne, and finally, echeloned in depth, thrust toward and across the Maas in the vicinity and south of Namur.

- The Panzer Lehr Division and Führer Begleit Brigade were, at first, to be held in readiness as Army reserves, and were to be launched for a rapid thrust toward the Maas as soon as one of the corps had succeeded in breaking through.

- Seventh Army: On X-Day, Seventh Army will cross the Our and Sauer, will break through the enemy front in the Vianden–Echternach sector, and its reinforced right wing will thrust toward the line Gedinne–Libramont–Martelange–Mersch–Wasserbillig in order to protect the southern flank of Fifth Panzer Army. Army will gain ground beyond this line, will advance up to the Semis sector and the Luxembourg area, and will – by fluid conduct of battle – prevent an enemy thrust into the southern flank of Army Group.

The following orders were issued for this purpose:

- The LXXXV Inf. Corps will start its attack at 0600 on X-Day, will cross the Our, and will break through the enemy front in the Vianden–Ammeldingen sector. The 5th FS Division on the right, and the 352 Volksgrenadier Division on the left, will relentlessly thrust to the west, and turn off toward the line Gedinne–Libramont–Martelnge–Mersch; there, their main forces will at first stay on the defensive.

- Mobile advance detachments will keep contact with the southern wing of Fifth Panzer Army which will be advancing via Bastogne to the north of Corps. These detachments will advance beyond the objective of the operation up to the Semis and block its main crossing points.

- The LXXX Inf. Corps will start its attack at 0600 on X-Day, cross the Our and Sauer, and will break through the enemy front in the Wallendorf–Echternach sector. The 276th Volksgrenadier Division on the right, and 352nd Volksgrenadier Division on the left, will relentlessly thrust toward the Mersch–Wasserbillig line, and their main forces will start on the defensive along this line. Mobile advance detachments will cross the Sauer, thrust into the Luxembourg area, and prevent the advance of enemy forces via Luxembourg. It is of vital importance that the enemy artillery positions in the Christnach–Altrier area be rapidly neutralised.

- During the course of the attack, the *Bewährungsbattallon* (penal battalion) which was committed on the Sauer front west of Trier, was to be held in readiness for the thrust across the Sauer.
- The LIII Inf. Corps was, at first, to remain available to Army.

MANTEUFEL: On 10 December 44 the Armies were ordered to designate their crossing points within their sectors themselves. From aerial photographs, I selected the crossing point of Dinant, in spite of the disadvantage that the Army would have to cross the Sombre west of Namur. It was my intention to reconnoitre with reconnaissance units of great striking power on a wide front towards the Meuse, in order to find one or more crossing points. In the sector of Sixth Panzer Army, the Skorzeny Group (code name Operation Grief) was to capture the Meuse crossing points by surprise, before the spearheads of the German forces reached them. When and where this unit jumped off, I never heard. I learned for the first time about the existence of this unit from a Sixth Panzer Army circular which, against my strict orders, was copied by 62 Volksgrenadier Division. (It was captured on the 16 Dec 44 by the enemy. This letter was of great importance for both sides.)

All three Armies had to carry out large movements of troops. Some of the troops attached to the Armies arrived by train from all parts of Germany; only a small part approached on foot from the area between Mönchengladbach and Koeln (Cologne). Because of the necessary secrecy, all these troops had to be assembled on a base line behind A Gp B. Beyond this line, an intermediate assembly area, which could be reached after three or four night marches, had to be found. From there, it was necessary for the troops to move to the assembly area in two nights. The jump-off positions were occupied in the last night before the operation, to prevent deserters from giving any information about the attack to the enemy. The disadvantage that the troops were unacquainted with the terrain could not be avoided, but – as I recognised afterwards – did not influence the operation, or at least not to the extent that commands had supposed.

Only the night before the attack were the troops informed of the operation. They were to approach the enemy positions as closely as possible during the night, when the terrain was illuminated only by searchlights. Then supported by artillery, they were to over-run these positions.

Sixth Panzer Army attacked only with some spearheads, which, according to statements of the division commanders, were not strong enough. Some of the tanks of my panzer divisions were subordinated to the infantry for the break-through, while Sixth Panzer Army kept its tanks together and brought its four panzer divisions up on two roads, one division behind the other. From the beginning, I was of the opinion – and I insisted on it at the conference with Hitler – that, in view of the enemy air and artillery superiority, the infantry could never make the breakthrough in daylight if the enemy was sitting in defence. OKW had ordered that the attack commenced at 1100 hours. I suggested, and finally my suggestion was approved, that the attack jump off at 0530 hours. This was of decisive importance, because if the infantry attack was carried out as planned, the armoured forces could cross the Our River during the first night and would be ready to attack at daybreak on 17 December 1944. I expected that the local tactical reserves of the enemy would be committed at the same time.

PRIESS: The written order to attack was issued by the Sixth Panzer Army on 10 December 1944. General hypothetical conditions for the attack were tactical surprise, and the striking of the initial blow during a period of bad weather. Artillery adjustment fire was not permitted, fire preparation was reduced to one hour, and artillery reconnaissance was to cease beforehand. The plan was that the Corps was to break through in its own sector of the enemy's main field of combat with the three infantry divisions: the 277th Volksgrenadier Division (right) to reach the area of Elsenborn, the 12th Volksgrenadier Division (centre) to reach the area of Nidrum–Weywertz, and the 3rd Fallschirmjäger Division (left) to reach the area of Schoppen–Elberdinge.

After the attainment of these objectives, the three infantry divisions were to be again subordinated to the command of the Army and to attack to the northwest. For this purpose, each infantry division was to have under its command a battalion of self-propelled guns from Army High Command.

Individual sections of the enemy's main front line were to be bypassed. At the two dividing lines of the Corps, for example, the neighbouring sectors were not to attack in the immediate proximity. It was believed that the tactic of cutting off enemy strongpoints and continuing our advance – which had proved so successful in the East – would be relatively unknown to the Americans, and that therefore these strongpoints would not resist for very long.

The 1st and 12th SS Panzer Divisions were not to be used in the initial breakthrough. The strength of these divisions was to be conserved for the thrust beyond this. The disposition of advance detachments had been arranged. These were to branch out in the course of the thrust, and to reach the Maas as quickly as possible without regard to their communications.

According to available information, the Corps sector was occupied by approximately 1½ American divisions. The German Command assumed there were three American Divisions in the area of Elsenborn. One American Panzer division was believed to be in the area north of Spa. The corps observation battery – which had been used since about the 28 Nov 1944 – had uncovered artillery posts in the areas of Elsenborn, Krinkelt, Büllingen and Holzhein. In order not to arouse enemy suspicions, these had been left quite unmolested.

The area assigned the Corps for attack was unfavourable. It was broken and heavily wooded. Wartime experience had tended to show that particularly good troops were needed for woodland fighting, and that – as a consequence of the state of the training of the infantry divisions – a rapid breakthrough in a terrain such as ours could be accomplished, was very doubtful.

In preparation for the coming battle armoured and motorised vehicles were overhauled and new ones broken in. The corps had found it necessary to employ drivers as infantrymen as they had suffered heavy losses. With the ever-present allied fighter-bombers it was not possible to create a driving school to train them and in some areas motor convoys had to be discontinued altogether and, when practical, driver training was given during precious supply runs. Provisionally, there was little time left for training. It was essential, therefore, to bring up replacements as quickly as possible, to place weapons and equipment in readiness for action, and to prepare for attack, those formations which had become exhausted by defensive fighting. Similar difficulties were encountered in the training of signal corps personnel, radio operators in particular. Every possible improvisation had to be taken the utmost advantage of, in order to break in substitutes and to prepare the signal corps units for their coming tasks.

In view of the air situation, this could only be carried out on a very limited scale up to the level of battalions. It had mostly to be done in the early hours of the morning or evening. In the interest of secrecy, it was necessary to cover all obvious tracks – particularly tank tracks – before dawn. The safety of the troops themselves was, of course, also involved.

An assault detachment was formed in every company, and a combat company was formed in every regiment of particularly good and specially trained men. Both of these formations were equipped with the necessary automatic weapons (submachine guns and fully automatic pistols) either from newly allotted equipment, or from existing supplies. Their mission was that of initial break-through, or the elimination of particularly stubborn points of enemy resistance. Each division possessed an armoured group for penetration by attack after the break-through. The advance detachments were made up of reinforced reconnaissance battalions. Upon penetrating, these were to fall out of line and, as far as possible, to reach the Maas by subsidiary routes without giving battle, and to take and hold a bridge. For this purpose, each of them was reinforced with a light battery.

The use of searchlights was demonstrated twice to the commanders of formations and units before the attack. This was done both with and without troops. The demonstrations proved that in favourable weather conditions – if sufficient searchlights were used, the terrain would be adequately illuminated. At this time of the year and in the prevailing weather conditions, the area was barely negotiable. Few roads were available, and at the time of the beginning of the offensive these were single track, in many cases woodland and field tracks. It had to be taken into account that they would be axle-deep in mud, and that the type of vehicle usually at our disposal for such purposes could be made to negotiate it only with difficulty.

Changes to the mission were suggested and on 10 December we received the following revised orders:

- On X-day at 0600 hours, the 1st SS Panzer Corps will break through the enemy positions in the sector Hollerath–Krewinkel with its infantry. It will then thrust to beyond the Maas in the sector Luttich–Huy, with the 12th SS Panzer Division on the right, and the 1st SS Panzer Division on the left. The Corps will so deploy itself as to be able – according to the situation – either to continue the penetration in the direction of Antwerp, or to be prepared for the defence of the right flank.
- Bridges in the sector Maas will be taken in undamaged condition by ruthless and rapid penetration. This will be accomplished by specially organised forward detachments, under the command of suitable officers.
- The following formations will be attached: 277th Volksgrenadier Division, 12th Volksgrenadier Division, 3rd Para Division. After breaking through the enemy's main field of combat, these divisions will be returned to the command of the Army.

Concerning the neighbours of the Corps, it was only known that the LXVII Army Corps – simultaneously – would attack Monschau on the right, and the LXVI Army Corps would attack St Vith on the left, but actual contact with the 1st SS Panzer Corps was not to be kept.

The strength, organisation and further objectives of the neighbouring formations was not known to the Corps. The area of operations for the Corps was determined by the Sixth Panzer Army. The Corps – and under corps command, the divisions – had freedom of movement within this area. Thus, march routes did not have to be rigidly adhered to. Each division had express permission to deviate from prescribed routes whenever the situation demanded, such as weak spots in enemy positions etc.

In order to preserve the mobility of the troops, there were defined limits set on the use of motor transport. Only vehicles used in the battle or for the supplies were permitted. All baggage trucks, etc were left in the concentration area.

At first only the commanding generals and the chief of staff knew of the orders. All detailed orders and instruction had to be worked out by the chief himself. About ten days before the commencement of the attack the Ia (Intelligence Officer) of the Corps was initiated, as well as the divisional commanders and the divisional Ias. The troop commanders were informed about two days beforehand.

A security line was set up about 8km behind the main combat line, which could not be crossed in a forward direction without a special pass signed by the Commanding General. Disadvantages of inaccurate reconnaissance had to be accepted. The troops themselves were only initiated the night before. In order that there should be no leakage of information by prisoners being taken, some of the scout troops were ordered not to operate.

After the departure of the Corps from its last quartering area, radio activity was maintained there at its usual height. In the areas of concentration and preparation, however, there was no radio activity at all.

A movement of troops in small groups was carried out in a northward direction during the day, whereas the actual movement of troops took place at night in a southward direction. To what extent the time chosen was determined by political questions and the general situation, is beyond the scope of my knowledge. Taking everything into consideration, the situation on our side probably made the time chosen the only possible one.

GENERALMAJOR (WAFFEN-SS) FRITZ KRAEMER

We knew that the American forces were weak in the Ardennes and while we did not know of General Patton's plans, we were aware of his concentration of troops in the south. Although for six days prior to the attack we had sent out no patrols for fear that captured members might give away the attack, we knew from our own interrogations that green troops were in the line. We also learned that your 2nd Infantry Division, because of its losses, was to be relieved by a new division.

We did not know anything about the location of your gas dumps, (although after the offensive started we saw fires in the direction of Francorchamps and suspected that you had gas there). Also, we could tell by intercepted radio messages sent by your military police that something was being evacuated from that general area. Your military police orders were very valuable to us all the way through, because by monitoring their broadcasts we could tell what type of unit (although not always the size) was moving where. The military police lacked security; many of their broadcasts were in the clear. We thus mapped out various roads which were being used to send troops to various areas.

The plan of attack

The over-all plan was for Sixth Panzer and Fifth Panzer Armies to fight shoulder to shoulder, moving west. Whichever reached the Meuse was to proceed westward. Because of the possibility of an attack from the north, Sixth Panzer Army was given enough troops to stop such an attack. If Sixth Panzer Army had reached the Meuse first, Fifth Panzer Army would have fought the holding attack in the north. If Sixth Panzer Army was attacked, it would speed the advance of Fifth Panzer Army. The principle was to hold the reigns loose and let the Armies race. The main point was to reach the Meuse, regardless of the flanks. This was the same principle we employed in the French campaign of 1940. My division in Russia employed the same principle, and we got beyond Stalingrad. I never worry about my flanks. I think this is the same principle that General Eisenhower follows. General Montgomery, on the other hand, builds up for a great power attack. I believe, as Clausewitz said: 'The point must form the fist.'

More than 200 searchlights had been assembled under the command of III Flak Corps and night training had been conducted for this manoeuvre. Fog, however prevented their use, and we had no occasion to employ them after the initial attack.

GENERALOBERST JOSEPH 'SEPP' DEITRICH – Sixth Panzer Army

On 12 December 1944 the Führer addressed us at a meeting and said that a winter offensive would be launched. He gave a long speech and said that they had to do something. At that time, however, Hitler did not give the time of the attack. He just said that they would have enough planes and tanks. I told Hitler that I wasn't ready to attack with my Army and that we didn't have the ammunition or fuel to carry it through successfully. The generals were all in a line waiting to speak to Hitler and I only had a minute to tell him this before the line moved on. He said that I would have all I needed.

Army commanders are not consulted very much. All of the higher leaders in the Army knew that I needed more time to get my Army in shape for an attack. The method in the German Army is for plans to come from above, based on reports from below. I knew about the attack too late and couldn't give my best advice to my division commanders. After we knew of the attack, no one dared talk about it for fear of reprisal.

12/13 and 13/14 December

PRIESS: During the nights of the 12/13 and 13/14 all vehicles were ordered strictly to keep to the roads during the forward advance. Movement was not begun until after dark, and by dawn, everything had to be under cover again. Vehicles that had broken down were either towed away or repaired by the fully operational repair and salvage services. Each unit commander was responsible for clearing the roads by dawn. In addition, officers both of the Corps and the Army were delegated to see that this was carried out. Each unit had a 'camouflage officer' whose special duty it was to see that all vehicles were either under cover or camouflaged by daybreak.

JODL: On 13 and 14 December, all army, corps and some division commanders conferred at Ziegenberg. We took aerial photographs and studied the condition of the Meuse bridges. We had to ascertain the location of the existing bridges, determine whether the bridges we had destroyed on our retreat had been rebuilt, and whether auxiliary pontoon bridges, etc, were in use. Bridges were vital to us, and we had to capture them by surprise.

Then, unknown to Model, we brought up two divisions, Führer Begleit and Führer Grenadier Divisions; the former was formed of men from Pz Div *Grossdeutschland* which had provided the guard for Hitler's headquarters. This division was fairly strong; its men had had combat experience and were good soldiers. The second was formed from the replacement unit of *Grossdeutschland*.

Rocket (Werfer) ammunition was saved for the offensive – we had very little. There was a shortage of ammunition for 150mm and 105mm field howitzers. Ammunition, therefore, had to be economised on other fronts. We found that more had been used up, proportionately, on the Eastern Front than on the Western, and we ordered economies in the East and in the sector around Aachen.

DEITRICH: On 13 or 14 December, I was told the attack would be 15 December. I said I couldn't get my troops there in two days, so the attack was postponed one day. At that, my units had to start the attack right from a march.

The general order of attack was for 1st SS Panzer Corps to be the attacking Corps and move towards Stavelot–Stoumont in the general direction of Liège–Huy. I instructed the commanders to secure a bridgehead any place between those two points along the Meuse. They were then to move in the direction St Trend–Hasselt–Antwerp. It was wishful thinking to hope that we could cut the British Armies off from the south.

JODL: Mid-Dec 44 was a very foggy, high-pressure period, and on 13 December an extended period of fog was predicted, broken only about midday. Schuster made the forecast at our Ziegenberg Command Post near Giessen, on 13 December after making meteorological observations. But weather was not really decisive in this offensive, as it was in some others. Of course we would not have attacked in perfectly clear flying weather, but we did not have to be assured of particularly bad weather. We could not have waited much longer, anyway.

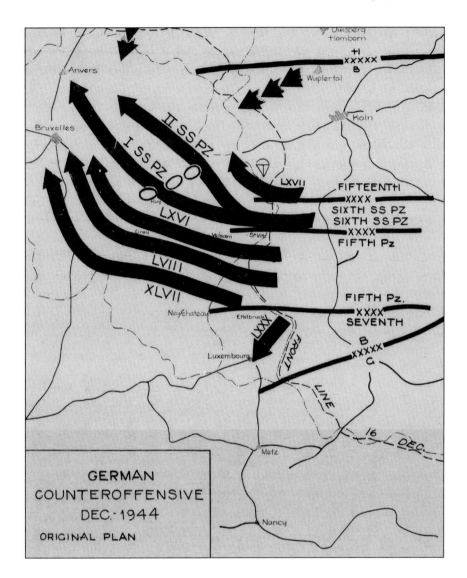

GERMAN
COUNTEROFFENSIVE
DEC.·1944

ORIGINAL PLAN

14 December

ZERBEL: The handing over of the command took place only on 14 December. Till that moment, the time was filled with conferences, map studies and reconnaissance. An order of the Army requested –

a thrust toward the northwest, without consideration of the enemy. Villages, which had a stronger enemy defence, were to be by-passed and later mopped-up by the troops which were following. I broached the subject concerning Bastogne during a map study in the presence of General v. Manteufel at Kyllburg. It was decided that the Panzer-Lehr Division, which would be the first in its sector to approach Bastogne, had to out-flank this town, if the resistance could not be broken rapidly. The 26th Volksgrenadier Division, which was following, was definitely to take Bastogne.

The text of the instruction I gave ran: 'Bastogne must be captured, if necessary from the rear. Otherwise, it will be an "abscess" in the route of advance and tie up too many forces. Bastogne is to be mopped-up first, then the bulk of the Corps continues its advance.'

PRIESS: On 14 December at noon, the Corps took over the command of its attack sector. Assembly and preparation of the artillery had to be completed by 0400 hours on 16 December and at 0300 hours Higher Artillery Command 6 (Harko 6) reported that all artillery preparations had been completed.

The three self-propelled gun battalions which had been promised us for the breakthrough, had not turned up. The motor fuel which had been promised by Genfm Model on 15 Dec 44 had not arrived. It had to be supplied by the II SS Panzer Corps, and the armoured divisions now had at their disposal 1.2 and 1.3 *Verbrauchssaetze* (100km fuel units) respectively.

On the day of attack, the Corps was composed of the following units:

1st SS Panzer Division
12th SS Panzer Division
277 Volksgrenadier Division
12 Volksgrenadier Division
3 Para Division

In addition, the following were attached for the breakthrough:

Harko 6
Arko 502
2 Volks-Artillery Corps
2 Volks-Werfer Brigades
SS Artillery Battalion 502

Motor vehicles were largely overhauled light commercial vehicles, so that there was a shortage of heavy transport. There was a particular shortage of prime movers and two trucks. Part of the light artillery was towed by light motor vehicles.

15 December

BAYERLEIN: The secrecy factors did not hinder the success of the offensive. All the preparations of the division, regiments and battalions moved smoothly. The troops were always prepared for anything (experienced, from their numerous unexpected commitments) and had just come from combat in the Saar. The commanders were all very well trained and ready for anything.

The following replacements were assigned to us up to 15 December:

a) 600 men, but almost all without weapons (more men came later, during the offensive), some 250 from convalescence.
b) 40 tanks and tank destroyers (later a further 15 tank destroyers). Guns: 18 Guns (88mm, 105mm and 150mm) but almost all without prime-movers – special weapons (mortars, machine guns and submachine guns).

Only individual allocations. One whole battalion had no mortars and very few MGs. One tank battalion of the tank regiment was being reorganised in Fallingbostel and equipped with the 'Sperber' (night aiming) device. [We were] 60 per cent of combat strength of troops; 40 per cent of tanks, and Tank Destroyer Battalions (1 battalion missing) 60 per cent of guns, 40 per cent of other weapons. In place of the missing tank battalion the division received: 539 Heavy TD Battalion (with Panther type TDs) 30 per cent equipped at the beginning of the attack; 243 Assault gun battalion, 70 per cent equipped.

Smoke guns and heavy artillery were not supplied; these were controlled by Corps and used principally to support the first attack over the Our.

KOKOTT: During the evening hours of 15 December, the final troop movements took place. It was cold and dark. The narrow paths of the Eifel, some of which were covered with ice, were densely crowded with troops and vehicles which were moving forward to their positions of departure and their firing positions. In spite of efficient traffic control, traffic jams were unavoidable. Efforts were made to drown out the noise of the motors of the heavy prime-movers by artillery harassing fire. After dark, the commanders informed the attack troops of the attack order. The troops accepted it with utmost seriousness. They were fully conscious of their decisive act. They were confident in their ability, their strength and the promise of strong air support as well as the effort by the war industries back home. Attitude and morale of the troops was good.

PRIESS: The morning (15 Dec) amounts of motor fuel were reserved for the attack; 3 fuel units (for 100kms) with vehicles; 2 fuel units (for 100kms) with the supplies; 5 fuel units (for 100kms) altogether.

At 0530 hours, the artillery opened its preparatory fire and the attack itself was at 0600 hours. At about 0730 hours word first arrived from all the divisions that the enemy outpost positions had been taken and the attack was making excellent progress.

On the afternoon of 15 December 1944, the Panzer Divisions had 0.4 and 0.6 *Verbrauchsaetze* (100km fuel units). On urgent requests to Genfm Model, who was at the Corps command post, the Corps received further supplies of motor fuel in the evening, so that on 16 December the Panzer Division had 1.2 and 1.3 *Verbrauchsaetze*. Thus, taking into consideration the difficulties of terrain and route, it was possible to reckon with a range of 60 to 70km

Food supply was available to the troops for seven days, apart from iron rations. The Corps had been told that supplies were assured. But, practically speaking, there was very little fuel and ammunition, either for heavy infantry weapons, or guns. Furthermore, supply and issue deposits were partly east of the Rhine. In view of the enemy air superiority and road conditions, this meant two to three days for delivery. With the issue of fuel promised, the Corps was not dependent on the capture of enemy gasoline depots. But when the armoured divisions found how little fuel they had to go into battle, the Corps *did* hope to come across some supplies of gasoline.

Movement from the rest areas to the areas of concentration was to be completed in a single night. Approach routes were about 80km and 100km respectively. Upon urgent request two nights were then allowed for this operation.

For movement, concentration and munitioning, the artillery – which also included the Panzer Division artillery – had been allowed five nights. This operation was begun on 10 December under command of the army. Each emplaced artillery battalion had counted positions and bridge-sites for three battalions of the reinforcement artillery, as well as surveying and preparing them. Gun positions for the reinforcement artillery had been chosen near roads offering camouflage in order to avoid visible tracks.

A security line was established about 8kms behind the main line of battle, which could only be crossed – even by reconnaissance units – by means of special passes issued by the commanding general. Some of the light artillery was brought up to its gun positions by horse beyond the security line. The remainder – including the heavy artillery – which had to be drawn by tractors, was brought into position during the last two nights. Low-flying aircraft were used to cover the inevitable noise. Ammunition was partly brought forward by horse, and partly carried by hand over the last, short distance.

MANTEUFEL: In order to move our vehicles into position on the night of 15/16 December 1944 we employed a transport regiment of Organisation Todt (OT) on all the roads leading to the attack areas. These OT people helped bring up all the equipment, pulled vehicles out of ditches, towed artillery and other heavy equipment up hills, moved up bridging equipment, and generally assisted us in the area from the autobahn up to the front.

Because we did not know the exact location of the American positions and because your lines were so thinly held, we decided not to have a long artillery barrage along the entire Fifth Panzer Army front. I felt that such a barrage was a World War I concept and completely out of place in the Ardennes, in view of the thinly held lines. We had artillery observers with all the attack companies, and we planned to lay down concentrated fire on known enemy strongpoints. I had a lengthy argument with Hitler concerning the artillery support, because he wanted to have a long barrage lasting until 1100 hours, when the attack would jump off. I finally convinced him that such a plan would merely be an alarm clock to the American forces and would alert them for the daylight attack to follow. I stated that our infantrymen were not of the same calibre as those who had invaded France, and that they did not meet the required standards to achieve a breakthrough in daylight. I pointed out that it was well known to us that American guards or sentries were usually asleep in the early morning hours, and therefore, the time to attack was before daylight.

Hitler agreed to this plan, and we formed assault companies in each division, picked from the best men available. These assault companies were then given additional night training so that they would be prepared for this attack in the dark.

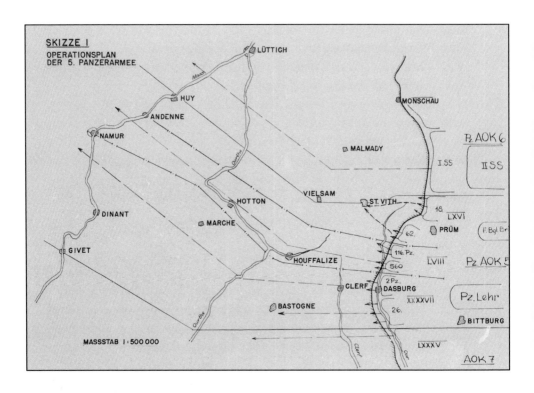

Dietrich (Commander Sixth Panzer Army), on the other hand, employed a heavy artillery concentration for approximately half an hour before his attack. Personally, I think this was a waste of ammunition.

Chapter 3

16–19 December: The Americans in Bastogne

WALTER STAUDINGER – Generalleutnant of the Waffen SS

We had a preparatory fire for one-half hour before the attack, although there were pauses in the firing during this time due to the shortage of ammunition. In all, we planned the following three types of fire for the first day: (1) fire on the main line of resistance, starting about 0500 hours; (2) fire on the command posts, road crossings villages in the neighbourhood of the main line of resistance, and other standpoints, thus cutting (US) lines of communication; and (3) fire on the more distant villages and standpoints, and especially roads on which we thought reserves would be brought up.

I wanted to concentrate the artillery in firing positions to cover the Eisenberg Ridge, where I thought we would encounter the heaviest opposition; however, I was over-ruled and we distributed the artillery almost evenly along the entire Army front.

Only the light battalions of divisional artillery were to move forward with the tank columns. The Corps Artillery was to fire from its positions as long as it could. As many of the large calibre guns required special emplacements, Army Artillery was not to displace until the Meuse River had been reached. Actually, the self-propelled artillery with Pepper task force (1st SS Panzer Division Leibstandarte SS Adolf Hitler) didn't get enough fuel and was recalled. Most of the Volksartillery battalions didn't move forward because of the lack of fuel and also because of the clogged roads. General Model found two or three of these battalions in their original positions and ordered me to court-martial their commanders. When I told him it was because of the fuel shortages and road conditions that they hadn't moved, he rescinded his order. We had sufficient gas for the attack, but it was just too far back. Our general policy was to capture gas and use it wherever possible.

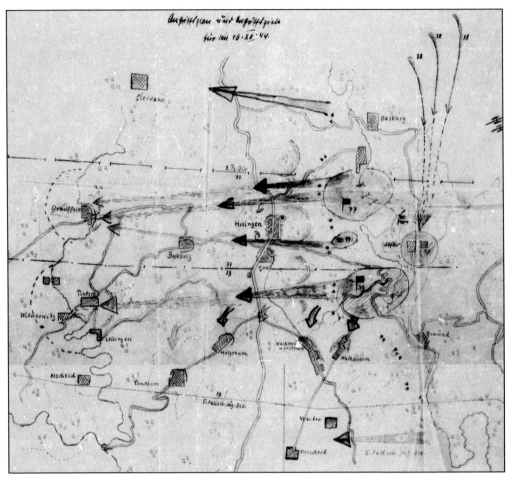

Plan of attack – targets to be attacked, 16 December.

KOKOTT: At 0500 hours on 16 December the elements committed for the attack and for the fire support reported to the division command post that they had completed their assembly. The division was facing the enemy ready to jump off. The front was still quiet. The nocturnal silence was interrupted only by the occasional salvo of an enemy battery or the sound of some individual guns or our own in normal harassing fire.

At 0530 hours suddenly all of the German barrels roared out with a raging fire, the sky vibrated with the glaring lights of the endless firing of anti-aircraft, mortars, howitzers, guns and the high trajectory weapons of the infantry, the infantry guns and heavy mortars. At a rapid rate of fire, the crews released shell after shell from the barrels. The fire was well regulated,

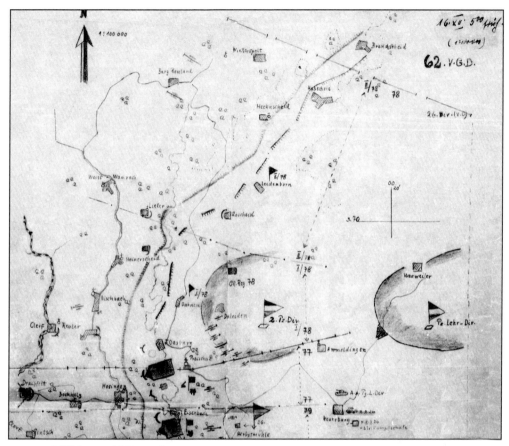

0500 hours, 16 December.

and as the first report soon indicated, its full impact everywhere reached precisely the designated target areas which were being turned upside down and pulverised by this hail of steel. Batteries of large anti-aircraft searchlights turned their beams toward the clouds thus illuminating the combat terrain with a pale white light.

The enemy artillery fire had ceased. One heard only the discharge of our own artillery which blended into one single whirl as well as the uninterrupted whistling and wailing of the trajectories hissing towards the west. The battle had begun.

It became evident already during the morning hours that the enemy, after the initial shock, was beginning to get hold of himself and was making efforts to delay and to stop the German assault with all available means. The day of fighting received its significance through a stubborn and mobile defence alternating with skilful and rapid evading movements as well as counter thrusts – supported by packs of tanks – against the flanks and rear of the pursuing attack groups, but also the occasional holding out to the last round of ammunition of some encircled pockets at important road junctions and defiles.

The (right) Regiment 77, for instance, by noon reported heavy engagements east of Bockholz and slow progress of the attack in the wooded terrain to the south thereof. Later on, the enemy, from the northern direction, conducted some solitary tank thrusts against the right flank and the rear of Grenadier Regiment 77. The regiment repulsed these attacks (several tanks were put out of action) and evading, whenever possible, all enemy pockets of resistance, continued its advance.

US FORCES: On the morning of 16 December, the VIII Corps front, which had been quiet since the latter part of September, suddenly flared up. For more than a month the enemy had been concentrating some twenty-five divisions without disclosing it. At 0500 hours heavy artillery concentrations struck along the entire VIII Corps front and were soon followed by tank and infantry attacks. The strongest attacks were in the north near the V and VIII Corps boundary.

JODL: In Sixth Panzer Army, the first wave was made up of 1st SS Panzer Corps, employing 1st and 12th SS Panzer Divisions; in the second wave was II SS Panzer Corps, committing 2nd and 9th SS Panzer Divisions. In Fifth Panzer Army, there were two divisions in the first wave and only one in the second. No special theory was involved in this arrangement. There were only a few roads along which we could advance, so we had to echelon in depth rather than in width. We had to seize bridgeheads through which we sent our troops. The third wave consisted of several divisions forming an OKW reserve, kept at its disposal.

In general, a period of two days between waves was a maximum. We expected the first wave to reach the Meuse on the first day, or at the latest on 17 December.

ZERBEL: Early morning of 16 Dec the Corps started the attack with infantry only and crossed the Our. The first enemy resistance was broken rapidly, so that the construction of the bridges which was of a particular importance could be started very soon. But the current was so strong that bridging was very difficult, and the bridges were ready at 1500 hours only. Some bicycles and Volkswagens were ferried across the river before that time.

2nd Panzer Division: The division reached rapidly the road Fischbach–Marnach, but Marnach was taken only after commitment of tanks. Urspelt and Reuler had strong occupation. Therefore, the arrival of the tanks which could advance only slowly across the bridge at Dasburg had to be waited for.

26th Volksgrenadier Division: The division advanced well in its sector and reached approximately the line Marnach–Bockholz–Holzthum. Only Hosingen could not be taken on 16 December, therefore it was impossible to bring up the Panzer Lehr Division during the night from 16-17 December past Hosingen. The removal of road obstacles took very much time. At dark the situation of the Corps was as follows: The enemy resistance, except at Hosingen, had not been very strong. Since further troops and tanks would cross the bridges during the night, the Corps calculated that Clerf would not be crossed later than in the evening of 17 December, and that the thrust towards the west could be continued rapidly.

BAYERLEIN: As the attack of 26th Volksgrenadier Division against Drauffelt did not succeed quickly and the American resistance in Hosingen and Rockholz on 16th December could not be crushed, units of Panzer Lehr Division, on orders from higher headquarters, were committed against Holzhum and Consthum to win the Kautenbach bridgehead, and from there to push on to the west. The Panzer Reconnaissance Battalion was committed first and, later, 901 Panzer Grenadier Regiment also was committed. The Panzer Reconnaissance Battalion took Hotzhum, while 901 Panzer Grenadier Regiment attacked Consthum, which was doggedly defended.

LÜTTWITZ XLVII Pz Corps:
On 16 December in the morning, an attack was ordered with 2nd Panzer Division on the right flank, 26th Volksgrenadier Division on the left flank and the Panzer Lehr in reserve. On 17 December Panzer Lehr Division moved in front of 26th Volksgrenadier Division. The engineer units of 26th Volksgrenadier Division had completed the necessary bridging to enable Panzer Lehr Division to break through, and it was hoped to push on to the town with this fast-moving unit.

The northern bridgeheads across the Clerf and the Our rivers had been built by 2 Panzer Division. These were the bridgeheads which controlled the movement of infantry on the Longvilly road. The two lower bridgeheads, built by the 26th Volksgrenadier Division over the same streams, made possible a sweep against the lines of communication south of Bastogne and the attack against the town from that direction.

The dividing line between 2nd Panzer Division and Panzer Lehr Division for the attack against Bastogne was on an east to west line about halfway between Noville and Bastogne. The objective of 2nd Panzer Division was the same road junction at Habiémont (northwest of Bastogne towards Tenneville) where 101st and 82nd Airborne Divisions had turned away from each other.

The mission of Panzer Lehr Division was to take Bastogne from the south. This was the initial plan contained in the original order for the Ardennes attack. The 2nd Panzer Division was moving fast. It had met heavy resistance in Clervaux from elements of the US 28th Infantry Division, but without further contact with the enemy it moved along rapidly to a point on the Longvilly Road.

On 12 December the Corps Commander had issued this order to his division:

'Bastogne must be taken eventually from the rear. If it is not taken, it will always remain an ulcer in our lines of communication, and for this reason it will contain too many forces. Therefore, first clear out the whole of Bastogne and then "march on"'.

The northernmost infantry regiment of 26th Volksgrenadier Division had orders after going through Longvilly to proceed through Foy towards Longchamps and it was elements of this division engaged in this movement which got into 505 Parachute Infantry Regiment's rear at Foy and threatened to split 506 and 501 Parachute Infantry Regiments along the railroad track.

At the road crossing immediately east of Allerborn (southwest of Noville), there was a panzer fight lasting about one hour with heavy losses to American armour. When this engagement terminated, 2nd Panzer Division again moved rapidly on to Bourcy, just east of Noville. It met resistance from the Bourcy roadblock and there swung around to the north-east of Noville with the intention of bypassing the heavy resistance there and getting over to Bertogne, which was on the road to the objective at Herbaimont. This decision however, was reached after it had made two heavy thrusts at Noville and had been turned back with losses as indicated in the American reports.

The orders called for 2nd Panzer Division to take Noville under any circumstances, as fast as possible, and it was the troops of that division who carried the attack throughout. The attacks of the two divisions had not been coordinated. Although each division was supposed to proceed with its divisional zone and the faster it moved the better, they were in radio communication at all times, and each division knew what the other was doing. In this phase of the attack they could not change the plan. Before they attacked, it was pretty clear that Bastogne would be difficult to take.

The point of 2nd Panzer Divison was at Noville, with the remaining elements of the division strung out along the road through Bourcy and back to the northwest of Allerborn. At this time, the Corps Commander got word that strong American armoured forces were moving from Bourcy to Longvilly and, therefore, were threatening his flank.

The forward elements of 26th Volksgrenadier Division were at this moment on Hill 499 southwest of Longvilly. The 2nd Panzer Division brought up its anti-tank battalion and stationed it so as to block the road at 64-65. At the same time, the anti-tank battalion of Panzer Lehr Division was pushed through 26th Volksgrenadier Division which took up positions on Hill 499. Also, at the same time, all of the artillery of 26th Volksgrenadier Division was ordered to fire on the area west of Longvilly, where the American armour had become entangled.

During the night, Panzer Lehr Division got on a country road to Margeret. The point of the division got to Neffe early in the morning and reduced the roadblock. When Panzer Lehr Division came to a halt in front of the Chateau Neffe, a regiment of 4th Grenadier Division was ordered to go immediately from Bizory to Bastogne. It thus was deployed in a manner which put its line directly against the deployed American infantry lines (101st Airborne Division).

When this combat team was stopped in the north, another combat team from Panzer Lehr Division was sent southward against Wardin and Marvie with the mission of getting to Bastogne. This combat team was brought to a stop about ½km southeast of Marvie. From this time on we were stopped on this line.

US FORCES: The infantry-tank attack on the north flank of the Corps began at 0800 hours and in three hours the enemy had penetrated the 14th Cavalry Group positions by 4km. Group reserves were committed and the 106th Division put out flank protection to the north. Through the right of the 106th Division the enemy advanced 2km rapidly but then as reserves were brought up their progress was slowed. The German gains threatened to isolate two regiments of the 106th Division. Captured documents showed that on this day the enemy hoped to take St Vith. This they did not do.

Against the 28th Infantry the enemy used two panzer divisions, three infantry divisions and one parachute division in an infantry attack on the 'Ridge Road' just west of the Our river. In operation, two enemy divisions assaulted each regiment. In the centre and right of the division the enemy advanced up to 7km and crossed the north-south highway at several points. In the southern part of the VIII Corps the 9th Armoured and the 4th Infantry Division were also attacked by the enemy. These attacks were diversionary in nature to prevent the shifting of troops to the north.

At the start of the German offensive VIII Corps reserves consisted of an armoured combat command and four battalions of combat engineers. The engineers were assembled during the first morning, and as the seriousness of the enemy thrust became apparent, additional troops were made available. In the north on the 17th, CCB of the 9th Armoured Division was released from V Corps and the 7th Armoured Division and ordered to close in an assembly area near St Vith. In the south 10th Armoured Division was moved toward an assembly area near Luxembourg. Orders were also issued to move the 101st and 82nd Airborne Divisions to the threatened area.

From captured documents and from the direction of early thrusts it became evident to Corps that the objective of the attack was Liège and possibly Namur. The number of divisions identified indicated that the enemy needed a system of roads greater than those in the area under immediate threat. To prevent the enemy from securing the road networks a Corps defensive plan of two parts was selected. The first phase was to cause a maximum delay by defending in place along the original line of the Corps. The Corps realised that both the extensive front and small reserves might not allow this phase to last very long.

The second phase of the defence was to deny the vital road networks to the enemy by building strong defences in front of St Vith, Houffalize, Bastogne and Luxembourg as rapidly as possible. Prompt assistance from the First and Third Armies would build up the defence of St Vith and Luxembourg; the attachment of two airborne divisions would make the defence of Bastogne and Houffalize possible. Unfortunately, no troops were ever made available to defend Houffalize.

Achieving considerable success in the first attacks, they obtained a breakthrough, penetrated 65 miles into Allied territory, halted the Allied offensive then going on, and threatened the entire front in the west. The failure of the enemy drive was due in part to American resistance at St Vith and Bastogne. At that time three American armies, forming the Twelfth US Army Group, were in position on the central portion of the western front. The First and Third US Armies were located along the Siegfried Line while the Ninth US Army was facing the Roer River in Germany. All three armies were heading for the Rhine over difficult terrain, across swollen rivers, and against determined enemy resistance. Except in the Aachen sector, where an advance was made to the Roer, the line did not move during October and November.

The Third Army fought near Metz, the First and Ninth Armies made the advance farther north, near Aachen. Between these two major efforts an extensive line of defence was maintained by the First Army; of this line the southern and major part was maintained by the VIII US Corps. Under the command of Major General Troy H. Middleton, VIII Corps had its headquarters in Bastogne, Belgium, and extended to Loshein, Germany, to a point where the Moselle River crosses the Franco-German border. Generally parallel to the German frontier along eastern Belgium and Luxembourg, it comprises a front of 88 miles. This section of the country, the Ardennes, has rugged hills, characterised by high plateaux, deeply incised valleys and a restricted road network. The mission which First Army gave VIII Corps was to defend this line in place.

New divisions were brought into this part of the front for battle indoctrination and battle-worn divisions were sent to the corps for re-equipment and rest. As divisions were rotated into the sector, they took over existing wire networks and other facilities. At the beginning of the German attack in December, the VIII Corps front was held by two battle-weary divisions: a green infantry division, part of a green armoured division, and a cavalry group. The battle-tested divisions were the 4th Infantry Division, which in November had fought a costly action through the Hürtgen Forest below Düren, Germany, and the 28th Infantry Division, which had sustained heavy casualties in the

Major General Troy H. Middleton in a jeep.

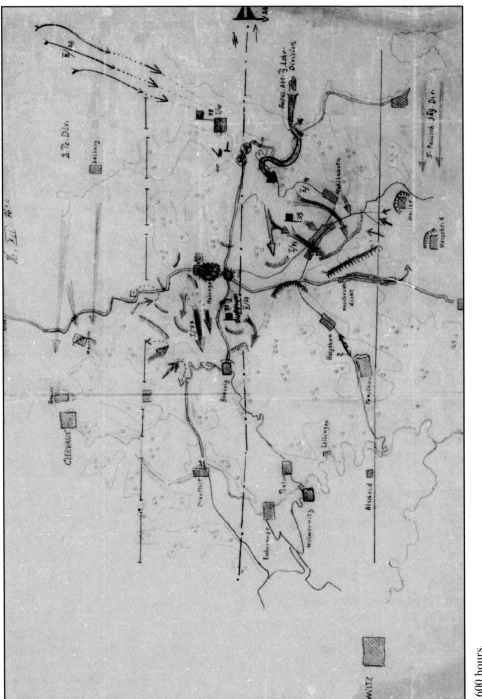

1600 hours.

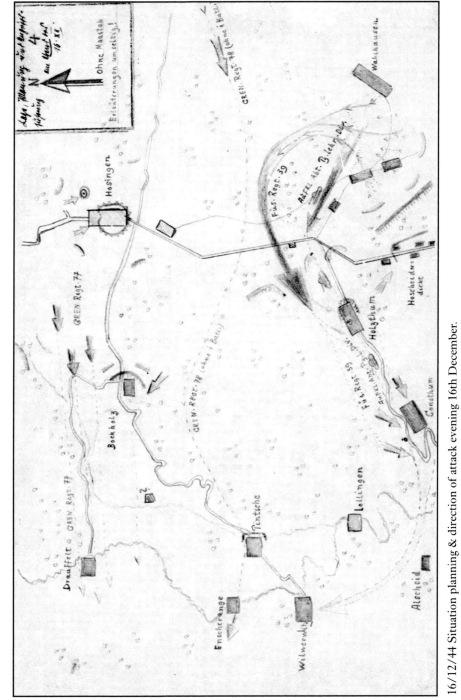

16/12/44 Situation planning & direction of attack evening 16th December.

First Army drive to the Roer. The 106th Infantry Division, newly arrived on the continent, entered the Corps line four days before the offensive began. The 14th Cavalry Group, consisting of the 18th and 32rd Can. Sqs, held the north flank of VIII Corps, and the 9th Armoured Division, minus CCB White, was with V Corps, and had the majority of its units attached to the divisions.

The enemy facing VIII Corps was estimated at four divisions. From north to south these were the 18th, 26th, 352nd and 212th. Early in December the 28th Division took prisoners and reaffirmed the presence of the 26th and 352nd Divisions, but the rumours of one or more panzer units in the rear of the German infantry divisions was not confirmed. From 12 December on the American outposts along the VIII Corps front heard sounds indicative of a great volume of vehicular motion behind the enemy lines.

KOKOTT: At the end of the first day of the attack, the objectives contemplated by the Army and aimed for by the troops were reached everywhere. On the evening of 16 December, the division had lost about 230 men and 8 officers.

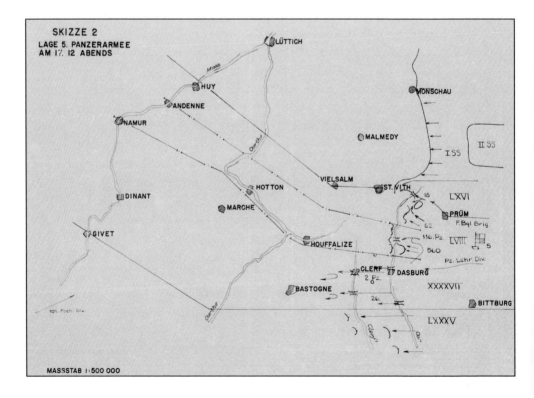

17 December

PRIESS: Despite the fact that the 12th SS Panzer Division and the 12th Volksgrenadier Division had thrown themselves forward recklessly, they had not succeeded by the 17 December in clearing the important road Bullingen–Malmedy. The enemy had received considerable reinforcements in this sector during the previous night. Nor had it gone any better with the neighbouring corps on the left; they had not succeeded in taking St Vith, so that the corps had nothing but the one-way, and in some spots very bad, road between Heeresbach and Heppenbach at their disposal and this had resulted in roadblocks. News coming in and the results of our own reconnoitring had shown that the roads were in bad condition and were also mined in spots and also blocked by obstacles. The fields on either side were deep in mud, so that it was out of the question for our wheeled traffic to take to them. It was therefore a matter of vital importance for the corps to free the road from Bullingen to Malmedy in order to regain a certain degree of mobility.

LÜTTWITZ XLVII Pz Corps: On 17 December we had intercepted a radio message to the effect that the 101st Airborne Division was ordered to Bastogne in a fast, motorised march. I personally heard this message and was trying to get into Bastogne before the 101st Airborne Division got there.

ZERBEL: 2nd Panzer Division: During the whole day, the division was engaged in heavy fighting. Upspelt and Reuler changed hands twice on this day. However, in the afternoon, the battalion at Monschau succeeded in crossing the Clerf near the station of Clervaux and penetrating the city from the north. Shortly after, at about 1700 hours, it was possible to take the big overpass at the south end of the town which remained undamaged.

The 26th Volksgrenadier Division: The division succeeded after heavy losses to take Hosingen at noon and during the night at Drauffelt; 22 officers and 400 enlisted men were taken prisoner at Hosingen.

Panzer-Lehr Division: This division was moving up. Before the 26th Volksgrenadier Division had built the bridgehead at Drauffelt, a message of the Army arrived, announcing that the 5th Para Division had succeeded in building a bridgehead at Krautenbach. The Panzer Lehr Division immediately was given orders to advance past Krautenbach and not past Drauffelt, as had been planned. The reconnaissance detachment, marching

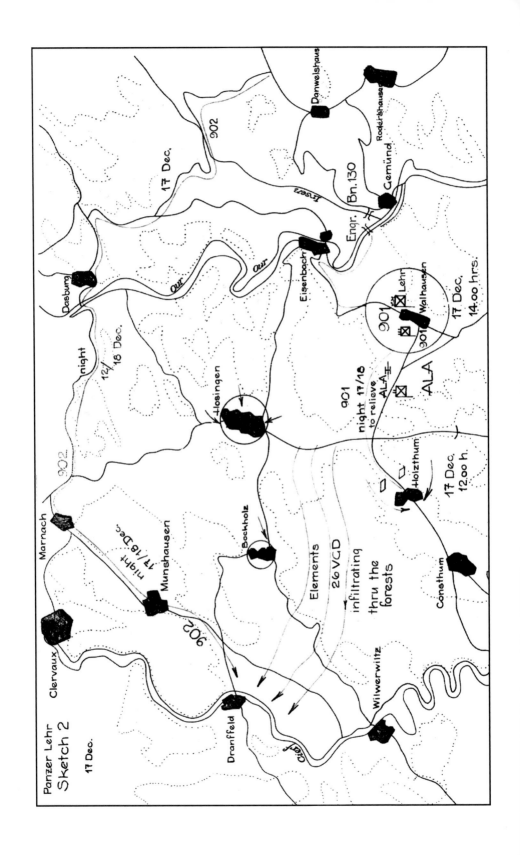

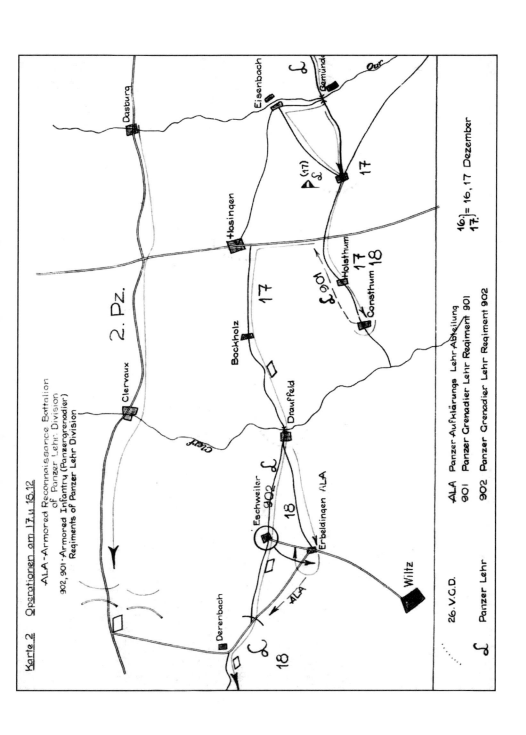

Karte 2 Operationen am 17. u 18.12

ALA - Armored Reconnaissance Battalion
of Panzer Lehr Division

902, 901 - Armored Infantry (Panzergrenadier)
Regiments of Panzer Lehr Division

26. V.G.D.

ALA   Panzer-Aufklärungs Lehr Abteilung
901   Panzer Grenadier Lehr Regiment 901
902   Panzer Grenadier Lehr Regiment 902

Panzer Lehr

16.] = 16,17 Dezember
17.]

in advance, met upon strong enemy forces at Kosthum, which could be repulsed only in the evening. During that time, the bridgehead at Drauffelt was built, which was used later by the Panzer Lehr Division.

KOKOTT: Early on the morning of 17 December, the following reports came in:

Right: Grenadier Regiment 77: 'Bockholz captured. Continued attack against enemy south of Munshausen and heights 1km northwest of Bockholz.'

Central: Grenadier Regiment 78: 'Advance elements of 1st Battalion moving forwards against decreased enemy resistance southeast of Bockholz – direction of Pintsche. Contact to the right, Grenadier Regiment 77, established.'

Left: 'Holzthum captured. Fighting near Consthum.' Regiment 77 and *Kampfgruppe Kaufmann* reported having taken prisoners and the destruction of tanks.

ZERBEL: At dusk, the situation of the Corps was as follows: The important crossings of Clerf and Draufelt were in German hands. Obstructed roads caused great difficulties, but there was much hope, that in the evening of 18 December the road Houffalize–Bastogne could be crossed. All divisions were instructed to advance with the greatest rapidity, especially, because it was known from an intercepted American radio message, that the 101st Airborne Division situated near Reims was on the alert, and that according to the calculations of the Corps it would probably arrive in the evening of 18 December at Bastogne. Who would be the first to reach Bastogne?

BAYERLEIN: Map 2 gives the attack of the 26th Volksgrenadier Division on the front in the sector Eisenbach–Gemünden. Mission: Formation of bridgeheads, first over the Our near Gemünden (bridge) on the line Hosingen–Wahlhausen, then over the Clerf near Drauffeld. After the creating of the bridgeheads, an attack of Panzer Lehr through the Drauffeld bridgehead towards Bastogne.

Support of the first attack of the 26th Volksgrenadier Division through artillery of the 26th and of the Panzer Lehr which was reinforced by further artillery and smoke-guns from Corps. Strong artillery fire was wasted, however, as it could not be exploited by the infantry of the 26th Volksgrenadier Division which was too far off. Bridge-construction near Gemünden by Lehr Engineer Battalion.

Course of battle: Wahlhausen was taken but an attack on Hosingen failed. Parts of Panzer Lehr were brought up and the reconnaissance battalion had to be thrown in to support the 26th Volksgrenadier Division. It was flung against Wahlhausen Colony and Holzthrun, reinforced by one tank company and one battery of 105mm guns. In the night of 16/17 December the 901 Panzer Grenadier Regiment was brought up and was committed at Consthum, where the attack was doing badly. The Lehr Reconnaissance Battalion was pulled out so that it might be committed for the thrust against Bastogne, which was to be captured by *coup-de-main*.

The 902 Panzer Grenadier Regiment was brought forward across the Dasburg bridge in the sector of the 2nd Panzer Division. The 26th Volksgrenadier Division succeeded in capturing Drauffeld on 17 December 44. On orders from higher headquarters, the attack of 901 Panzer Grenadier Regiment was immediately discontinued, and the Regiment also moved through the Drauffelt bridgehead in order that a divisional attack could be launched against Bastogne.

Consequently, the stubborn resistance in Consthum was not the first, but the second reason for giving up this plan. In general, the plan was to thrust forward where it could be done quickest and easiest, and to commit our troops at the first point we succeeded in establishing a bridgehead over the Clerf.

In my opinion the following points were already decisive for the unfavourable development of the offensive:

1) Premature employment of the ALA and Panzer Grenadier Regiment 901 in engagements with heavy casualties, so 901 was not available in time for Bastogne.
2) Long resistance of US troops at Hoesingen, which was not attacked with sufficient energy by the 26th Volksgrenadier Division on 16 December. So Panzer Lehr crossed the Drauffeld bridge too late and arrived too late in the Bastogne area. That was decisive for the battle of Bastogne. It was then a question of only a few hours. When the advanced troops of Panzer Lehr arrived at Bastogne – they were not strong enough to break the resistance, which had just been built up.

The 901 Panzer Grenadier Regiment was committed near Consthum, which was taken in the afternoon. The Lehr Reconnaissance Battalion attacked on Erpeldange; 902 Panzer Grenadier Regiment attacked via Drauffeld (on the Clerf) against Eschweiler, Derenbach, Neider Wampach.

MANTEUFEL: I wanted to take St Vith on 17 December. Although I had expected that Bastogne would be defended, I did not think the Americans would be able to defend St Vith. I had assigned LXVI Infantry Corps the task of capturing St Vith, with the exception of its several attached panzer battalions. I did not feel that the area around St Vith would be suitable for tanks, and my idea was that LXVI Inf. Corps would 'eat' its way through, slowly clearing out resistance.

BÜCHS: When Manteuffel broke through and bypassed Bastogne, then the question of what to do about Bastogne arose for the first time. Should he use parts of the divisions in the first wave to take Bastogne or not? He decided to go on and try to secure bridges between Namur and Dinant.

MANTEUFEL: By the night of 17 December our troops were in front of St Vith, and on the evening of 18 December, I ordered the final attack on St Vith, which was to begin at 1000 hours on 19 December. However, LXVI Inf. Corps was not composed of our best troops; 62nd Volksgrenadier Division was an especially poor unit and did not seem to be able to organise itself for the attack, because of a lack of leadership at all levels.

My first order to 62nd Volksgrenadier Division was to move on St Vith by the shortest route, but when it was apparent that the division was moving too slowly, I ordered it to hit just to the south of St Vith. We wanted St Vith very badly; in fact, it was vital to us in the first days of the attack. If St Vith had fallen earlier, we would have been able to move on much more rapidly and very probably would have been able to aid Sixth Panzer Army, by preventing the American forces from forming a defence line along the Amblève and Salm Rivers. St Vith was much more important than Bastogne at that time, and those four days of waiting in front of St Vith were of great disadvantage to Dietrich, on our right.

My original plan was to move Panzer Lehr Division through Bastogne, if Bayerlein (Genlt, Cmdr of Pz Lehr Division) could reach that town before your expected reinforcements arrived. However, when we discovered your 101st Airborne Division there, I told Bayerlein to move south of Bastogne and not attempt to attack it, because we had OKW reserves coming along behind who could take the town.

US FORCES: Orders were received by the Third Army from 12th Army Group on the 16th directing the 10th Armoured Division to be temporarily attached to VIII Corps, First Army, to counter a serious attempt at a breakthrough on the part of the enemy.

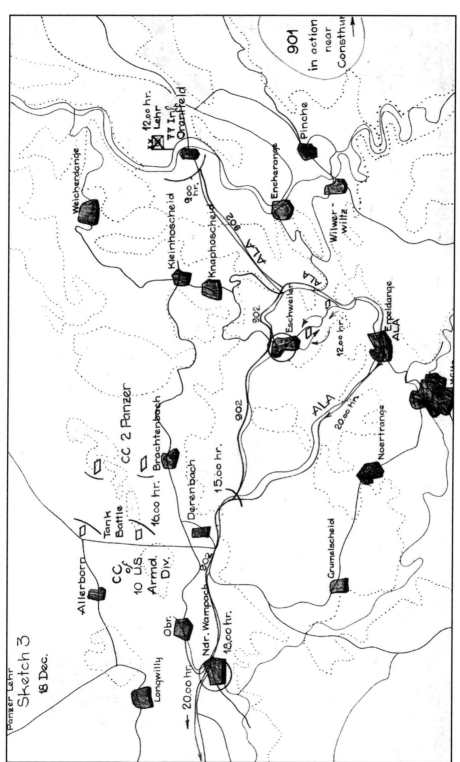

BAYERLEIN: 2000 hours Neiderwampach reached without resistance.

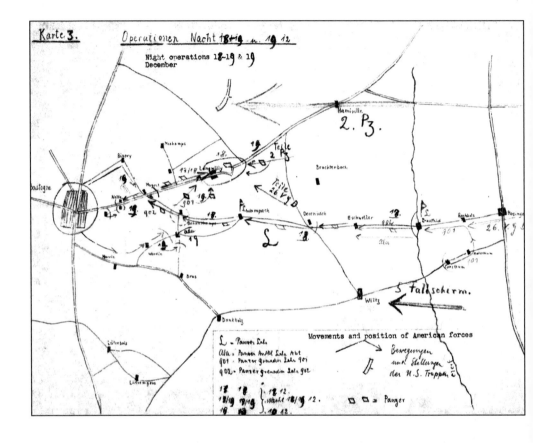

At 1320 hours on 17 December, in compliance with the order, CCV, 10th Armoured Division, took its first step towards Bastogne when it moved from a rest area at Remeling, France, to the vicinity of Merl, Luxembourg. That evening at 2030 hours the 101st Airborne Division, which was then re-outfitting in a training area at Camp Mourmelon (near Reims, France) received telephone orders from Headquarters XVIII Airborne Corps that it was to go to Bastogne.

The enemy increased the pressure along the entire front, especially in the north. The V Corps' right flank was forced back and in the VIII Corps, infantry and armour had by 0900 hours cut off two regiments of the 106th Division. To stem the advance on St Vith the 168th Engineer Combat Battalion fought a

McAuliffe.

delaying action north and east of that town, CCV, 9th Armoured Division, was put into the line and the 7th Armoured Division was committed piecemeal as it arrived in the evening.

In the 28th Division sector the Germans began their attacks early and made large gains. The left flank was forced to withdraw to the west bank of the Our River and the right was pushed back an additional 2 to 6km. But it was in the centre of the division, where one salient of 13km and another of 10km existed, that the enemy made their largest gains. Everywhere the American withdrawal had been 7km to 10km kilometres. At some points the enemy was within 18km of Bastogne.

On the southern flank of VIII Corps the 4th Infantry Division defended against strong attacks, but the enemy did not make the effort here that they did further north. The 10th Armoured Division reached the Luxembourg area in time to assure its defence.

At Camp Mourmelon, 101st Division was short of many of its soldiers who were on leave in Paris. The Division Commander was in the United States. The Assistant Division Commander was giving a lecture in England on the airborne operation in Holland. The Artillery Commander, Brigadier General Anthony C. McAuliffe, got the division staff together at 2100 hours on 17 December and outlined the prospect in these words, 'All I know of the situation is that there has been a breakthrough and we have got to get up there.' He directed the division to move out in combat teams without waiting for the men on pass.

Ten minutes after the advance party had left Mourmelon, McAuliffe started for Werbomont, taking with him his G-3, Lt. Col. H.W.O. Kinnard, and his aide, 1st Lt. Frederic D. Starrett. They drove as rapidly as they could, passing many elements of the 82nd Airborne Division along the route. At Neufchateau, General McAuliffe was informed by VIII Corps that the division was attached to VIII Corps at Bastogne. Officer guides were left in the town to see that the column received the new route. On reaching Bastogne at 1600 hours, McAuliffe's party went directly to the command post of VIII Corps, which was located in the former German barracks at the western edge of town and reported to General Middleton.

At that same moment Colonel Roberts, who had arrived ahead of his column, presented himself to Middleton and reported that Combat Command B was on the road and would soon be in Bastogne. Middleton asked Roberts, 'How many teams can you make up?' Roberts replied, 'Three.' The general then said, 'You will move without delay in three teams to these positions and counter enemy threats. One team will go to the southeast of Wardin, one team to the vicinity of Longvilly and one team to the vicinity of Noville. Move with the utmost speed. Hold these positions at all costs.'

Robert accepted the order without demur through at that moment he believed that the distribution of his force over so great an area would make it ineffective. But he made the mental reservation that the Corps Commander must know the situation much better than himself. Middleton's decision was the initial tactical step which lead finally to the saving of Bastogne. CCB continued on its way moving north and east to carry out its orders.

While McAuliffe and his party were on the road, at Mourmelon the division was working with the problems of the move. The few hours before the division began its march were utilised in preparation for departure and in partly providing those combat supplies which had been lost in Holland. Such things as mortars, rifle ammunition, entrenching tools, Arctic overshoes, blankets and gas masks were far below requirements.

In the great emergency, Transportation Corps and Oise Base Section acted with utmost dispatch and rallied truck groups from Rouen and Paris. Many of the truckers had already been long on the road when they were ordered to Mourmelon. They were intercepted, unloaded on the spot, and directed to their new destination. The first trucks arrived at 0900 hours. The last of the 380 trucks needed for the movement of 11,000 men arrived at the camp at 1720 hours. At 2000 hours, eleven hours after the arrival of the first vehicles the last man was outloaded. As far as Bouillon, Belgium, the column ran with lights blazing. It was a calculated risk taken by the 101st for the sake of speed. The night was clear and the stars shone brightly. Had the Luftwaffe come on then, the story of Bastogne might have taken a different turn.

In Bastogne, Middleton sketched the situation to McAuliffe and Kinnard very roughly, telling them, 'There has been a major penetration ...' and '... certain of my units, especially the 106th and 28th Divisions, are broken.'

In the absence of the advance party Kinnard tried to function as an entire division staff during the conference. But after discussing matters with both the G-2 and G-3 sections at Corps, he had only the vaguest picture of what was happening and felt altogether uncertain about both the friendly and enemy situations. He gathered that some armoured elements – the 9th Armoured Division and 10th Armoured Division were mentioned – were out in front of Bastogne, but he could not pinpoint where their roadblocks were located. Because of their own uncertainty, both he and McAuliffe became acutely concerned over plans for the night bivouac. Further than that, they worried that the column might be hit while it was still on the road or that it might even be caught by the German air force while far back.

While the light remained, they took a quick swing out over the area west of town and McAuliffe pointed out to Kinnard where he wanted the division placed. It was a snap decision, yet it importantly influenced the campaign because it placed the division in a sheltered forward assembly area until it was ready to strike. In the emergency Kinnard grabbed an MP private from Corps and sent him to the crossroads at Sprint to meet the division as it came on. He and McAuliffe then went to the junction of the Arlon and Neufchateau roads in Bastogne to make another attempt to find the advance party.

Kinnard had with him nine 1:100,000 and six 1;50,000 maps of the area. This was all that the Corps staff could give him to fight the operation. When he returned from the reconnaissance, Kinnard searched at Corps for more maps but found that the map section was already moving out. From Corps he obtained an administrative order telling the location of ammunition dumps, water points, evacuation hospitals and other installations.

At this time two officers from 502nd Regiment, who were supposed to have accompanied the advance party but had fortunately missed it, showed up at Corps headquarters. They joined Kinnard and Starrett and drove west to Mande-Saint-Étienne. Here they met a jeep load of 327th Regiment officers who had also missed the advance party. Kinnard now had enough personnel to set up the assembly area. An officer guide was posted on the Mande-Saint-Étienne road to direct the incoming column and Starrett went to work setting up a division CP in a nearby farmhouse. The remaining officers reconnoitred their regimental area and made their plans for the night dispositions. The hour was a little after 1800 hours and there was not yet any sound of combat in the vicinity. A heavy maintenance company from 28th Division was already in Mande-Saint-Étienne. The commander told Kinnard this was his area and he would not leave.

Kinnard had to return to Bastogne to get an order from the Corps Commander to clear the area. Around General Middleton in the Corps CP there were now only six or eight officers. Major General Matthew B. Ridgway, the Commander of XVIII Airborne Corps, came to VIII Corps Headquarters about 2030 hours. Ridgway and Middleton were each under the impression that his Corps was responsible for the 101st. They called First Army Headquarters and were told that the division would operate under VIII Corps. McAuliffe decided to stay at Corps to get his mission for the next day. During the conference of the corps commanders, Brigadier General Gerald J. Higgins, Assistant Division Commander of the 101st, who had been called from England by McAuliffe, arrived. Higgins and Kinnard went out to the division assembly area. Lt. Starrett had found that the local school house was a better CP than the dwelling which Kinnard had designated and on his own initiative had made the change. He already had telephone lines strung to Corps and to 501st Regiment. An officer from the 506th Regiment who had missed the advance party reported at the CP and was given his sector. Things were now beginning to look a little more snug.

That night in Bastogne was quiet, largely because the 28th Infantry Division was holding on, commanding ground around Wiltz and fighting the enemy off for a few vital hours. Many stragglers were falling back through the town and the roads were jammed to the south and west. No attempt was made to hold any of these men at the time.

Corps was busy with its evacuation and CCV and 101st were engrossed in their own problems. Colonel Roberts, who had set up his CP in Hotel Lebrun at 1800 hours, found that it was difficult to persuade the organisations who were about to withdraw to give up their motor parks so that he could get his own vehicles off the streets.

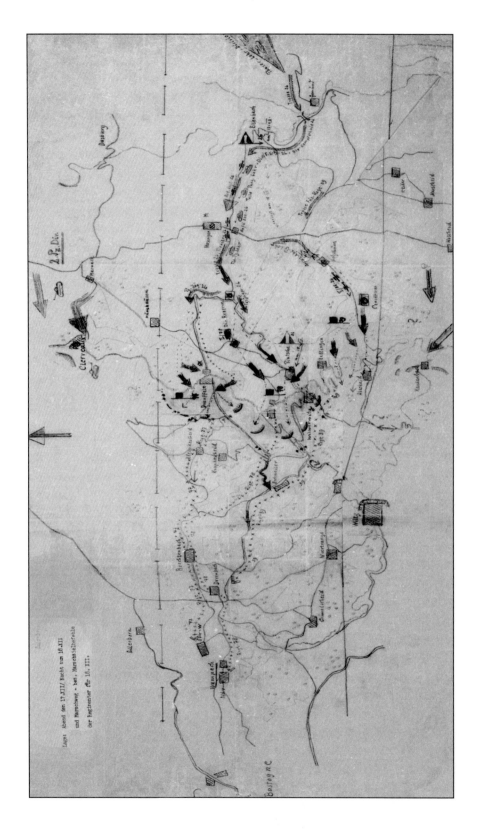

Lage: Abend den 17.XII./ Nacht zum 18.XII und Marschbefehl - bez., Marschteilbefehle der Regimenter für 18.XII.

18 December

WAGENER: The enemy had occupied Bastogne and crossings over the Our and would probably soon open counterattacks against both flank armies. It was reported that forces had been withdrawn from the Third American armies and were being shifted north. Enemy air activities against railroads and villages were increasing in rear areas.

Sixth Panzer Army had been able to thrust as far as Trois Ponts, despite weak advance guards; in all other sectors it gained no ground whatsoever. The right flank of Seventh Army was still alongside XXXXVII Panzer Crops; however, developments on its left flank were causing the army anxiety.

The Fifth Panzer Army ordered the LXVI Army Corps to go on to take St Vith. The XLVII Panzer Corps received the mission to attack Bastogne only if opportunity offered favourable conditions, otherwise it was to push past it further to the west.

The LVIII Panzer Corps was exhorted to speed things up as much as possible. The Volks Artillery Corps and Werfer Brigade were placed under the immediate command of the Army, since they were not able to keep up with the Corps, lacking as they did the necessary fuel and towing vehicles. Their vehicles were mostly used to move anti-aircraft guns, bridging equipment and to supplement the supply columns. The military bridges over the Our were replaced by emergency bridges.

ZERBEL: At Clervaux, some pockets of resistance continued to defend themselves till the late afternoon, so that the passage through this town was only possible with armoured vehicles. The division advanced with two combat teams (*Kampfgruppe*), met upon weak enemy resistance only (American 9th Armoured Division) and reached Hamiville as night fell. At midnight, the division, at the road crossing at 1km each of Allerborn, met upon a strong enemy armoured group, which was assembling. It was almost entirely destroyed (more than 20 tanks were put out of action).

The 26 Volksgrenadier Division: The division was advancing with two regiments past Drauffelt in the direction of Over-Wampach. The third regiment screened toward the south. The advance part of the Dive (reconnaissance detachment) reached Over-Wampach at about 2000 hours.

Panzer-Lehr Division: The division crossed the Clerf at Drauffelt in the morning, and meeting weak enemy resistance, reached Niederwampach at about 2000 hours. From there, the division advanced on the almost impassable road past Benonchamps on Mageret.

At dark the position of the Corps was as follows: All divisions advanced well. Strong enemy resistance was met in no place, new enemy forces had not yet arrived. The message, announcing that the road Houffalize–Bastogne was reached, was expected from hour to hour.

BAYERLEIN: In the morning of 18 December the bridgehead at Drauffeld was established. The commander of the division took over the command of this Task Force. At the road fork, 3km southeast of Derenbach there was an engagement with US Panzers who were located behind an abatis.

Advancing south of Derenbach–Schimpach, one could notice a heavy Panzer battle in the area of Brachtenbach and north of it. (2 Panzer IV against a Combat Company Reconnaissance of the US 9th Armoured Division). Only a few kilometres away Panzer Lehr, with their barrels turned northwards, passed by this impressive spectacle, in the twilight which, cut by the tracer bullets of the Panzers, took on a fantastic aspect. The enemy did not notice us and we reached Neiderwampach unmolested at 1800 hours.

Decision to attack Bastogne: the question was, which way to choose: via Benonchamps–Mageret or Bras–Marvie. The corps recommended the southern way but did not order it. The road via Benonchamps was ascertained as usable by our own reconnaissance and by statement of inhabitants. Moreover, it was the shorter way and the enemy probably did not expect the Germans to come by this side road. (This was confirmed later). For these reasons I decided to choose this way. During the night, however, the way got worse and worse because it was not paved and the constant rainfall softened it. Bringing up the bulk of the division was delayed by some hours.

We dwelt at such length on the question of the choice of the road because the timetable in the first days of the Bastogne battle was decisive. To use that road delayed the movements of Panzer Lehr so that the 101st Airborne arrived by some 1-2 hours ahead of the first parts of Panzer Lehr east of Bastogne. But in my opinion the 26th Volksgrenadier Division was to blame for the delay, because it took too long to capture the bridgeheads; the 47th Panzer Corps, too, because it committed parts of Panzer Lehr, contrary to all original plans, east of the Clerf – completely shattered as they were – so that Panzer Lehr was unable to reach the area of Bastogne on time and in sufficient strength.

US FORCES: The third day of the offensive; the enemy increased the momentum of his drive in the centre of VIII Corps. The Corps' north flank was bolstered by the arrival of the 7th Armoured Division but remained extremely critical because of the deep penetrations in the V Corps sector. But the weight against the 28th Division was so overwhelming that its thin defences disintegrated and the enemy achieved a breakthrough.

101st: An advance party was set up to precede the division to Bastogne. In the party was a representative from each major unit and a company of engineers who were to be used as guides to lead the combat teams into their Bastogne assembly areas. Just as the advance party was pulling away from Camp Mourmelon at noon of the 18th, the Acting Chief of Staff of the Division, Lt. Col. Ned D. Moore, ran out of the CP and told the party that XVIII Corps was to handle the operation, that they should go to a rendezvous with XVIII Corps at the crossroads in Werbomont, 30 miles north of their original destination. This they did. It was an error that might have been fatal through in the end it cost nothing. The right flank, which had pulled back across the Our River the previous night, was unable to stabilise its lines. In the withdrawal a wide gap was created through which the enemy pushed a great deal of armour. In the centre enemy thrusts between strongpoints encircled companies and destroyed or captured them one by one. To division the picture was obscure throughout the day because of lost communications, but the appearance of many enemy columns behind the regimental sectors and the tragic tales of stragglers indicated a complete disintegration of regimental defences. The 28th Division command post was itself attacked when the enemy approached Wiltz. The 44th Engineer Combat Battalion, the 447th Anti-Aircraft Artillery Battalion, and miscellaneous headquarters personnel from the division were used to defend the town. Communications remained with only one regiment.

Directly behind the 28th Division on the St Vith–Bastogne road were roadblocks established by Combat Company Reconnaissance, 8th Armoured Division. One block, known as Task Force Rose, was attacked in the morning and overrun by the enemy by 1400 hours. A roadblock on the Wilts–Bastogne road, known as Task Force Hayze, came under heavy enemy attack by 1815 hours. The Germans overran this roadblock and came within 3km of Bastogne. The defence of Bastogne now became the task of airborne infantry and armour which had been ordered into the sector.

On 18 December at 1800 hours, the 705th Tank Destroyer Battalion, then in position at Kohlscheid, Germany, was ordered by the Ninth Army to march to Bastogne and report to VIII Corps, Bastogne, then the headquarters of VIII Corps, was an important place for rendezvous. The town is a normal point in the highway system of the eastern Ardennes – a countryside forbidding to the movement of mechanised forces except when the roads are under control. By holding at Bastogne VIII Corps could unhinge the communications of the Germans who were striking south and west toward the line of the River Meuse.

Combat Command B closed in the vicinity of Merl at 2155 hours. On the following morning it was ordered to move independently of the 10th Armoured Division to join

VIII Corps and took the road through Arlon to Bastogne. On the way Colonel William L. Roberts, the commander, received a request from Major General Norman D. Cota, commanding the 28th Infantry Division, to support his force at Wiltz by putting CCB into position south and southeast of the town. But this Roberts could not do and comply with his Corps orders, so he took his column on into Bastogne and reported to Major General Middleton at 1600 hours.

On reaching Werbomont on the night of 18 December, we were told that the operation was being handled by VIII Corps and that they were even then due in Bastogne. (In this way the advance party failed in its mission and did not reach the objective until 0300 hours on the morning of 19 December.)

The third major part of the Bastogne garrison, the 705th Tank Destroyer Battalion, under the command of Lt. Col. Clifford D. Templeton, got its marching orders at 1800 hours on 18 December. It left Kohlscheid, Germany, at 2240 hours, but could not proceed by the shortest route – Liège, Houffalize, Bastogne – because the enemy was already around Houffalize.

On the evening of 18 December, Roberts ordered Team Cherry to move out along the road leading east and go into position near Longvilly. It thereby became the first of the Bastogne reinforcement to move out and engage the enemy. The force, under the command of Lt. Col. Henry T. Cherry (CO 3rd Tank Battalion, 10 Armoured Division) included the 3rd Battalion, Co C of the 20th Armoured Infantry Battalion, the 3rd Platoon of Co C of the 55th Engineer Battalion and 2nd Platoon of Troop B of the 90th Cavalry Squadron. They went on into the darkness, knowing only this of their situation, that some parts of Combat Command Reconnaissance (CCR) of the 9th Armoured Division were supposed to be in the vicinity of Longvilly and that the enemy was reported advancing toward that town from the east.

The march was uneventful. 1st Lt. Edward P. Hyduke (Co A, 3rd Tank Battalion), commanding the advance guards, came to a halt just short of Longvilly at 1920 hours. The town is on low ground and its streets seemed already jammed with the vehicles of CCR. Leaving the main body, Cherry went forward to the CP of CCR to learn their intentions. But they had no plan and did not know whether they would stay or get out. So Cherry returned to his force which was then refuelling on the road, and told Hyduke to make a reconnaissance and occupy ground west of the town before dawn came. The main body was to remain 1000 yards west of the town until there was a change in CCR's situation.

At 2300 hours Cherry returned to headquarters in Bastogne to tell Reports how things were going. As he went through Mageret he noticed that CCR's train were headed for the rear. Roberts told him that he was to cover CCR's main body if it withdrew, but in any case he was to hold at Longvilly. The road was already packed with stragglers, most of them moving in trucks and half-tracks back toward Bastogne. They

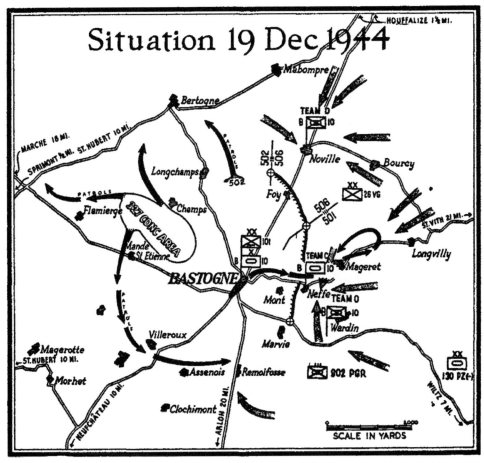

1. 501 ENGAGE ENEMY IN BIZORY – NEFFE – MONT AREA. TEAM CHERRY ENGAGED AT NEFFE & MAGERET
2. TEAM DESOBRY & 501 HOLD NOVILLE AGAINST HEAVY OPPOSITION
3. TEAM O'HARA & CO 1, 501 MEET ENEMY AT WARDIN

knew nothing except that they had last seen the enemy about 6 miles east along the main road. When asked what the Germans had, they repeated: 'Tanks, tanks, tanks,' and then moved on to the rear.

CCR was set up with roadblocks to the north and east of Longvilly, with one battalion of infantry and another of tanks supporting the blocks, and two batteries of artillery helping to cover them from a position next to the town. But there was no close-in defence around the houses. Looking these dispositions over, Hyduke decided there was danger that the enemy might come in from the south. So, he sent his platoon of cavalry in that direction with instructions to withdraw quickly if the pressure became heavy.

Seven light tanks were placed forward with four medium tanks covering to the right. Infantry were in outposts north of the position. One of the field artillery batteries from CCR tied in with Hyduke's party and shortly thereafter opened fire to the eastward, though Hyduke never learned at what they were firing.

At 2340 hours, CCR started its withdrawal from Longvilly, though it was not until two hours later, while Cherry was returning to his team, that he got word by radio from Hyduke that Team Cherry was not holding alone. The next few minutes brought more distressing news to the commander. In Neffe he met a wounded enlisted man who said that his vehicle had been shot up near Mageret. Then a sergeant told him that a strong German patrol had entered Mageret just before midnight. This meant that the Germans were across the road between Cherry and his team. Cherry radioed Captain William F. Ryerson (CO of Co. C, 20th Armoured Infantry Battalion, 10 Armoured Division), who had been left in command at Longvilly, to get a patrol to Mageret and reopen the road. Two squads of infantry were sent in a halftrack on this mission. They dismounted before reaching the village and approached stealthily. Within a few minutes they had located three enemy tanks and an infantry force, which they guessed to be about one company in positions around the crossroads at Mageret. They had come in along the side of the town which was not being covered by an enemy tank, and while they waited there, they heard another armoured vehicle coming up behind them. For a few seconds they were in a cold sweat, thinking they were about to be trapped by a fourth tank. Instead, it proved to be an American Tank Destroyer.

The infantrymen and the TD crew discussed their chances and decided they weren't strong enough to attack Mageret. So they returned to Ryerson. By then Ryerson had heard from Roberts that he was to commandeer any American men or equipment which he could use, so he drafted the TD into his outfit.

The discovery that the enemy was across the team's rear, quickly followed by Ryerson's report of the enemy strength which his patrol had found at Mageret, convinced Cherry and Roberts that the situation was such that Longvilly could not be held.

BAYERLEIN: 18 December 2100 hours: Departure of Task force 902 from Neiderwampach. Strength: 1 Battalion Panzer Grenadier, 12 Panzer, 1 Battery Artillery. Without contact with the enemy and unnoticed, the Task force reached Mageret via Benonchamps. A Belgian civilian gave information that two hours before a US Task force of about forty Panzers and many other armoured and unarmoured motor vehicles as well as artillery had passed Mageret in the direction of Longvilly. At once, I blocked the road on the northeastern end of Mageret with mines and Panzers.

I myself was in Mageret. Still more US armoured units and motor vehicles came from Bastogne, as it was not known that the Germans were already in Mageret. But we did not know either that Mageret was occupied by US troops. Only during the search of the place did an engagement take place; then the search went on until dawn.

A US Dispensary in the Bois St Lambert was left to carry on and treat wounded American and German men.

After some US armoured cars, which came back on the road from Longvilly, had been put out of action, the advance on Bastogne was continued at 0600 hours. In the twilight, I saw US troops preparing for defence on the mountain chain southwest of Mageret. The halting place at Neffe was captured after a roadblock had been removed at 0700 hours: Neffe, the village, was captured at 0800 hours by an all-embracing attack from the south. The next thrust against Mont was repelled. American resistance grew incessantly.

Reconnaissance reports show that Bizory and Marvie are occupied by the enemy and US patrols are reported to be in Wardin. Enemy pressure makes itself felt from the north via Arloncourt and the woods west of Longvilly. At about 1200 hours those parts of Panzer Grenadier Regiment 902 that had arrived are thrown in from Benonchamps to the north to eliminate the envelopment of Task Force 902, then beginning.

At 1400 hours, the woods were mopped up and the anti-tank guns had big success, when, in cooperation with parts of the 26th Volksgrenadier Division, they put out of action a great number of US tanks and armoured motor vehicles between Longvilly and Arloncourt. They completed the envelopment of the CC of the 10th US Armoured Division from the west and contributed essentially to the annihilation of the CC.

19 December

BAYERLEIN: ALA was committed to attack Wardin in the morning of 19 December, to eliminate the incipient envelopment of Task force 902 from the south. In the evening, Wardin was captured, but the next attack (against Marvie on 20 December) failed. In the meantime, more artillery and the Flak Battalion of Panzer Lehr had arrived from behind. They were employed at Benonchamps.

KOKOTT: It was obvious the enemy had made good use of the time! They had brought reinforcements and dug in and prepared for the defence. The original target, the order: Attack! On to Bastogne! remained, of course, in effect. At the same time, however, it was now evident that the enemy could be thrown only by means of a systematic attack and that it would only be possible to advance in phases.

WAGENER: The LXVI Army Corps was again unsuccessful in its attack on St Vith. After four days, the left wing of the Corps had finally crossed the Our sector near Steinbrück. A large enemy group surrendered in the Schnee Eifel.

LVIII Panzer Corps joined up with 116th Panzer Division and crossed the road Houffalize–Bastogne continuing westward to the Salle. The 560th Division followed on the right, echeloned to the rear. With this, the left division of the Corps had come over into the XLVII Corps sector. It was not desirable to crowd its roads more than they were already, and it was undesirable to let the weak 560th Volksgrenadier Division advance in the middle corps sector. Commitment of the 116th Panzer Division in the attack against Bastogne was definitely rejected. However, withdrawal of the division by way of Houffalize into the corps sector, as the LVIII Panzer Corps had ordered, was not in accordance with the plans of Army.

The XLVII Panzer Corps was tied down in front of Bastogne on the line of Noville– Bizory–Neffe, where it appeared that the enemy had succeeded in erecting a strong barrier at this important road junction.

The *Heeresgruppe* had ordered us to take St Vith. XLVII Panzer Corps' mission could only be to bypass Bastogne and push forward to the Maas. We were so far behind our schedule that only a desperate push towards the ultimate objective could assure us success for the whole operation. St Vith was to be an example to us, of how a fortified and occupied village can disrupt a whole operation. Once Sixth Panzer and Seventh Army had to be used to clear up enemy strongpoints in the rear where resistance had not been wholly broken. Nevertheless, these two armies had so tied down the enemy, despite the fact that general progress was hardly being made, that the Fifth Panzer Army could now push further to the west without having to worry about its flanks, exposing itself in these engagements. The Fifth Panzer Army stuck to its original plan; a choice had to be made between two alternatives: either to mop up the principal enemy strongpoints east of the Maas or to gain bridgeheads over the Maas. The decision handed down to attack Bastogne, therefore meant, nothing other than to execute the whole mission simultaneously.

On 19 December it became more evident, that enemy counter measures had begun. The enemy command had thus regained a measure of control.

By tapping radio conversations of an M.P. network, it was determined that a defensive line was going to be set up on the western bank of the Maas, while special units were to delay our advance east of the Maas. More forces were sent from north and south to counterattack both flanks of the German attacking force.

An order was issued by the *Heeresgruppe*, stating that the 2nd SS Panzer Division was to be brought up to the sector of the LXVI Corps. The 9th Panzer Division and the 15th Panzer Grenadier Division were assigned to the Fifth Panzer Army, although they had to refuel first!

ZERBEL: 19 Dec. 2nd Panzer Division:
At 0530 hours, the division attacked Bourzy and reached at 0830 hours the end of the forest 800m east of Noville. The started attack had to be discontinued at 1130 hours, because of the strong enemy resistance, and the arrival of reinforcements had to be expected. It seemed impossible to outflank Noville because of the bad condition of the roads. Early in the morning, the division was attacked in the flank by an armoured group, 1km northeast of Longvilly. This armoured enemy group (about 100 vehicles), with the cooperation of the Panzer-Lehr Division, was entirely destroyed (at about 1400 hours).

Panzer Lehr Division: The division penetrated Mageret at 0300 hours. Delayed by the muddy road at Benonchamps, only a small part of the forces of the division had arrived. They took the station and the castle of Neffe at about 0600 hours and continued their advance on Bastogne. At Mont and north of it, they met upon a stronger enemy resistance. Enemy infantry was advancing from Bastogne eastward.

26th Volksgrenadier Division: The division attacked with the leading regiment (77th Regiment) from Oberwampach past Longvilly on Bizory, where it was contained. The 78th Regiment on the right side of it reached the railroad, and the 39th Regiment on its advance west reached Donkholz.

KOKOTT: On the evening of 19 December it became apparent that the enemy had thrown reinforcements at least into the area Foy–Neffe. This could only have been elements of that enemy group which had been in the process of moving up to Bastogne. Their method of fighting, the concentration of the fire and their systematic defence gave all indications that these were not only tough and tested troops, but that they were solid, well-coordinated units which had been prepared for commitment. During the night of 19 December, the right neighbour was fighting for Noville.

Panzer Lehr Division: At dark, the situation of the Corps was as follows: The Corps was contained on the line Noville–Bizory–Neffe. The enemy resistance had increased during 19 December. The question had to be decided, whether all the forces of the Corps were to be committed for the capture of Bastogne or whether – as planned – the two Panzer Divisions were to outflank Bastogne and leave the capture of this town to the 26th Volksgrenadier Division.

The Army decided to advance with the two Panzer divisions towards the west. Accordingly, the divisions received orders, the Panzer Lehr Division was to try once more to take Bastogne on 20 December, but keep forces in readiness, in order to continue the advance past Sibret toward the west.

In the forces east of Noville a big ammunition dump was captured: 23 Sherman tanks, 30 jeeps, 25 trucks, 14 armoured cars, 15 self-propelled guns, about 20-30 vehicles were destroyed.

US FORCES (705 TD Bn): The column proceeded via Laroche where it went into a defensive position along the heights 6 miles south of the town at 0915 hours on 19 December. Templeton looked Laroche over and was thoroughly alarmed at what he found. American units were sprawled along the road. They were making little or no effort to adjust themselves to the situation or to set up a local defence, so in midmorning Templeton sent two platoons with four TDs to set up a roadblock to the north of the town. Leaving the battalion at Laroche, he then went to Neufchateau, where VIII Corps was newly established. Middleton told him to get on into Bastogne and attach himself to the 101st Division. An officer was sent back to Laroche to bring the battalion on, but to leave the roadblock force in place.

Templeton and his command section, after reporting to McAuliffe, started northwest to meet the oncoming column. At Bertogne the section was ambushed by a German party armed with two machine guns, one self-propelled gun and several small anti-aircraft guns. The opening fire wounded three men, destroyed a jeep and forced the abandonment of the armoured command vehicle. Templeton's men withdrew along the road about ½ mile with all their weapons engaging the enemy. This action took place about 1500 hours and was over in twenty minutes.

Templeton radioed to his battalion to expect the roadblock at Bertogne. He then told them, however, that the roadblock could be overwhelmed and the battalion was to 'come any way possible to Bastogne but get there'. He did not know that the Bertogne

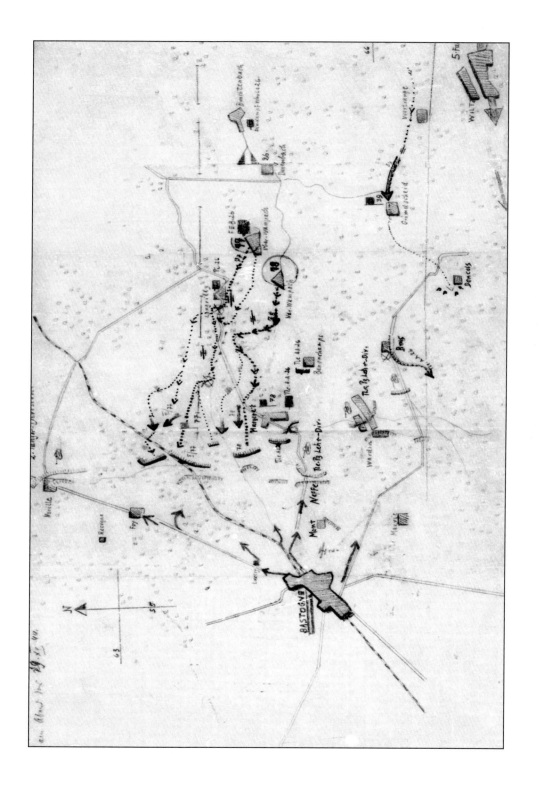

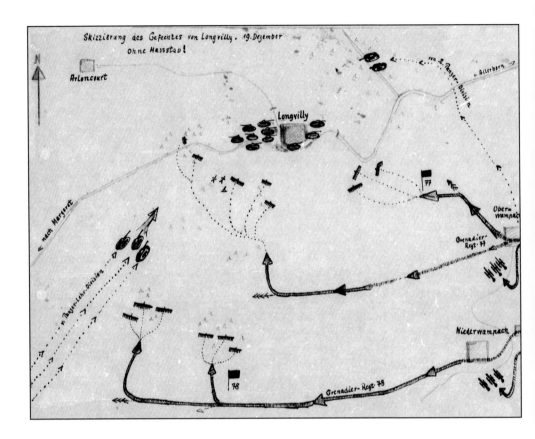

road was impassable as the bridge above the town was out. In the late afternoon the command section returned to Bastogne to establish its CP. Templeton then radioed the commander of the supply train to 'find a haven in the west and hook up with some big friends'. He felt quite certain that his train would get through safely because the one M18 accompanying it was capable of dealing with any roving enemy tank or infantry group along the way. The 705th Tank Destroyer Battalion reached Bastogne at 2030 hours, by the route Laroche-Champlon-Ortheuville-Bastogne.

With the arrival of the 705th Tank Destroyer Battalion, all the organisations present in Bastogne during the siege were gathered. The 101st and CCB had begun the fight that morning and the TDs were now ready to link their power with that of the armour and the infantry. Men of every unit had morale of the highest quality and with their weapons each was capable of stiffening the other. It was a matter of finding the way through courage, resource, and good will.

Cherry ordered the advance guard under Hyduke to hold its ground at Longvilly while the main body tried to beat its way back through Mageret. These orders, which arrived at 0830 hours, turned the advance guard into a rearguard. Cherry went back to his CP which was in a stoutly walled chateau 300 yards south of Neffe and stayed there awaiting developments. The CP force, the rearguard and the main body were each engaged during the entire day in widely separated actions.

By daybreak Hyduke was set up on three sides of Longvilly and ready to defend the rear. However, the closing of the road at Mageret by the Germans had kept many of CCR's vehicles from withdrawing and, after taking to the road, they sat there, blocking all traffic. There was a heavy *nebelwerfer* shelling of Hyduke's lines in early morning and the area then quieted until 1000 hours. The position was reasonably safe from frontal assault as the ground to the north of the main road was marshy for 10 yards, while facing toward the marsh was an embankment much too steep for tanks to cross. On the right of the road the ground fell away too sharply for tanks. A large culvert a short distance ahead of the position was set for demolition.

The morning engagement opened with the sighting of two enemy tanks about 1500 yards southeast of Longvilly, but with the visibility so poor because of fog that they could be seen only in vague outlines. A shot from the Germans hit a tank in the CCR group along the road, locking the turret. All of the American armour returned the fire and both enemy tanks went up in flames. After this there was a prolonged shelling of Longvilly. At 1300 hours the enemy armour put direct fire on Hyduke's position from front and left flank, disabling two half-tracks and one light tank at the tail of the column. Five minutes later the enemy knocked out two more medium tanks 150 yards in front of the burning halftrack. An enemy anti-tank gun on the left hit a CCR tank which had remained in position with the lone artillery battery; the battery then promptly took off. The groups on the road were now almost in a state of panic and when some of the vehicles tried to swing around the column, the road became more jammed than ever.

One group of stragglers which had been organised to cover the left flank deserted their position, leaving that part of the group to only twenty-three infantrymen of Co C. Hyduke who had been given authority to take over any portion of CCR which withdrew, but found that it was impossible to do so. However, despite the panicky state of the stragglers he was able to maintain close control of his own force and continued to engage the enemy until 1330 hours when Cherry ordered him to fall back on Ryerson. The order couldn't be carried out. The road was absolutely blocked. He couldn't order his men down from their vehicles because enemy foot troops were now moving in on his flanks and the whole area was under heavy bullet fire.

Some of the tanks turned around on the road and tried to get back to the ground which they had defended. In this period of threshing round five of his seven light tanks were destroyed as well as one tank dozer and a tank recovery vehicle. The halftracks at the front of the column had to be abandoned, and right after their personnel dismounted, two more medium tanks were hit by artillery fire. One medium tank became cut off and when last seen was trying to fight off an attack by German infantry. The last medium tank received a direct hit on its track as it tried to get out. The three remaining light tanks, including one which had belonged to an artillery forward observer, were destroyed by their crews to prevent capture.

By 1500 hours the survivors had escaped the scene of wreckage and joined Ryerson. That commander had had a difficult time carrying out his mission because of the traffic jam along the road, but by 0945 hours his column had progressed to 300 yards east of Mageret. As his lead tank came round the last bend in the road, a shell from an enemy AT gun in Mageret hit it frontally, burning the tank and killing or injuring all members of the crew. The road ran through a cut at this point and the burning tank plugged it completely.

The stalled column then became a general target for intense shelling and small arms fire from the German armour and infantry force in the village. Ryerson's infantry then dismounted and proceeded forward to reconnoitre the enemy position. The high ground on both sides of the burning tank protected them for a little way but they could not go past the ridge because the down-slope was getting heavy bullet and mortar fire. Two 105mm assault guns manoeuvred up to the ridge and shelled a tree line where they thought the German infantry was hiding.

The small arms fire from the village then slacked off a bit. From the rear two AA halftracks from the 9th Armoured came on past Ryerson's force moving toward Bastogne. Ryerson's men tried to stop them but they drove on heedlessly until they turned the curve and saw the burning tank. The crews jumped for safety without trying to save their vehicles. The Germans shelled both vehicles and the road became doubly blocked. Next, the gun crews along the ridge saw an American command car and a Sherman tank, complete with cerise panels, whip out of Mageret and move north. They were quite startled for a moment and held their fire. By the time they had decided these vehicles were being used by the enemy, it was too late; they had moved out of range.

Two batteries of the 73rd Armoured Field Artillery came up behind the column and on finding the road blocked they moved out north and west and proceeding via Bizory got into the line of the main American position. By about 1400 hours the fire from Mageret had subsided so appreciably that a force composed of 18 infantrymen, 2 medium tanks and a 105mm assault gun were sent against the village, moving through the fields on the right flank. One of the Shermans got hung up on an embankment, drew a great deal of fire and returned to the column. The rest of the force worked its way into the northeast portion of the village, receiving some shell fire from the southeast of the village while so doing.

At the main crossroads they could see a roadblock with one German tank and an American M IV. This armour did not move or fire and the party concluded that it was already destroyed. In the southern part of the village they could see two more German tanks, an American halftrack, a jeep and a German ambulance. The heavy guns with the party could not find a position from which to fire and the infantry could not do anything effective. From the rear of his column Ryerson was called by his AT officer, 2nd Lt. Earl B. Gilligan, and told that 20 halftracks loaded with men had just come in. Ryerson told him to get the men forward dismounted and send along any tanks that he might see. Gilligan got the men – about 200 stragglers, mostly tankers – out of the halftracks but only 40 of them, with three captains and two lieutenants from CCR and a few officers from Hyduke's section, moved up toward the fire fight. The others fled across the fields to the north.

The 40 men were organised into four squads and at 1600 hours this force moved against the southeast part of the village supported by a section of medium tanks. But the tanks could not get over the ground which lay south of the road and the men were not inclined to go far beyond the tanks.

Within the village several of the German vehicles which had been to the south started to move north toward the main crossing. To the amazement of Ryerson's men, the German tank forming the roadblock, which they had thought to be dead all the time, suddenly came alive and moved out of the way. Ryerson's force had spent hours sitting within plain view of this tank at range 600 yards without receiving any attention from it. The American tank now put it under fire at once and the German tank burned.

There was still so much shelling from the south of the village however that the American guns had to remain immobile and the small force of infantry could not get forward. Prisoners which they had taken said that the enemy infantry group comprised about 120 men. The 40-man force which had attacked toward the south of Mageret had no communication with Ryerson's main body and later that evening somewhat less than half of them returned. They had made no real progress. Since noon Ryerson had been aware that infantry forces were coming to his aid from Bastogne. He didn't know what units were coming but the expectation of relief encouraged his efforts to take Mageret.

Through these misadventures and decisions, Team Cherry had come to the point where it could no longer confront the on-coming enemy anywhere; most of its strivings would be directed toward keeping itself in being and covering its own flanks and rear. Whether the German advance into Bastogne from the east could be checked and thrown into recoil now depended on the forces of 101st Division.

They played in luck from the beginning and their luck began weeks before the siege started. In the early part of November a young lieutenant colonel commanding a regiment on the Neder Ri in Holland took a busman's holiday and spent two days' leave in Bastogne. He was possessed of an eye for ground and keenness for the study of it far beyond the powers of the average regimental commander, and he spent his two days roaming over the ridges east of Bastogne and reflecting on their military significance. This was Julian Ewell, commanding the 501st Parachute Infantry.

It was luck that in giving the march order prior to leaving Mourmelon, McAuliffe had put 501st Regiment at the head of the column. It was luck again that Ewell got away well in advance of the column and was the first commander to arrive in the vicinity of the bivouac. He ran into a wire-stringing detail, asked what they were doing, found that they were men from 101st and then followed their wires into the Division CP. Then he got ready to guide his men in. All down the route over which he had come he had found the traffic blocking and stopping, and he didn't expect 501st to come up to him before 2300 hours because of this backwash. But it beat that schedule by one half-hour and Ewell was closed in his area by 2400 hours. McAuliffe knew at midnight that he had one regiment ready.

Earlier in the night Ewell had talked to McAuliffe and Higgins. The one thing on which all of the commanders agreed was that no one could be certain of anything. Ewell said of himself that he was as much in the dark as any man present. But he presented to his commander that he should be given a definite assignment. It was a large request, the situation considered.

The index finger pointed out along the road running eastward – toward the ridges where Ewell had walked in November – although neither Middleton nor McAuliffe ever knew that he had seen the ground. The enemy was coming that way. At Corps the 9th Armoured was thought to have a roadblock somewhere around Longvilly and the 10th Armoured had a block farther west toward Neffe. The 9th's block was thought to be surrounded; the 10th's block was supposed to be engaged but not yet surrounded. Middleton had described the situation at these blocks when McAuliffe reported to him and had said: 'There is a battle now going on for Bastogne.' He spoke of the block out along the Longvilly road as 'surrounded' and he described the position of three other blocks which CCB of 10th Armoured was maintaining to the east, northeast and southeast of the city.

The Corps Commander had no specific plan for the employment of 101st Division, and at first McAuliffe could think of nothing. At 2200 hours he suggested to Middleton that a combat team be sent east to develop the situation. That idea appealed to McAuliffe simply as a 'good old Leavenworth solution of the problem'. It was wholly consistent with Middleton's concern for the preservation of the other elements of his command.

Middleton and McAuliffe sent for Ewell. He had been spending a part of his time unprofitably on the road intersections trying to get information from the Americans who were straggling in from the north and northeast. All talked vaguely and dispiritedly. Man after man said to him: 'We have been wiped out,' and then stumbled away through the dark. They did not know where they had been. They had no idea where they were going. Ewell and his officers tried several times to draw out these men, then gave up as a bad job and paid no further attention. Ewell reached his separate conclusion that any quest for information concerning the enemy, other than going out bodily after it, was useless.

The exact mission given Ewell was to 'seize the road junction at 676614 and hold it'. That would put him out in the east road well beyond Longvilly. Middleton told him that CCR of the 9th Armoured had a roadblock at that point which was supposed to be 'isolated' and that the 110th Infantry was supposedly still maintaining a CP at Allerborn. From 501st's assembly area it was 9½ miles to the road junction. However, that distant point did not enter into McAuliffe's instructions to Ewell or what he anticipated the regiment would be able to accomplish. McAuliffe was not sure where the enemy would crown him first, but he thought it most likely that they would roll on him from the east. That had as much to do with his assignment of Ewell as did the involvement of the armoured roadblocks. He simply pointed to the map and moved his finger along in the direction of Longvilly, he said: 'Ewell, move out along this road at six o'clock, make contact, attack and clean up the situation.'

Ewell didn't ask a question. He said: 'Yes, sir,' saluted and went on his way.

Recalling that scene some days afterward, McAuliffe was to remark: 'There were many men and commanders in my operation who did outstanding things. But Ewell's was the greatest gamble of all. It was dark. He had no knowledge of the enemy. I could not tell him what he was likely to meet. But he has a fine eye for ground and no man has more courage. He was the right man for the spot I put him in.'

Of the few maps which Division had obtained from Corps, twenty went with Ewell's combat team as it started to march. It wasn't enough to go around. Lt. Col. Clarence F. Nelson, commanding the 907th Field Artillery Battalion, had only one map scaled 1:100,000 from which to provide his firing data. So, as the movement got underway, he had sketches drawn up for the forward observers. On the sketches all control points and critical features – such as crossroads, bridges, woods and towns – were marked and numbered. The observers knew the locations of the batteries. In this way the artillery operation was coordinated.

The offensive mission was limited to the one combat team. McAuliffe had decided right at the beginning that a successful defence of Bastogne depended on the utmost harbouring of his reserves at every stage of the operation and having sent Ewell forth, he proposed to sit on Bastogne with the rest of his division until something new developed.

That same idea – conservation of his force – guided Ewell in his opening moves. In giving his battalion commanders the march order, he told Major Raymond V. Bottomly, Jr, who was leading out with the 1st Battalion, that he was not to put out flank security until he reached Mageret, otherwise the progress of the column would be much too slow. But in line with the governing principle he added the instructions to all commanders that if they met opposition, they were to 'take it slow and easy'. Being familiar with his men and their method in past campaigns, he knew that they tended to throw themselves direct on the target. These methods had worked in Normandy and Holland. But from what he had seen of the Bastogne terrain in November, he had concluded that his main chance lay in 'fire and manoeuvre' rather than in shock action. He felt that his whole operation should be guided by this principle. He said to them: 'I don't want you to try to beat the enemy to death.'

The regiment took off at 0600 hours, passing its CP exactly on the minute. Battery B of the 81st Airborne Anti-Aircraft Battalion – seven 57mm guns – moved out behind 1st Battalion. The Division Reconnaissance Troop, which had been attached to 501st, started through the town ahead of Bottomly's men. The observers and the liaison party from the artillery moved out with the lead infantry company. The artillery battalion remained in the bivouac area 2 miles west of Bastogne waiting for the infantry to find the enemy.

Ewell went forward at 0700 hours. The light was just beginning to break. Already, he felt vaguely familiar with the terrain and the first incident strengthened his confidence. At the first intersection past the town, he found the 1st Battalion proceeding down the wrong road – toward Marvie. He saw, without referring to the map, that they were misled, and he recalled them and got them pointed towards Longvilly. The Reconnaissance Platoon, having proceeded furthest along the wrong road, thus got behind the battalion column, and raced to catch up.

The column passed on down the road which follows the line of the creek toward Neffe. To their left the hills rose evenly from the edge of the right-of-way, fairly easy slopes up which an infantryman might run without undue exertion. Ahead, they could see very little. The road dipped and turned around the hill facing the little valley and the morning fog lay so thick that the visibility toward the south, where the land opens up beyond the line of the creek, was limited to 500 yards.

First Battalion had been on the march for a little more than two hours, and the advance party was being passed through by the Reconnaissance Platoon, when the body was fired on by a machine gun stationed along the road and just short of Neffe. The first burst of fire did no damage, but the battalion hit the dirt. They needed to, for they were looking straight down the groove toward the enemy position; for the last 700 yards the road runs straight and almost level into Neffe. To right of the road, the ground fell off sharply to the creek; to the left were the gently sloping hills.

Bottomly deployed his men that way. Ewell told him to go ahead and develop his situation. Shells began whipping along the road and Bottomly sent word back to Ewell that he thought he was being opposed by two tanks and two platoons of infantry. Ewell took himself off, leaving Bottomly to direct his own fight. He had already tasted the shell fire and he didn't want to tempt it, unnecessarily. Back beyond the road's first

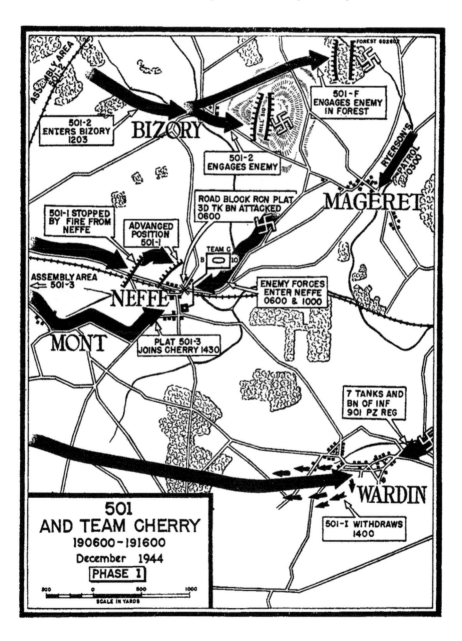

FOREST 602602

501-F
ENGAGES ENEMY
IN FOREST

501-2
ENTERS BIZORY
1203

ASSEMBLY AREA
501-2

BIZORY

HILL 510

501-2
ENGAGES ENEMY

RYERSON'S PATROL 0300

MAGERET

ROAD BLOCK RCN PLAT
3D TK BN ATTACKED
0600

501-1 STOPPED
BY FIRE FROM
NEFFE

ADVANCED
POSITION
501-1

TEAM C
B 10

ASSEMBLY AREA
501-3

NEFFE

ENEMY FORCES
ENTER NEFFE
0600 & 1000

MONT

PLAT 501-3
JOINS CHERRY 1430

7 TANKS AND
BN OF INF
901 PZ REG

WARDIN

501
AND TEAM CHERRY
190600-191600
December 1944
PHASE 1

501-1 WITHDRAWS
1400

SCALE IN YARDS

turning, about 1000 yards from Bottomly's skirmish line, there was a pocket in the hillside to left of the road where a stone house fitted snugly. Ewell set up his CP there.

It soon became clear to him that 1st Battalion would not be able to reduce the roadblock because of the German tanks – they were firing from a defilade close into the hillside where the road runs down to Neffe from Bizory. Bottomly couldn't bring the 57mm to bear because of the straightness of the Neffe–Bastogne road over the last half mile. About 1000 hours, being convinced that 1st Battalion was stopped, Ewell decided to bring the rest of the regiment out of Bastogne. But it was easier said than done. VIII Corps was rushing the evacuation of its last units and their troops were streaming through town across the regiment's line of march. Second Battalion fought its way through this traffic during the next hour and Ewell ordered them on to an assembly area on the reverse of the gently sloping ridge north of Bottomly's position. He figured that he would put them out to the left closed up, so that they could be deployed as the occasion arose.

Lt. Col. Nelson, CO of the 907th Glider Field Artillery Battalion, and Captain Gerald J. McGlone, CO of Battery B, had gone forward to Ewell the minute the radio flashed word that 1st Battalion had met fire at Neffe. McGlone got his battery into position 500 yards northeast of Bastogne on the left of the Longvilly road, and opened fire as soon as he was in position, which was only a few minutes after 1000 hours. The atmosphere was still thick with fog and the battery was working under several other handicaps – its radios had never been tested and five of its guns had never been fired. But they spoke now from a distance of only 1000 yards behind Bottomly's skirmish line. Having weighed the risk that the enemy might flow on around Ewell's narrow front – and accepted it – Nelson decided that one battery was enough in that particular position. He put Battery A, under Captain Lowell B. Bigelow, into the action from a position near the Battalion CP, 1000 yards west of Bastogne. Luck rode with him. The defilade where he had placed Battery B on the spur of the moment was so well chosen that the guns were to work there for almost a month without receiving one round of counter-battery fire.

This day, however, the batteries had no need to worry about anything coming in on them. The only heavy support for the German attack was from their tanks and it was all close-up fire directed against Ewell's line. The American artillery fire was turned mainly against the tanks and the small groups of German infantry; there were many such targets.

Ewell sized up his situation. In 1st Battalion, Companies B and C were in skirmish line, while Co A was collected in reserve. Bottomly had deployed most of his strength to the north of the highway, but he had managed to find room for one platoon in the ground south of the creek and the rail line. The battalion had put two mortars into operation almost immediately and their fire was shaking down the houses around the enemy roadblock in Neffe.

But an attempt to get 1st Battalion's left flank forward had failed. From Neffe, the north road climbs gradually through a shallow draw to the small farming community of Bizory. The country hereabout is absolutely barren grazing land except for the small, but thick, tree plantations and clusters of farmhouses which appear as villages on the map. The dominant terrain features are the long and quite regular ridges which run generally in a north-south line. These hills are gently undulating and the hillsides are quite smooth. From the tops of the commanding ridges one may see great distances on a clear day. The reverse slopes are smooth and are usually accessible from either end of the hill, making them highly useful to artillery and armour. The roads are close enough together that vehicles may move to the ridges from either direction. When the country is covered with snow, nothing obtrudes on the landscape except the small black patches of forest. The ridges fall away in gently sloping draws which provide a clear field of fire to the front and enable an easy coverage of the main lines of communication.

The road from Neffe to Bizory rises gradually for a distance, providing a perfect slot for fire from the low ground around Neffe. Bottomly had made one pass in this direction and shells from the tanks had fairly blistered the little valley. Ewell decided that as long as the enemy tanks were in Neffe, 1st Battalion couldn't move in any direction. He ordered 2nd Battalion to seize Bizory. That hamlet is in the same draw up which the tanks had shot at Bottomly's men, but the ground flattens out at Bizory so that the place can't be seen from Neffe. This detail, however, Ewell couldn't see from the rear, but he was curious to find out about it. The map told him that the ridge adjacent to Bizory was the high ground and wouldn't be of use to him. He wanted to see if the enemy force east of there was holding a continuous position and he sent 2nd Battalion forward to find out.

His decision, so casually made, probably contributed as much to the salvation of Bastogne as anything that happened during the first few critical days. Ewell was still strongly of the opinion that he was being opposed by only a minor roadblock. But when he determined to extend and sweep forward, he made it a certainty that the oncoming Germans would suddenly collide with Americans who were attacking along a broad front. These were things they least expected. Until that time they had been meeting small or disorganised units, which they quickly encircled and overcame. The shock discovery threw them off stride. They recoiled, hesitated and lost priceless, unreclaimable hours and opportunity because of their own confusion.

In that action, a few platoons hardened the fate of armies. Ewell thought of none of these things as he ordered the 2nd Battalion to seize Bizory. He reflected on them later in his CP in the Bastogne Nunnery which the German artillery had made one of the best ventilated buidings in Belgium.

East of Bastogne

The 3rd Battalion of the 501st Regiment had become caught in the traffic snarl west of Bastogne and was at a standstill. Ewell checked on them at 1200 hours and found that they had moved scarcely at all. After trying to get out of town, the battalion had backtracked, only to find that the auxiliary routes were likewise clogged with out-going troops. Yet even the delay had its benefits. Some of the infantrymen lacked helmets, rifles and ammunition. They begged them from the armoured troops of CCB who were in town, and in the interval the battalion became better equipped.

Ewell ordered Lt. Col. George M. Griswold, commander of 3rd Battalion, to march the battalion to Mont, a little hamlet lying south of the Neffe road. It seemed like the best opportunity to get the battalion out of Bastogne. However, Ewell directed that one of Griswold's companies be sent down the Wiltz road to cover the battalion's right flank. Griswold was told to send the company to the bend in the road lying directly east of the village of Marvie. Ewell planned to send the 3rd Battalion against Neffe from the southwest after it had reached Mont, but he issued no orders to the effect at the time. He followed his usual plan of giving his subordinate commanders only a limited objective.

At 1203 hours the 2nd Battalion took Bizory without opposition except for unobserved fire from the tanks in Neffe. Still convinced that the Neffe roadblock was the only immediate threat to his front, Ewell ordered 2nd Battalion to advance and seize Mageret. By this move he figured he would box the tanks and could then proceed against them from either front or rear according to the advantages of the ground. But he specified that Major Sammie N. Homan, commander of 2nd Battalion, send one company to seize the patch of woods directly north of Mageret. This wood was a small plantation of very tall spruces. Ewell saw that the long ridge running across to the spruces dominated Mageret in the valley. It seemed to him that putting one company there might cover the approach to Mageret.

Homan started out by road from Bizory to Mageret, but his route march ended quickly. At the crest of Hill 510 he collided with German infantry in dug-in positions: they were the Reconnaissance Platoon of the 26th Volksgrenadier Division. Homan took the first jolt almost without loss; not so, the enemy. Their line was moving forward from the foxholes and coming over the hill when the battalion mortars and Nelson's artillery caught them with full blast. The paratroops saw a number of the enemy fall before the survivors ran back. Deploying the rest of the battalion, Homan sent Co F to the left to seize the coveted wood. When this extension was completed he reported to Ewell by radio that his hands were full and he was not engaged along his entire front. 'For the time being,' he said, 'I cannot think of taking Mageret.'

Third Battalion reached Mont and found one of the ring of roadblocks outposting that point, but the further assignment of the main body of the battalion was compromised by the nature of the ground between Mont and Neffe. The two villages are little more than a mile apart and from Neffe one may look right down the little valley and see Mont clearly. The tanks of Panzer Lehr which were at Neffe were shipping a few shells toward Colonel Griswold's infantry; It seemed possible that a small party might work its way toward Neffe but the ground was much too naked for the exposure of any large force. Griswold stopped where he was.

Company I, which had drawn the assignment on the extreme right flank, was instructed to prowl the three large woods west and northwest of the village of Wardin. At 1330 hours Co I reported that it had checked the three woods and had found no enemy. Ewell then told Co I to advance to Wardin and make contact with a friendly armoured roadblock which was supposed to be there. Ewell had not been told officially of the existence of this force but had heard of it quite casually from someone walking down the road. The company went on to the contact which Ewell had ordered, but for all practical effect, the stranger who had mentioned that there were friends at hand might just as well have left his words unsaid.

This was Team O'Hara of CCB (10th Armoured Division) which on the night of 18 December had taken up position on the high ground out of Wardin just short of the woods. The night had been quiet except for the stragglers coming through – mostly rear echelon people from 28th Division whose idea about the enemy situation was wildly confused. The morning opened with fog. About 1000 hours the trickle of stragglers failed altogether. This worried the force as they figured it must mean that the enemy was coming on. They put out a reconnaissance screen to the east which moved slowly along the road to Bras. At 1140 hours they engaged and destroyed a Volkswagen on the Wilts-Bastogne highway. Just as they opened fire, they saw the head of the enemy column break through the fog a few hundred yards away – two Mark IVs and a personnel carrier. The platoon had nothing with which to fight armour and so it cleared out rapidly, reporting its findings by radio.

As a result of the message, unobserved fire was put on Bras by the 420th Armoured Field Artillery Battalion. At about the same time Captain Edward A. Carrigo, Team S-2, and 1st Lt. John D. Devereaux, commanding Company B of the 54th, were entering Wardin from the southwest and finding it unhealthy. The town was wrapped in fog; they could scarcely see anything at 50-yard range but they prowled on through the town and just as they got beyond it a projectile of anti-tank size hit the front bumper of the jeep. Nothing was hurt, but the two officers increased their speed and reported that there were people moving into Wardin who were quite unfriendly.

By noon the visibility lengthened to 800 yards. Second Lt. Theodore R. Hamer, observer for the 420th, moved forward to the top of a small hill (609555). There were five tanks of Team O'Hara on the crest when he got there. Before he had a chance to observe for fire, his own tank was hit twice from the left by a high velocity gun. Hamer

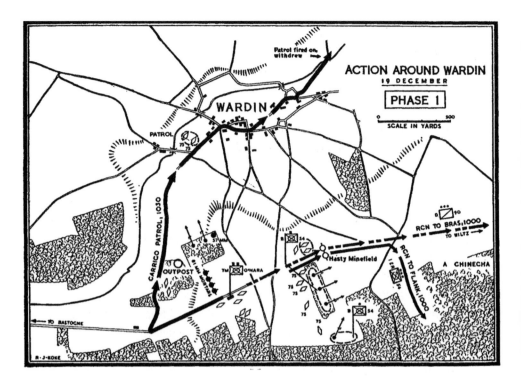

and three other crew members were wounded. One man was incinerated inside the tank. A second medium tank was hit in the turret by a shell which killed the gunner. The driver backed the tank down the hill wildly, not stopping until the vehicle became bogged; the tank could not be salvaged and later had to be destroyed. The other tanks cleared away from the hill as rapidly as they could. Direct fire artillery began to hit the force's main position from north across the valley.

On the road ahead, the team had hastily set up a minefield. At 1300 hours a few Germans jumped from a Volkswagen and tried to remove the mines. From only 200 yards away to the west, five of the infantry halftracks and five medium tanks opened fire on the party. But they jumped in their car and made a clean getaway. Shortly after, an outpost at the south of the position saw another enemy group moving through woods northwest toward Wardin. One of the Medusa tanks moved up and put them under fire.

These were the things which had happened prior to the time when Team O'Hara saw men coming towards them from the woods at their rear. They were in a patrol formation and wore an unfamiliar green uniform, which looked tight around the legs. The tankers were just about to fire and then someone in the approaching party yelled. They were the point of Co I, 501st Infantry. Their green jump suits had almost been their undoing; the main body of the company was right behind them in the woods.

They were on their way to Wardin. It was good news to the tankers; the first infantry support had arrived and they could now withdraw their own patrol which had been reaching out toward the town. Some fateful minutes passed and nothing was done to unify the action. With many crowding in on them, the forces acted like two ships passing in the night. The paratroopers went on. Two medium tanks were placed so as to cover the exits from Wardin. That was all.

Lt. Col. James O'Hara, commanding 54th Armoured Infantry Battalion, 10th Armoured Division, had thought that the enemy would push on the Wilts–Bastogne highway, but he was wrong about it. They bypassed his group – except for a few who squeezed a little too far over to the west and got themselves killed for their pains – and went on to Wardin, moving along a deep gully where O'Hara's tanks couldn't bring their fire to bear. The tankers could see the German infantry infiltrating by twos and threes, moving northwest toward the town, until a hundred or more had passed. They asked that artillery be put on the gully, but the artillery was occupied with the defence of Noville. Then the enemy began to fret O'Hara's immediate front again: one trophy came close enough to fire at a tank with a rocket which fell 5 yards short. Halftracks sprayed the area with machine-gun fire and the tanks pounded away.

With their 75mms thus preoccupied, Team O'Hara paid no mind to Wardin. They knew there was fighting going on but the situation was 'obscure'. At 1415 hours,

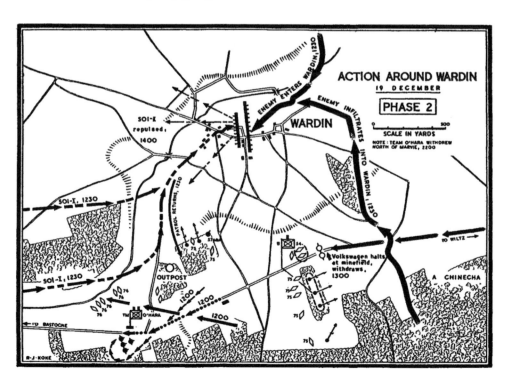

Ewell heard that Co I was being fired on in Wardin. The reports trickling in during the next few minutes indicated that the company was doing pretty well. Armour was not opposing them, but they had already knocked out two tanks and were pushing the enemy infantry from the town. By 1600 hours, Ewell was pretty content with his general situation. He had three battalions approximately abreast; he was in contact all along his front and there was a friendly roadblock – Team O'Hara – on his extreme right flank.

But he felt that he had gone as far as he could with his offensive action and that such strength was now being committed against him that he could no longer think about his specific mission. He therefore ordered the battalions to make plans to break contact at dark and draw back to defend a general line along the high ground to the west of Bizory–Neffe and in any approximate extension of this line to the south of the creek. At Division Headquarters, McAuliffe and Kinnard looked over his plan and approved it.

As he was walking back through Bastogne he met a sergeant from Co I who said to him, 'Have you heard about Company I? We've been wiped out.' Ewell got to his radio; he didn't believe the sergeant, but the story was nearer right than he thought. Company I had lost 45 men and 4 officers at Wardin and the survivors had scattered so badly that it was no longer possible to form even a platoon. The news was a shock. Upon hearing that Co I was becoming involved in Wardin, Ewell had ordered it to disengage and withdraw; however, before the company could comply, it had come under the full shock of an attack by seven tanks and one battalion from 901 Regiment of Panzer Lehr. The survivors got out as best they could.

The incident simply strengthened Ewell's conviction that he must abandon all offensive intention and tighten up his position. O'Hara had reached the same conclusion and for much the same reason. Four of the walking wounded who had got out of Wardin had come into his lines and told him the news. He saw himself in an exposed position with no one on his right, an aggressive enemy on his left and pressure along his front, and he asked CCB for permission to withdraw.

By radio he received his reply, 'Contact friends on your left, hold what you have.' That showed that Headquarters still didn't understand the situation. So he sent his S-3, Captain George A. Renaux, to Bastogne to explain what he couldn't put over the air, and then he took himself to the rear to reconnoitre a better position. At 1715 hours he was ordered to withdraw to the high ground north of Marvie – the same place he had already chosen as the best defensive line in the area. The HQ Co, heavy weapons and engineers were first to start digging into the new slope; when they were in place, the rest of the force came along, except for four medium tanks and one platoon of infantry which covered the withdrawal. Throughout the whole move, the 420th put a heavy covering fire into the ground where the enemy had been seen during the day. But not a shot was fired in return.

Because of the loss of Co I and the feeling that the enemy was building up on his right, Ewell asked Division to attach one battalion to his regiment for a right flank and reverse. He was given 1st Battalion of 327th Glider Infantry under Lt. Col. Hartford F. Salee. They were put in behind Ewell's 3rd Battalion which put them next to Team O'Hara.

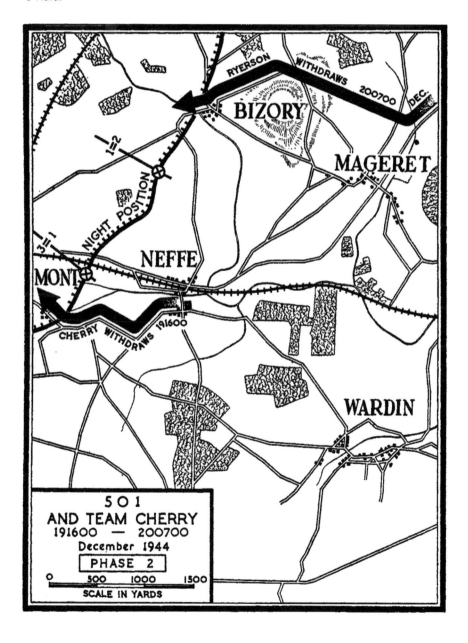

501 AND TEAM CHERRY
191600 — 200700
December 1944
PHASE 2
SCALE IN YARDS
0 500 1000 1500

Between 1700 and 1800 hours, the 501st fell back to the new defensive line. Estimating his gains and losses, Ewell didn't give the regiment too much credit. He thought that Co I had probably killed some Germans at Wardin, but since the enemy still held the town, he couldn't be sure. His impression was that the execution done by his own right and centre had not been very good. Ewell said, 'Any actual killing of the enemy that day was due to artillery.'

Captain Ryerson's force, having spent the day hoping that the infantry would get up to them, clung to three houses in the northwest edge of Mageret after dark. The enemy shot up flares and blazed away at Ryerson's vehicles with AT guns; three of them were destroyed. Their infantry then came on but were driven back by the fire of the 420th Battalion.

At 0030 hours, CCB sent orders for Ryerson to withdraw before dawn, and to make contact with Ewell at Bizory. One line in the special instructions said, 'The head vehicle will inform outpost line of number of vehicles in his column to ensure that no Germans follow column into our lines.'

Ryerson got leave to move his wounded to a point beyond the crest of the first hill – the first step on the way out.

Col. Cherry had been sitting on the hot seat. Having failed to get to his forward elements that night of 18 December, he went to his CP, which was set up in the chateau 300 yards south of Neffe. A signal company from VIII Corps which had hastily pulled out of this building had scribbled signs on the walls saying, 'We'll be back – The Yanks'. One of Cherry's men read it and snorted, 'We'll be back – Hell: We're here to stay.'

At 0600 hours on 19 December – just as Ewell's men were passing the CP – Cherry's Reconnaissance Platoon of the 3rd Tank Battalion, which was outlasting the road junction at Neffe, was hit by enemy tanks and infantry from the east. The platoon knocked out one tank with a bazooka, but the enemy kept coming; and after taking some losses, the line broke back under a storm of fire, machine-gun and direct artillery fire. Most of the outpost fell back along the Bastogne road up which Bottomly's men were coming, but three of them were able to get through to Cherry in the chateau; they carried the word that the enemy had come to Neffe with two tanks and two infantry platoons.

At 1000 hours, while Ewell was committing his 2nd Battalion, Cherry saw four more German tanks – one, a Tiger Royal – an armoured car and 97 more infantrymen enter Neffe from the direction of Mageret. Right after that, they hit him, and they spent the rest of that day trying to crush him with their left while poking at Ewell's troops with their right. The chateau was stoutly built and this somewhat compensated for Cherry's depleted numbers. He had to see it through with his headquarters personnel who moved from one side of the building to another as the attack shifted. The automatic weapons had been taken from the vehicles and placed in the windows and at other points where they could cover the chateau yard and walls. From three sides, the enemy infantry pressed in against the building; the west side of the chateau was raked with 20mm and machine-gun fire. But though some died within 5 yards of the walls, not one German got into the chateau.

There was only one sombre note in the defence. A depleted platoon of engineers which had arrived from the direction of Mont early in the morning was ordered to the south of the chateau at the height of the action. The enemy was moving through woods toward the high ground in that direction. The engineers started on their mission but kept on over the hill and Team Cherry never saw them again.

Sometime around mid-afternoon a platoon from Ewell's 3rd Battalion in Mont worked its way carefully forward, taking advantage of the cover by the forest patches and the rise and fall of the ground, and entered the chateau. It turned out this way, that whereas the fire of the German tanks had kept Griswold from closing on Neffe, his infantry fire had compelled the Germans to release their tight hold on the chateau. Too, the enemy must have felt mounting concern for what was occurring on their right. The platoon had come as reinforcement – to help Cherry hold the fort. But by that time the roof was blazing over his head and his men were being smoked out by a fire lit by the enemy's HE Shell. Such was the confusion of battle that 101st CP had the impression that Cherry had burned the chateau before withdrawing in order to keep it from falling into enemy hands. He waited until the approach of dark and then he led all hands out of Neffe and back to the infantry lines at Mont. Before leaving, he sent CCB this message, 'We're not driven out … we were burned out. We're not withdrawing… we are moving.'

Team Desobry at Noville

The contemporary accounts which attempted to apportion the credit for the saving of Bastogne had much to say about the 101st and relatively little about anyone else. It was irony that a paratroop outfit which had done equally brilliant work in Normandy and Holland won world recognition for the first time and in so doing eclipsed the splendid help given by the other victors at Bastogne.

It was the belief of the commanders at Bastogne that the 28th Division had absorbed much of the shock of the attack before the enemy reached their front on that first day and that the harassing of the German rear by the armoured forces which had gone out the Longvilly road further lightened the burden to their men. In those critical hours the armour out along the roads leading north and east was to the infantry in Bastogne like a football end throwing himself in the path of the interference so that the secondary defence can have a clean chance to get at the man with the ball.

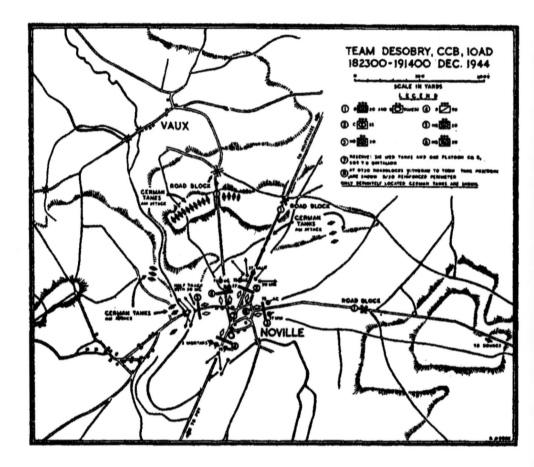

One of the most desperately placed of these small armoured forces was Team Desobry which assembled in the Noville area at 2300 hours on 18 December. The town of Noville is on relatively high ground yet it is commanded by two ridges from about 800 yards, one in the south-east and the other running from north to north-west. Because the team arrived in the darkness, full advantage of the natural defences of the area could not be taken immediately. Major William R. Desobry (CO, 21st Armoured Infantry Battalion, 10th Armoured Division) set up a perimeter defence of the town under Captain Gordon Geiger of Headquarters Company. Three outposts, each consisting of a depleted platoon of infantry and a section of medium tanks, were sent forward. One went east on the Bourcy road, one went northwest on the Houffalize Road and the third set up its roadblock at some cross trails on the road to Vaux.

This outpost line was about 800 yards from the main body. The engineers were instructed to install minefields in support of the roadblocks but found it impossible to comply with the order because of the flow of American stragglers back over these same roads. They came on all through the night, men from scattered engineer units, from CCR of the 9th Armoured Division and from the 28th Division. Roberts had told Desobry to draft into his organisation any men he could use. Every vehicle which came down the road was halted and searched for infantry soldiers. At the end of the search Desobry had collected many individual riflemen but only one organised group – an officer and 14 men from CCR. This group filled the gap in Desobry's ranks and maintained itself courageously during the next few days, but it was Desobry's experience that the strays were little use to him and took to the cellars when the action became warm.

Chapter 4

19–20 December: Tank Battles in the Fog

US FORCES: At 0430 hours the flow of strollers abruptly ceased and Desobry's men grew tense, anticipating an enemy attack. At 0530 hours a group of halftracks could be heard and dimly seen approaching the block on the Bourcy road. In the darkness the outpost could not tell whether they were friend or enemy. The front sentry yelled 'Halt!' four times. The first vehicle pulled to a grinding halt within a few yards of him. Someone in the halftrack yelled something in German. From a bank on the right of the road, Desobry's men showered the halftrack with hand grenades. Several exploded as

they landed in the vehicle. There was loud screaming as some of the Germans jumped or fell from the halftrack and lay in the road. The rest of the column quickly unloaded and deployed in the ditches along the road. There ensued a 20-minute close-up fight with grenades and automatic weapons and although the roadblock crew was greatly outnumbered, the bullet fire did them no hurt because of the protection of the embankment. S.Sgt. Leon D. Gantt decided that too many potato mashers were coming into the position and ordered his men to withdraw about 100 yards. There one of the Germans turned their halftrack around and ran for safety; they were apparently a reconnaissance element and had completed their mission.

During the action the two tanks had done nothing although they were within 100 yards of the German column. Sgt. Gantt went to 2nd Lt. Allen L. Johnson and asked him why. Johnson replied that he wasn't sure what to do. He then fired a couple of Parthian shots down the road, but the enemy had already disappeared into the fog and darkness. At dawn the outpost fell back on Noville according to instructions.

Twenty minutes after the fighting had died on the Bourcy road, three tanks approached the outpost on the Houffalize road. The sound of their motors seemed familiar to S. Sgt. Major I. Jones who was out by himself 75 yards in front of the roadblock. He thought they were American. When the tanks were 75 yards away Jones yelled, 'Halt!' and fired a quick burst with his BAR over the turret of the lead tank. It stopped 50 yards from him. He heard the occupants conversing in English. Then fire from the tank's .50cal broke around Jones' foxhole in the sloping bank on the side of the road. He flattened quickly and the fire missed his back by inches. The men at the roadblock fired on the tanks. Suddenly a cry of, 'Cease fire, they're friendly troops!' was heard. Jones was not certain whether the cry came from the force in front or behind him. The small-arms fire ceased but the two medium tanks which were supporting the roadblock and were standing about 100 yards from this new armour, were less sanguine. The tank on the right side of the road fired its 75mm; the first round hit the bank 15 yards from Jones and almost blew him out of the hole. The foremost tank confronting Jones fired six quick rounds in reply. The first round knocked out the American tank on the right. The second round knocked out his companion. The succeeding rounds also scored direct hits, yet none of the tankers were killed through several were hard hit. One man had his right leg blown off and his left badly mangled.

Pvt. John J. Garry, an infantryman, moved over to the ditch to help the wounded tankers and was hit in the shoulder by a shell fragment. Jones and the other men in the advanced positions were pinned to their foxholes by the grazing fire from the enemy guns. The American halftracks were in line behind the Shermans. The position of the ruined armour not only blocked the enemy from coming down the road but gave the halftracks partial cover so that they could turn their machine guns against the enemy column. A bazooka team tried to get forward but couldn't find an avenue by which they could bring the rockets to bear. Under these conditions of deadlock the two forces continued to slug it out toe-to-toe while the fog swirled around them and at last closed in so thick that they could scarcely see the muzzle flashes of the guns. At 0730 hours the platoon disengaged and withdrew to Noville, acting on the orders given by Desobry the night before.

They had held to the last minute and so complied with the order, but they were about through in any case as enemy infantry was now coming up around the flank. The roadblock on the Vaux road was not attacked. But while that party likewise was withdrawing at 0730 hours they heard the enemy coming down from the north.

During the night Captain Geiger had set up roadblocks on all roads entering Noville and had placed a thin screen of infantry in a circle just beyond the buildings. The position was particularly weak on the south and west – the sides which the enemy seemed least likely to approach. One tank was posted on the road leading to Bastogne and two were put on the other main exists from the town. In addition, one 57mm gun and a 75mm assault gun were placed to cover each of the roads which had been outposts during the night. The survivors of the two opening skirmishes had just drawn back within this defensive circle when 88mm fire from the north ripped out of the fog which by this time completely enveloped the town. From Noville's main street the north-running road is straight for miles: the defenders figured that German tanks were sitting out on the road somewhere and firing right down the slot. The fire was very heavy for half an hour. It destroyed three halftracks and a jeep and blew the machine gun from an M8 car, but miraculously, no one was hurt.

At 0830 hours two Tiger tanks nosed out of the fog and stopped within 20 yards of the machine-gun positions covering the northern sector. The 57mm gun to the right of the road was within 30 yards of the tanks. A medium tank with a 75mm gun was looking straight at them. The machine gunners alongside the road picked up their bazookas. All fired at the same time and the two Tiger tanks became just so much wrecked metal; later, all hands claimed credit for the kill.

A few Germans jumped out of the tanks and started to flee. Machine gunners and riflemen in the outposts cut loose on them but they could not be sure whether the fire found the targets because the fog swallowed the running men within 30 yards.

Some German infantry had come along behind the tanks and Desobry's men had caught only a glimpse of their figures, but they turned back the moment the skirmish opened. About 0930 hours the enemy began to press against the west sector with a series of small probing actions which lasted until 1030 hours. The officer in charge of this ground, 2nd Lt. Eugene E. Todd, was new to action and he felt that he was sustaining the weight of a major attack by the whole German Army. When he asked

Captain Geiger for permission to withdraw, Geiger replied, 'Hell, hold your ground and fight.' He did.

The real thing started at 1030 hours. The defenders had heard the rumblings of tanks and the puttering of smaller vehicles out in the fog as if a tremendous build-up were going on. Quite suddenly the fog lifted like a curtain going up revealing the stage: the countryside was filled with tanks. From the second storey of his CP in the Noville schoolhouse, Captain Omar R. Billett, (CO of Co B, 20th Armoured Infantry Battalion, 10th Armoured Division) saw at a glance more than 30 tanks. Others saw as many more from different points of vantage. In an extended skirmish line along the ridge short of Vaux were 14 tanks; Desobry's men looked at this scene and knew that they were standing in the road of an entire Panzer division. At that moment they might all have uttered the words of [The Song of] Roland, 'Great are the hosts of these strange people,' but instead they picked up their arms.

The leading enemy formations were 1000 yards away. The distance made no difference even to the men working the .50cal machine guns: they fired with what they had. When 800 yards out, the 14 tanks on the ridge halted and shelled the town. Other tanks were swinging around the right flank within 200 yards of the American position when the curtain went up.

The events of the next hour were shaped by the flashes of the heavy guns and the vagaries of the ever-shifting fog. The guns rolled in measure according to a visibility which came and went in the space of only a few seconds. But it was never any infantryman's battle. Little knots of men on foot were upcoming behind the German tanks, and the 420th's batteries hammered at these forces; it is doubtful if the American artillery stopped a single tank.

About the time that the enemy array became fully revealed, a platoon from the 609th Tank Destroyer Battalion rolled into Noville and added the gunpowder of its four TDs to the guns already engaging. The sudden, sharp focus given the line of Mark IVs and Mark Vs on the ridgeline, made them like ducks in a shooting gallery. Nine were hit straightaway, three of them exploding in flames. One came charging down the highway and was turned into flaming wreck 500 yards out. Two tanks which had been in the foreground, ahead of the ridge, also charged the town at a speed which wrought momentary confusion in Desobry's CP. At 30 yards range, a 105mm assault gun fired its first round, stopping one tank, but not disabling its gun. The German fired but then tried to withdraw; the assault gun finished him off with a quick round. The other German had been stopped by one of Desobry's mediums at range 75 yards. Looking in the direction from which they had come, observers in the taller buildings of Noville could see four more tanks lying in a draw – almost concealed.

The ground cover was good enough that the Noville guns couldn't get at them – until one tank made the mistake of pulling out onto the road. It was a shining mark,

300 yards away; a TD fired and the tank exploded in a blaze. The fog swirled back, screening the draw, and the other three tanks ran. To east of town, the run down the flank by the enemy armour ended with the destruction of three of the tanks. German infantry had appeared on that side in fairly large numbers but when the lifting of the fog exposed them, they turned and ran, and bullet fire from Noville thinned their ranks while they were running. In Noville, the defending infantry company had lost 13 wounded, 4 vehicles had been wrecked and one TD smashed, mainly from indirect artillery fire which had harassed the town while the tanks came on. By 1130 hours the fight had died, though intermittent shelling continued to worry the garrison.

In Bastogne, McAuliffe got the news at the crisis of the first attack and decided that Team Desobry needed help. At 1050 hours he ordered the 1st Battalion of 506th Regiment, under Lt. Col. James L. LaPrade, to reinforce Noville, putting 2nd and 3rd battalions in division reserve just north of Bastogne on the Noville road. At the same time, he detached 1st Battalion from the Regiment and put it under Division control. LaPrade and his staff got up to Desobry at 1130 hours and told him the battalion was on the road. It was not quite clear to either of the local commanders whether there had been an attachment of one force to the other, but they decided that for the time being they would keep it a 'mutual affair'.

LaPrade and his command had just one 1:100,000 map to serve them for the forthcoming operation. The commanders agreed that the next order of business was to attack due north and seize the high ground which the enemy had tried to use as a springboard during the morning. Infantry and armour would jump off together at 1400 hours. However, LaPrade's battalion didn't arrive until 1330 hours and couldn't make ready that soon; the jump-off was postponed until 1430 hours, since meanwhile there was a small matter of supply to be finally adjusted.

The 506th had left Mourmelon in such a hurry that may of the men did not have helmets and others were short of weapons and ammunition. LaPrade told Desobry about his embarrassment and the armoured force's S-4, 2nd Lt. George C. Rice, was sent packing to Foy to bring up ammunition. En route, he met the upcoming battalion and asked for their supply officer; but the latter was in Bastogne beating the woods for weapons and ammunition, so Rice asked the company officers what they needed most and found that rocket launchers, mortars and all types of ammunition were the critical shortages. He then dashed on to Foy and loaded the jeep with cases of hand grenades and M1 ammunition. The jeep was turned around and the stuff was passed out to the paratroopers as they marched.

On his next shuttle, Rice got back to the moving battalion with a jeep and a truck overloaded with weapons and ammunition. The *matériel* was put alongside the road in five separate piles so that the men could pick up the things they needed as they went by. He made one more trip and caught the head of the column just before it reached the limits of Noville. A load of 81mm mortar ammunition came into town after the battalion got there. These details caused a slight delay in getting the battle under way again.

Colonel LaPrade and Major Desobry wanted the high ground and this was their plan – that three tanks would strike northward along the Houffalize road and four tanks would head east toward the high ground west of Bourcy. With this group of tanks would go 1½ platoons of infantry for their close-in support. In between these two armoured groups moving along the road, LaPrade's paratroopers would spread themselves over the middle ground. One company would advance south over the Bourcy road, another off to the left of it would extend to the Houffalize road and the third company would go toward the high ground at Vaux. In this way, armour and infantry would spread out fanwise as they left Noville and started for the commanding ridges.

However, the preliminaries were not propitious. Noville was already taking a pounding from the enemy artillery. The Germans were firing by the clock and dropping 20 to 30 shells into the defensive position every ten minutes. The houses and several of the vehicles were afire. A proper reconnaissance became impossible; the assembly went off badly. Still, the attack got away at 1430 hours, 19 December, though somewhat unsteadily.

The line had scarcely moved out from the houses when an artillery concentration landed in the middle of Company C of the 506th Parachute Infantry, which was on the right flank. A number of men were hit but the company kept moving. Bullet fire from enemy positions on the high ground bit into the infantry ranks and slowed their advance. The little groups worked their way along, dashing on to favourable ground, stopping there to fire, then making a rush on to the next point of cover.

But elsewhere along the line, except on the far left where Company B kept moving, the attack was already flagging. The tanks and armoured infantry decided the attack was impossible so moved back to their holes, not even realizing that the paratroopers were continuing to attack in any strength. Company A was blocked by heavy tank fire immediately and, after a small advance, was forced to return to the village. But on the flanks, B and C went on until they reached the lower slopes of the objective ridges and started to climb. At that moment the enemy tanks came against them, supported by some infantry. A few of the paratroopers kept going; their snow-covered bodies were found on the ridges weeks later.

But the greater part of the two companies went to earth and sought whatever cover was at hand. Then they continued to slug it out with their small arms as best they could. They could hardly see the enemy at any time. The fog was closing down again and it was mixed with the smoke drifting over from the fires of Noville.

They held the ground until dark then Colonel LaPrade's men fell back on Noville. The fighting on the slopes had cost the battalion heavily, but the men thought they had caused equal losses to the enemy. From the town itself three tank destroyers had exchanged fire at about 1500 yards with the enemy tanks and had kept them from coming on, but whether they had done any real hurt to them could not be seen.

For about an hour after the return to Noville the front was deathly quiet. LaPrade's men had had no chance to dig in prior to the attack so they sought refuge in the houses. Colonel LaPrade improved his command post by moving a heavy clothes closet in front of the window. The Germans resumed their bombardment of the town and, in the middle of the shelling, a platoon of tank destroyers from the 706th Tank Destroyer Battalion reported for duty. Further tightening the defence, General Higgins, having arrived at Noville just as the American counterattack was fading, took the essential steps toward unifying the local command. Major Desobry and Colonel LaPrade were in agreement that one man should be in control, and LaPrade, being the senior, drew the assignment. LaPrade told General Higgins that he thought he

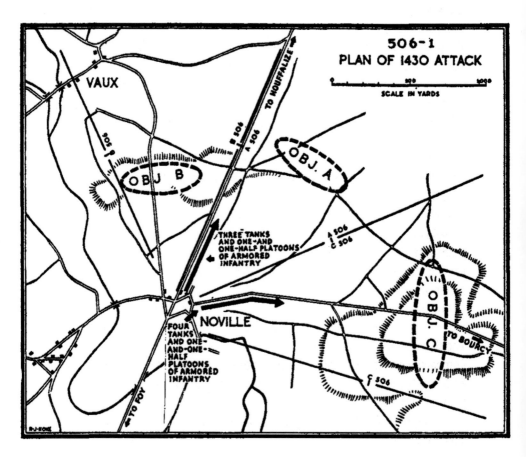

could hold on until dark but that he was convinced that the enemy would attack in strength shortly thereafter.

Soon after that, Colonel Sink got up to Noville for a personal reconnaissance. He talked to LaPrade and the latter shortly issued his orders for the combined defence. The plan was for Company B to defend to the northwest and Company A to the northeast and Company C was to cover the southern half of the perimeter, while the armoured group was held in the centre of the town ready to strike out in any direction. A few minutes after LaPrade was placed in command, an 88mm shell landed in the street outside the command post. The explosion shattered the clothes closet and both commanders were struck down by fragments. Colonel LaPrade was killed and Major Desobry wounded. Major Robert F. Harwick, LaPrade's executive, who had rushed back from a leave in Paris to join his battalion and had arrived in Noville just at the close of the afternoon fighting, took command of the combined force. The armour passed into the hands of Major Charles L. Hustead.

For the men of Combat Command B who were within the town the rest of the night (December 19-20) was comparatively quiet. Their peace was punctured at times by the dropping of a few artillery shells and out beyond the wall of fog they could hear the noise of an enemy build-up. There was little quiet, however, along the infantry perimeter. Enemy tanks in twos and threes, supported by infantry, probed toward them. When warned by small-arms or bazooka fire, they checked and blazed away at the positions from which they had seen the flashes. The accompanying German infantry tried to infiltrate through the lines. These small penetrations and the resulting fire were such that it was almost impossible to maintain wire communication with the outposts. For the paratroopers those hours were a nightmare of surprise fire, ominous noise and confusion. But when morning came the light revealed that two of the enemy tanks had been knocked out by bazooka fire.

These opening blows in the first round at Noville had been enough to convince General McAuliffe that the enemy was full of fight. After that first day they would never seem as strong to him again and the impression would deepen that their attacks were coming on in diminishing volume. But on the first day he looked toward his northern sector with increasing concern.

In the afternoon of December 19, the 3rd Battalion of 506th had been ordered to move up to Foy between Bastogne and Noville and establish a line there, with the 2nd Battalion moving to Luzery as a regimental reserve. When this move was made, Company H on the right made contact with the 501st Parachute Infantry by patrol and Company G on the left joined with the 502nd Parachute Infantry, maintaining a strong point in Recogne.

That night all platoons of Company C of the 705th Tank Destroyer Battalion were attached to the 506th Parachute Infantry and General McAuliffe got ready to employ as much of the strength of 502nd along his northern flank as the morrow would prove necessary. This small, confused action had reverberated all the way back to Corps. On returning to Bastogne, Higgins had reported to McAuliffe as follows: 'I think we're way out on a limb. There is too much distance between LaPrade in Noville and Strayer in Foy. It is my judgment that the Noville force had better get out.'

Colonel Sink, having carried out his independent reconnaissance, had reached exactly the same conclusion. At around 1820 hours he called Division and said that it was getting very hot at Noville; he urged that his forward battalion be withdrawn to a point north of Foy. But in view of the fact that General Middleton had ordered that Noville be defended and that the armour which had gone forward in response to that direction was still acting under Roberts' orders, it looked like a matter for decision by the higher headquarters.

General McAuliffe called General Middleton and relayed Higgins' and Sink's reports of the situation, adding his personal recommendation that the force be withdrawn. Middleton said, 'No; if we are to hold on to Bastogne, you cannot keep falling back.' Sink was called and told that the Noville force would have to stick. By then, Major Desobry had ceased to worry about the local problem. He was unconscious when they removed him from the CP to the nearest field hospital. He was still out, when, a few hours later, the Germans overran the hospital and took him prisoner.

On the whole, that first night in Bastogne, the situation was good, and it was largely the intuition and hunch and driving energy of the leaders that had made it so. The day of the 19th had proved that in the few minutes allowed him the night before, General McAuliffe had sized up the position properly. He had been tossed into a battle in which nearly all the major facts about the movement of forces were either unknown or obscure. He had rejected Corps' idea that the 101st Airborne Division be assembled to the southwest of Bastogne. It was a point that didn't give particular concern to General Middleton so long as General McAuliffe got his troops in where they were best placed to defend the town. However, VIII Corps Headquarters' reasoning was based on the long-range thought that after the enemy found he could not get through Bastogne, his next important move would be to the southwest.

In his hasty reconnaissance out to the west with Colonel Kinnard, his G-3, late in the day on the 18th, General McAuliffe had selected the ground for his camp from the short-range point of view. He wanted an assembly area which would place him at maximum advantage with respect to his own immediate deployments and the movements of the enemy in the immediate future. Though he had no way of knowing it at the time, his centre of equilibrium was on the ground furthest removed from the early dangers of the encirclement, although his two eastward-facing regiments were pointed directly toward the avenues along which the Germans would make their first approaches. The first day's results proved that the angels had been with him as he made his first decisions.

In the opening arrangements one decision was taken which worked out adversely. Lieutenant Colonel David Gold, the surgeon of the 101st Division, and Lieutenant Colonel Carl W. Kohls, the Division supply officer, had picked out a conveniently located crossroads to the west of the division assembly area and decided that this must be the rear, if there were such a thing. The division hospital was set up on the crossroads. Near midnight of 19 December the 327th Glider Infantry was told to send a motorized patrol to crossroads X – the site of this evacuation centre. The patrol was to investigate and clear up reports of machine-gun fire in that vicinity. They encountered no fire but the hospital was gone. Colonel Gold, all his officers and the men of the clearing company had been captured by the enemy. The 327th patrol decided that there must have been a fight, for dead Germans dressed in civilian clothes were found strewn over the ground, though there were no bodies of American soldiers. The bulk of the division medical supplies had been captured or destroyed.

Division then called on VIII Corps for medical help, and all 101st Division units were notified that casualties would be evacuated to the aid station of the 501st Parachute Infantry in Bastogne itself. One platoon of the 429th Medical Collecting Company, then located at Jodenville (about a mile west of Sibret), was made available to the 101st. Until the night of 21 December the platoon used its five ambulances and two weapons carriers to carry some of the wounded back to the 635th Medical Clearing Company. Then the Germans cut across the road and contact was lost with the clearing unit. An abandoned medical supply dump and the chance discovery of another depot in Bastogne containing blankets, litters, splint baskets and other hospital items helped the situation. Yet there continued to be a critical shortage of bed clothing, litters, penicillin, surgical instruments and surgeons.

The losses of the first day of battle had not, however, put any unusual stress on the medical facilities. But later in the fight when Bastogne became encircled, many of the wounded would have to lie on concrete floors with little or no cover. The blankets of the dead were collected so that there would be a chance for the living, and the shattered homes of Bastogne were searched for any kind of quilting.

Colonel W. L. Roberts, commanding Combat Command B, 10th Armoured Division, had been at Château-Thierry in 1918 and he well remembered the things that happen during the rout of an army. In his first conversation with General Middleton in which the VIII Corps commander had outlined the missions that sent the three combat teams of Combat Command B to Wardin, Longvilly and Noville on the night of December 18, Colonel Roberts had foreseen one of the main problems.

General Middleton said to him, 'The 28th Infantry Division and the 9th Armoured are ahead of us. They are badly cut up. The situation is fluid.'

Colonel Roberts replied, 'Sir, there will be stragglers. I want authority to use these men.'

Middleton agreed orally and later confirmed it with a written message: 'Major General Middleton directs that you have authority to take over all or any part of Reserve Command, 9th Armoured Division, in case they show the slightest inclination to retire. Anything you do to prevent falling back in that area will be given fullest backing.'

Colonel Roberts set his net to catch those drifting back. His Headquarters Company was instructed to keep hot food ready all day at a central point in Bastogne. A detail stood by to get these men from other units into billets around the town square. MPs were stationed at the road crossings in the south of Bastogne with instructions to stop every soldier who was trying to get away from the battle and turn him back to the Combat Command B area. About 250 stragglers were thus reorganized in Bastogne on 19 December. Some were men from the 9th Armoured; most were from the 28th Division. In this way Team Snafu was born, and within the next week it came to include 600 men, led by casual officers; but this outfit was severely handicapped by the fact that they were short of equipment and transportation as long as the siege lasted. Team Snafu was mainly a reservoir for the defending force. The stragglers went into it, the regular units drew from it as they had need.

Any organized units heading south were also commandeered. At 1400 hours on 19 December the 73rd Armoured Field Artillery Battalion of Combat Command Reserve, 9th Armoured, moved through Bastogne. Colonel Roberts watched it go by before suddenly realizing that it was his for the taking. He sent a staff officer to bring the battalion back and within a few minutes the battalion commander reported at his command post. Roberts told him to put the battalion in position with the 420th Armoured Field Artillery Battalion. The commander returned to his battalion but found that there was insufficient fuel for his vehicles and could not make the return trip. The 58th Armoured Field Artillery Battalion was stopped and put into position with the 420th, where its twelve guns fired during the next day. Just before the Germans closed the roads to the south, this unit heard that it had been cut off from Bastogne so it moved to the west.

Colonel Roberts had worried a lot about the security of the town itself for he had only part of his Engineer battalion and the Anti-aircraft Artillery battalion as reserve. General McAuliffe wanted to keep his own reserve as mobile as possible and couldn't see assigning one of his battalions to garrison the town. A task force from Combat Command B, 9th Armoured Division, entered Bastogne to learn the situation but was ordered by higher authority to withdraw to Léglise, 6 miles southeast of Neufchâteau. A request to 10th Armoured for the use of the Reserve Command was turned down. So, finally, Colonel Roberts committed Team Snafu, under command of Captain Charles

Brown of 110th Infantry, to the close-in defence of Bastogne. Team Snafu's complexion was somewhat changed on the following morning, 20 December, when Brigadier General George A. Davis of the 28th Division arrived in Bastogne with a request that Combat Command B attack toward Wiltz. It couldn't be done, for by that hour all of Colonel Roberts' forces were fully committed. Not long after General Davis departed, Combat Command B was ordered by Corps to release all 28th Division stragglers to their own command.

SCHRAMM: According to news received from our neighbour on the right, Bastogne was now surrounded and was being called upon to surrender. Gen. Pz Brandenberger, Commanding General of Seventh Army, was now able to link up with the troops of Gen. Pz von Lüttwitz's XLVII Panzer Corps in Berlé. The latter declared the situation of his corps to be favourable; he expected the early fall of Bastogne. It was true that the most forward elements of his corps – 2 Panzer Division – had reached only midway between Laroche and Saint-Hubert, although, according to plan, they ought to have reached the Meuse on the fourth day of the offensive. (19 December).

However, the enemy in front of this corps appeared to be completely defeated and no enemy reserves of any significance had made their appearance, so that there appeared to be nothing to prevent them from reaching their initial objective, the Meuse. To be sure, at this point the spectre of a fuel shortage made its appearance.

Up till now, Seventh Army, in spite of difficulties, had completely fulfilled its mission. It now received an order from Army Group B that, in addition to its mission of protecting the southern flank of the offensive, it would form a front to the north and prevent any escape of the trapped garrison of Bastogne, in the direction of Martelange; Panzer Lehr Division and elements of the 26 Volksgrenadier Division would secure the front at Sibret in the direction of Neufchâteau. The strengthening of the front south of Bastogne, where – owing to the failure of our troops to take Bastogne – meant it had to be ready for attacks of enemy reserves moving in from the south and south-west to relieve the town.

US FORCES: Throughout the first day of battle there had been losses and a few minor gains in the 101st Division's already strained supply situation. In the 907th Glider Field Artillery Battalion, Lieutenant Colonel Nelson, worried because his ammunition supply was rapidly reaching the vanishing point, dispatched searching convoys toward what he thought was the division rear. They moved westward and had been gone about six hours before Colonel Nelson grew aware that he had actually sent his trucks into enemy ground and that they were cut off. A second convoy of five trucks and trailers was sent toward Neufchâteau under Staff Sergeant Vincent Morgan, a supply sergeant. Sergeant Morgan was told that if he could not get M3 ammunition (standard for the 105mm. M3, a gun especially adapted for glider use) he was to bring back some M2 ammunition which the manual said could be used in an emergency.

The fortitude with which this young noncom carried out his assignment was one of the finest things of the siege. He returned late that night through heavy shelling and small-arms fire about one hour before the Germans cut the road of his inbound journey. He had first gone to Neufchâteau and on being disappointed there he had driven far to the northwest, covering in all about 75 miles. On his trucks were 1,500 rounds of M2. It was the only resupply of ammunition received by the 101st Airborne Division before the air resupply came in.

That partly compensated for a stroke of bad luck. The two convoys of the Division Quartermaster and Ordnance companies reached the division rear area late at night and were told to remain at a crossroads in the woods (P448630). Lacking time in which to reconnoitre the area, the two companies left all trucks parked on highway N4 facing west. Shortly after midnight on 20 December, Division headquarters was notified that the service area was receiving machine-gun fire and a few minutes later came the message: 'Evidence indicates service troops have disappeared.'

That alarm was enough; within five minutes a message was on its way to Corps headquarters asking for Quartermaster and Ordnance help. After being flushed by the fire the two companies had headed west and then south. Most of the trucks got through to the Corps rear and on the next day Captain John L. Patterson of one of the units, the 801st Ordnance Maintenance Company, taking a different route, got into Bastogne with two trucks bringing 500 gallons of gasoline. He then turned south again to bring the rest of the convoy forward. But by that time the Germans had already closed the road. Such was the shortage of gasoline in Bastogne through most of the siege that vehicles were fuelled only just before they went out on a run so that there would be no loss of gasoline if any standing vehicle was hit.

The German thrust from Neffe coincided with an assault on the 3rd Battalion's position at Mont, though here the battle took a quite different form because of Major Templeton's tank destroyers. The 1st Platoon of Company B, 705th Tank Destroyer Battalion, under command of First Lieutenant Robert Andrews, had arrived to reinforce Colonel Griswold's 3rd Battalion position on the evening of December 19. One tank destroyer was posted at the bend in the road. From here it could cover both the dirt road winding across the valley from Neffe and a draw leading off to the south.

A second tank destroyer took position by the last house, which put it somewhat behind, but in line with the tank destroyer blocking the Neffe road. The other section was placed on the north side of Mont to check any tank advance from directly across the valley. The tank destroyers held these positions until the hour came when they were most needed, on the night of December 20. Between 1900 and 1930 hours on that night the enemy struck through the fields lying between Neffe and Mont, advancing against Colonel Griswold's left. But the presence of the tank destroyers had intimidated the German armour. It took refuge in the little wood lying just west of the Neffe château and from the grove it shelled Mont. The German infantry advanced under this fire.

Enemy self-propelled guns moved along the railway line from Neffe a short distance (the rails here ran through a cut) and went to work on the same target. These two lines of fire converged on Griswold's positions almost at a right angle; the men in the forward line had to give ground, falling back on the village. The most forward of the tank destroyers, commanded by Sergeant George N. Schmidt, became their rallying point. Schmidt unloaded most of his crew and told them to join the fight with small arms. He then joined the infantry machine gunners who were already searching the down slopes with every automatic gun the battalion could bring to bear; in the next few minutes he threw 2,000 rounds of calibre .50 at the enemy.

Lieutenant Andrews used a radio-equipped jeep as his command post and central control station and used his security section as ammunition carriers to feed the stuff up to whichever tank destroyer was calling for it most urgently. The other three tank destroyers, under Sergeant Darrell J. Lindley, were shooting at the railway line. They tried at first to spot the self-propelled guns by firing at muzzle blasts; when that failed, they put flares up over the valley.

The fighting died about 2300 hours. By that time, the three self-propelled guns were out, and lines of German dead littered the hillside. Because of the dark, the defenders of Mont had no clear idea of why their automatic fire had made such a clean reaping of the German attack or of where the attack had broken.

On left flank of the 506th Parachute Infantry, the 502nd had passed a quiet night. In mid-afternoon of 19 December the 502nd had moved to Longchamps and established a perimeter defence there. Its 3rd Battalion deployed on a high hill to south of the village; its 1st Battalion was in the Bois de Nibermont, which was south of the hill. Initially, the 1st Battalion had held half of the front, but at 2400 hours on the 19th General McAuliffe told Lieutenant Colonel Steve Chappuis, commander of the 502nd Parachute Infantry, that inasmuch as his regiment was the division reserve, he could leave one battalion on the north-facing line. The 2nd Battalion drew the assignment. It made no difference in any case, for though the battalion was stretched 7,000 yards, there was no action anywhere along its front that night.

On December 19 Captain James E. Parker, of the Ninth Air Force, reported into Bastogne as air controller for the defence. His equipment consisted of a pocket full of radio crystals; what he needed was a high frequency radio that would give him contact with American planes. He searched the whole 101st Division without success, then found that the attached 10th Armoured Division units had two radios of the type needed – one in a tank and the other in a jeep. The tank could not be spared but the jeep and a technician from Ninth Air Force, Sergeant Frank B. Hotard, were given to Captain Parker. By 21 December his radio equipment was complete and he was ready to work with supporting planes. But the fog still enveloped Bastogne to keep the planes away. Parker had to wait two more days.

So, on 19 December the Germans, having gained contact with the 501st Parachute Infantry on a wide front, at first drew back to defensive positions. On 20 December the enemy made three attacks and the infantry, armour and tank destroyers in Colonel Ewell's sector beat them down. One of these fights was tactically less spectacular, but strategically more useful than the others. During the period of the fighting at Noville and Neffe there had been an action between the flanks of the 501st and 506th Parachute Infantry regiments which, although just a minor affair in itself, was to have an important effect on the general situation.

When the two regiments moved out to their positions on December 19, one going east and the other going north, they could not initially form a common front. In theory they were joined somewhere along the railroad track below Lahez (11 miles south of Foy) but in fact there was a considerable gap between their closest elements. Each became so closely engaged in its local situation that the matter of contact was neglected. Colonel Sink was alarmed about the peril to his right flank from the

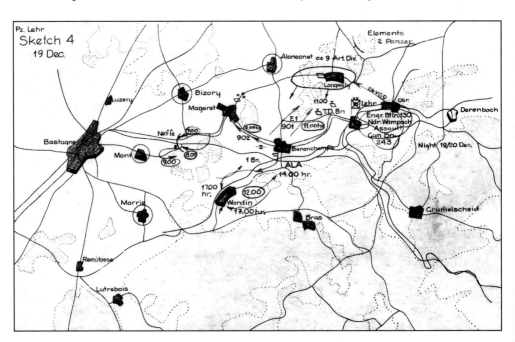

beginning, but it was not until late on the night of December 19 that Colonel Ewell fully shared his apprehension.

Company A of the 501st was in reserve in a small wood just north of the quarry on the Neffe road, which made it the most rearward element in the 501st's general position. Several hundred yards to its rear were the guns of the 907th Glider Field Artillery Battalion's forward battery. At 2300 hours on 19 December, a German patrol of 30 men came in between the company and the battery, moving from out of the northeast. A man on outpost duty for Company A saw the patrol and alerted the company. The patrol was permitted to come on. As it drew near the wood where the company had bivouacked, both the artillery and the infantry opened fire. The enemy dispersed into a nearby wood, though one member of the patrol was taken prisoner. Upon being interrogated he said that the patrol had come forward through the gap between the two infantry regiments and that its mission had been to get in behind and cut the Bastogne road.

The incident gave the artillery grave fears about the security of their base and it also called Colonel Ewell's attention to the most vulnerable sector of his front.

The night of December 19-20

As the darkness grew, more men from the elements which had been shattered to the east of Bastogne came moving back through the regimental lines of the 101st. Few of them stayed. Colonel Ewell and his officers talked to these men. They could tell very little of what had happened to them. Many of them were inarticulate. Infantrymen from units of the 28th Division still trickled into the area in groups of three or four. They made no attempt to organize themselves and they did not for the most part wish to be organized by anyone else. Some of these straggling infantrymen would ask Ewell's men, 'What are you doing?' Upon being told, 'We are fighting Germans,' they would look at the paratroopers as if they were stark mad.

But not all were like that. Some who seemed utterly wretched and spent when they came to within the lines, upon being handed a K ration, would eat it and look around and ask where they could get a rifle. They were ready to fight again. But to others food and companionship made no difference. They had been shocked so badly that they wanted only to keep on drifting. They were allowed to do so. This disorder had no ill effect on the combat force. The demoralization did not seem to bother the nerves of the men who were still fighting and they accepted it as the natural product of battle it often is.

A battalion of Field Artillery, the 109th of the 28th Division, came through as a unit and attached itself to the 907th Glider Field Artillery Battalion. Those groups from the 9th Armoured Division, which had been compelled to withdraw from the advanced ground along the Longvilly road, were in good order and high spirits when

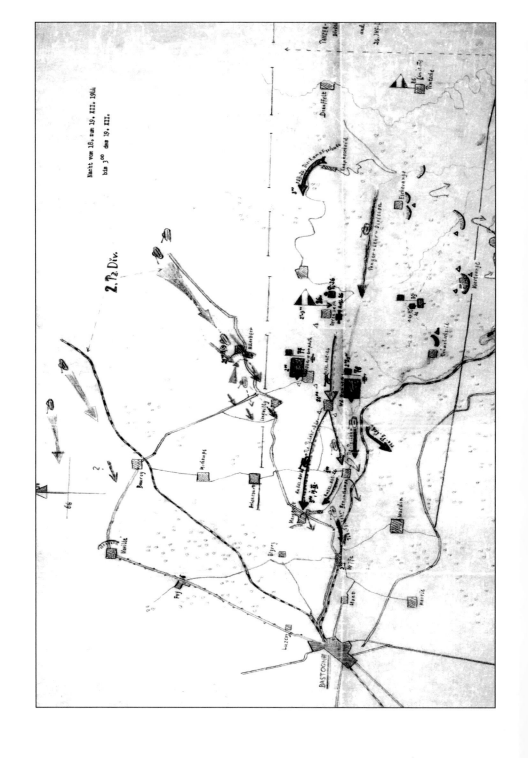

they reached the lines around Bastogne. One platoon of armoured infantry attached itself to Major Homan's battalion (2nd Battalion, 501st Parachute Infantry) and helped them carry the fight during the next several days. Seven tanks arrived from the 9th Armoured Division and constituted themselves a small task force operating in support of the battalion. At 0200 hours the 2nd Platoon of Company B, 705th Tank Destroyer Battalion arrived with four tank destroyers and took position on the south edge of Bizory. These reinforcements got there in the nick of time.

Chapter 5

Closing in on Bastogne

BAYERLEIN: On 20 December, the Infantry Regiment 78 of the 26th Volksgrenadier Division was subordinated to Panzer Lehr to carry out an attack on Luzery, via Bizory. Eight anti-tanks were subordinated to the regiment for this purpose. But the attack of Inf Regt 78 came to a halt before Bizory. The attack of Panzer Grenadier 902 on the road via Neffe towards Bastogne in the evening of 20 December was repelled with heavy casualties.

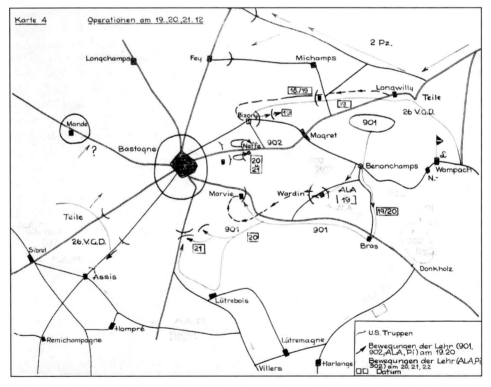

Bayerlein: Pz Gren Regiment 901, reinforced by one Panzer Company and one Artillery Battalion was employed to attack Marvie via Bras. ALA was by order of the Corps withdrawn from Wardin on the night of 20-21 December, to thrust, together with the Engineer Battalion south of Bastogne, towards Saint-Hubert. This task force advanced in the night via Lutremange–Hompré–Sibret into the area Gerimont–Tillet.

The resistance and the fighting strength of the enemy in this sector had increased considerably; artillery fire was notably intensified.

The attack of CC 902 and one regiment of the 26th Volksgrenadier Division against Bastogne from the east failed – with heavy losses. (See map 4 on the previous page).

KOKOTT: Upon the arrival of the combat instructions by corps, division, during the early hours of 20 December, its orders were issued to the regiments. Regiment 78 had the additional mission to clear, before the start of the attack, the situation at Magaret, as some enemy nests were still holding on in the southern part of the village. With assault troops – supported by the forces of Reconnaissance Battalion 26 – the situation there was to be cleared by dawn and positive contact was to be established with the Panzer Lehr Division fighting near Neffe.

The main point of effort of the two–division attack was to be in front of the Regiment 78. The terrain (affording good view for observation) as well as the intention to get hold as quickly as possible of the dominating heights west of Bizory, were the decisive factors for selecting this sector as the central point of effort. The main attack was to begin as soon as the customary morning fog would have lifted sufficiently to safeguard a clearly observed support by artillery and heavy infantry weapons.

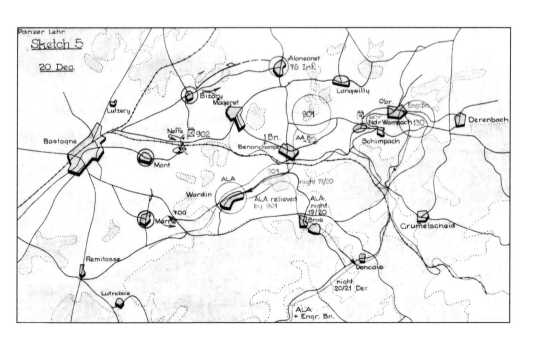

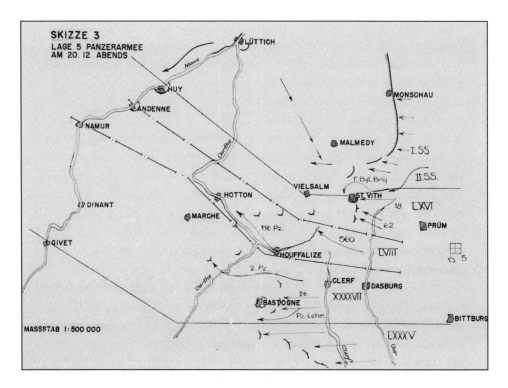

Rifle Regiment 39 had been ordered to proceed from its assembly area at Grumelscheid via Niederwampach to the area south of Arloncourt where it should be at the disposal of the division. Complete assembly of the entire regiment near Grumelscheid was not to be awaited, however, but as the various elements of the regiment would arrive there, they should be formed into 'mixed combat units' and be brought up speedily.

WAGENER: Portions of the Sixth Panzer Army were crowding the roads of the LXVI Corps and were choking them so that they prevented the artillery reinforcements destined for St Vith to be brought up. The C.I.C. of the *Heeresgruppe*. Field Marshal Model, for example, needed eight full hours to travel from Auw to Schoenberg. Favourable weather enabled the enemy Air Force to take a heavy toll of our troops in this sector. Consequently, the attack against St Vith was delayed until 20 December and achieved no success. An attempt by the Corps to break through according to orders, south of St Vith with units of the division on the left, started out well at first, but was brought to a standstill, however, near Lommersweiler and north thereof.

LÜTTWITZ XLVII Pz Corps: The 2 Panzer Division, after attacking and taking Noville without resistance about 1500, on 20 December moved its reconnaissance elements on westward as far as Salle, north of Flamierge. They then drew fire from the roadblock directly to the west. [This was the roadblock sent far to the northwest by one of Allen's companies – Editor]

These reconnaissance forces then turned northwest of the roadblock. At 2400 hours the reconnaissance team reached the bridge by Ortheuville. We then proceeded to build up the bridgehead in front of Tenneville. We had assumed from the beginning that 101st Airborne Division would remain in Bastogne and fight. Having been given their zones, we assumed that both divisions could proceed in good style and could keep together without too much difficulty. When we found that 2nd Panzer Division could not continue with its advance westward past Tenneville, I proposed to the Army Commander (Manteuffel) that we change the plan and concentrate all our effort against Bastogne, using all our forces to take the town. This was disapproved; instead, we were ordered to continue in the general line of advance given in the first order, with Panzer Lehr Division advancing south of Bastogne and 2nd Panzer Division advancing north of Bastogne. As they advanced, 26th Volksgrenadier Division was to close in behind, invest the town from the east, and subsequently take Bastogne when the occasion became favourable.

I knew that VIII Corps (US) had no reserve and therefore, for the first time, I was not afraid of being hit in the flank. Further, Seventh Army was supposed to be on my southern flank, and I was assuming that with their right flank they would take Libramont. At this time, 116 Panzer Division was reaching Nadrin on my right flank.

The reconnaissance group of 26th Volksgrenadier Division had a very efficient commander; therefore, he ordered his troops to advance from Bras to Lutrebois and on to Sibret. From Sibret, they were to advance to Chenogne, and from there to Mande. This reconnaissance group, consisting of 600 to 800 men and some anti-tank guns, was given the task of encircling Bastogne on the south, while the three infantry regiments of 26th Volksgrenadier Division moved to encircle the town from the north. In the meantime, however, some of the elements of Panzer Lehr Division had become engaged in the close-in fighting near the town, and I could not get them out. The reconnaissance group met very slight resistance en route to Sibret and up to the railroad track. There was heavy fighting around Sibret, but after it was taken we captured many American vehicles. The reconnaissance group then moved south of Mande where it again became engaged. [This was with Allen's battalion – Editor]

WAGENER: The LVIII Panzer Corps maintained its steady advance westward on 20 December and reached Cherain (northeast of Houffalize) with its 560th Volksgrenadier Division and Samree with the 116th Panzer Division. The division captured large stores of motor fuel there.

The XLVII Panzer Corps thought it necessary, to make still another attempt to take Bastogne. It was not successful, however. The 2nd Panzer Division then succeeded in crossing the Ourthe near Ourtherville, without interference from the enemy by taking the road bridge there, undamaged. The Panzer Lehr Division started to go around Bastogne from the south. The 26th Volksgrenadier Division had been assigned the mission of either taking Bastogne or encircling it. Prisoners confirmed that elements of the 101st Airborne Division were in the city.

It seemed that the way to the Maas was still open for the Army. Army was determined to let nothing interfere with its intension of searching this goal, neither the situation of the neighbouring armies, nor St Vith and Bastogne, nor any ideas of the lower commanders or of higher echelons. Bastogne had been encircled and that was enough. If the Seventh Army, could not accomplish its mission of protecting our flank against enemy forces arriving from the south then the southern flank of Fifth Panzer Army would be gravely threatened, even if the Bastogne pocket were liquidated. And if Sixth Panzer Army did not start something soon, the endangered northern flank would cause our advance to be stopped.

The Sixth Panzer Army again requested that strong reinforcement be sent down from the *Heeresgruppe*. The supply of motor fuel for the troops was long delayed, owing to the terrain difficulties and traffic congestion. Because the troops had not been furnished with enough provisions, they had to live from hand to mouth. The unloading of motor fuel had to be done at frequently changed places, due to enemy air activity. These changes prevented us from doing anything at all on scheduled time.

US FORCES: At 0530 hours, 20 December, while the 501st Parachute Infantry was patrolling toward its front, the 2nd Battalion got an attack over the same big hill to the east of Bizory where they had been stopped by the German reconnaissance force the day before. At a range of 3,000 yards, the tank destroyer men saw six enemy tanks rolling toward them from the southeast. Sergeant Floyd A. Johnson led his section to the hill north of Bizory and put the two tank destroyers on either side of the road. First Lieutenant Frederic Mallon led the second section to the higher ground southeast of town and waited for the German tanks in an open field.

The firing opened at 0730 hours, the tank destroyers withholding their fire from the enemy infantry so as not to compromise an engagement with the enemy armour, which by this time comprised one Mark IV, one Mark V and two 75mm self-propelled guns. These were following the infantry line by 400 yards; it was a full battalion of infantry, the 2nd of the 76th Regiment, 26th Volksgrenadier Division. In the first long-range exchange of fire, one tank destroyer was disabled and its loader killed by a direct hit on the turret; it limped away to the rear. The second tank destroyer in this section, after knocking out the Mark IV tanks, pulled back into Bizory where, in taking up another position, it damaged the tube of its gun by running against a building and became incapacitated. The other tank destroyer section opened fire at 600 yards on the Mark IV tank and one self-propelled gun, destroying both.

This was the crux of the engagement: most of the in-fighting of that morning of 20 December was done by the heavy guns. Major Homan's machine guns had opened up on the German infantry while the tanks were coming on and by so doing had kept them at a distance. Within a few minutes of this first body check to the German battalion, all the artillery that General McAuliffe could turn eastward from Bastogne blasted them.

1. ANDERSON'S FORCE WITHDRAWN FROM MAGERET. 501 HEAVILY ATTACKED DURING DAY & AT 1900
2. TEAM HUSTEAD & 101 WITHDRAWN FROM NOVILLE 504 REGT ENGAGED AT FOY
3. ENEMY ATTACKS MARVIE AT 1123
4. CHATEAU ROAD CUT BY ENEMY

Homan's infantry along the ridge were too far distant to do much bullet damage to the advancing German formations, but his men had a clear view of the German ranks coming on slowly, of the automatic fire making them hesitate, of the shells falling among them, of the attack gradually spending itself and of the enemy that was left then breaking away to the north to escape the fire.

KOKOTT: Toward 0700 hours on 20 December, Grenadier Regiment 78 reported that Mageret was 'enemy free' and that combat-fit reconnaissance troops were on their way to the west. It was very foggy day and at first all observation was impossible. Towards 0800 hours the Artillery Regiment reported that one battery of the Second Artillery Battalion was about to go into position. Towards 1100 hours the entire artillery could be expected to be ready for action.

After 0800 hours, the commander of Rifle Regiment 39 arrived at the division command post and reported elements of the regiment as being moved up. He was hoping to have, at the latest between 1000 and 1100 hours, at least 1½ battalions ready for commitment in the assembly area, including heavy infantry weapons.

Despite the tidying up of all measures for assembly and march, delays had occurred due to communication difficulties, road conditions and vastly extended grouping of the regiment's forces. Between 0900 and 1000 hours, 20 December, the commander of XXXXVII Panzer Corps appeared at the division command post. He pictured the situation about as follows:

'The 2nd Panzer Division has taken Noville. The enemy is in flight-like retreat from the 2nd Panzer Division via Foy to the south. The 2nd Panzer Division is in pursuit. The fall of Foy – if not already taken place – is to be expected at any moment. After the capture of Foy, the 2nd Panzer Division, according to orders, turns to the west and drives into the open terrain.

The Panzer Lehr Division is still outside of Neffe, but has taken Wardin and is advancing quickly via Marvie. The enemy there apparently weak and unprepared. Marvie possibly already taken by now?

Impression of enemy: The enemy feels himself beaten, is retreating and is merely trying to cover his withdrawal through delaying resistance in the sector south of Foy–Bizory–Neffe. It is now the primary mission of the 26th Division with all its available elements to proceed via Wardin–Remoifosse for an encirclement of Bastogne from the south, then to penetrate Bastogne from the southwest or west. The Panzer Lehr Division, with main effort on the left near Marvie, will close in on Bastogne from the southeast.

According to information from Army, forward sections of the 5th Parachute Infantry Division are quickly thrusting forward to the Bastogne–Martelange highway via Lutremange–Harlange. No enemy forces opposite the right wing of the Seventh Army.

Utmost speed is imperative for exploitation of the initial success.'

This unfortunate change of the situation came as a surprise to the division; all the more since Regiments 77 and 78 had not detected or reported any signs of weakening on the part of the enemy. They only had to record unchanged heavy enemy resistance and powerful artillery and mortar fire. The same impression had continuously been reported by the Reconnaissance Battalion 26 which was facing the enemy.

The divisional commander submitted these impressions to the commanding general and pointed out the present distribution of his units. Two of them, Regiments 77 and 78, were engaged with the enemy, one (Regiment 39) with combat group was at the moment marching up, with forward elements on about the level of Niederwampach. The regiment commander had gone forward to Arloncourt. The artillery was in firing position or also on the move and the only mobile unit of the division, Reconnaissance Battalion 26, was still subordinate to Panzer Lehr Division and most of the battalion was committed in the front.

He proposed that the approaching Regiment 39 – in the order of its arrival – should relieve Panzer Lehr Division in the area on both sides of Neffe and thus to enable the motorised Panzer Lehr Division to carry out the southern encirclement of Bastogne and the thrust from the south. This would also simplify the command as the 26th Division in its entirety would then cover the sector Foy–Neffe and the entire Panzer Lehr Division the southern sector Marvie–Isle-le-Pré–Isle la Hesse; this aside from the fact that the southern encirclement could be carried out much quicker with the motor vehicles of Panzer Lehr Division than by the elements on foot of the 26th Infantry Division. This proposal was rejected, partly with the reasoning that such a relief movement might possibly take up too much time and the objective would be reached much quicker if all marching elements of the 26th Division would immediately be turned into the new direction.

On the road stretch between Bras and the intersection of the road leading south from Wardin to the Bastogne road, tanks of the Panzer Lehr Division had taken up a covering position. Burned out and destroyed enemy tanks were scattered about on both sides of the road. Some of our own armoured groups were rolling back along the highway from the west towards Bras. The fog, which until then had been almost unnaturally thick, began to disperse. It was cold, the roads were slippery and muddy.

Having arrived at the intersection 4km west of Bras, the division commander had a hazy view towards the west through the threads of fog and discovered motor vehicles and guns rolling along the mountain road from north to south. This could only be enemy vehicles, probably it was the road from Neffe to Marvie. These vehicles were rolling forward with irregular intervals and apparently in great haste.

To the north – area Mageret, Neffe – the deep rumble of artillery could be heard. In the wooded sections west of Wardin, in addition to the crashing impact of the mortars, readily to be discerned, the quick and bright German and the slower American machine-gun fire was audible. The men themselves were not visible at all. Inside the village of Wardin there was not a single soldier. This may have been toward 1030-1100 hours.

At that moment a road reconnaissance officer arrived with the report: 'Forest paths 1200 metres west of intersection (road Wardin with Bastogne highway) and 1600 metres northeast of intersection passible only for pedestrians, impassable for all vehicles.' It was therefore ordered: 'All elements on foot use the western forest path to Lutrebois. Machine-guns and medium mortars, as well as the necessary ammunition, are to be taken off the vehicles; the weapons are to be stripped and carried. Guns, heavy mortars and all the vehicles turn around and move on to Lutrebois via Doncols-Lutremange.'

Mission for Rifle Regiment 39: Immediate thrust via Lutrebois–Remoifosse towards Assenois, attack out of Assenois area towards north against Bastogne. Objective: Capture of Bastogne from southwest. Replacement Training Battalion, Engineer Battalion and two artillery battalions are subordinated for that purpose to the Rifle Regiment.

Division Combat School – improvident mobile by means of bicycles – moves at first via Donclos-Lutremange to Lutrebois where it will be at the disposal of the division.

<u>Intentions for Reconnaissance Battalion 26</u>: The division intended, as soon as the reconnaissance battalion will have been drawn out of the fighting and its present subordination to Panzer Lehr Division, to pull the battalion around into the north of Assenois from where it would then be committed for the drive into Bastogne out of the area Senonchamps–Mande–Saint-Étienne from a westerly direction. The division command post was first at Wardin, with the intention of bringing it up later to Lutrebois.

The commanders reiterated their respective missions. Everything was clear. The rifle companies and the engineer company which had arrived in the meantime, unloaded their combat vehicles without delay. As they were approaching, they remained in the march and – after the equipment had been taken off the vehicles – disappeared in 'single file' loaded down heavily with weapons and ammunition, in the forest heading for Lutrebois. With exemplary calm and matter-of-factness, weapons, ammunition and equipment were unloaded, stripped and picked up, with the steady flow of the arriving units continuing smoothly to the west and southwest. There was no enemy fire on the Bastogne road. The fog had disappeared and the view was fairly good.

Regiments 77 and 78 in the sector Foy–Bizory had been informed about their tanks and the intentions of the division through a liaison officer. The returning officer reported that the regiment had begun the attack at 1100 hours despite the reduction of supporting artillery. The men passed by with a firm and confident attitude, bent down by the weight of the stripped heavy weapons and ammunition, proud of their previous successes and of unwavering determination to fulfil their soldierly duty to their beloved country. Whether they were old and battle-proven soldiers – there was hardly anyone that had not been wounded several times – or young replacements who had been facing the enemy for only a few weeks, whether officers, NCOs or men, they all shared their love of their country and the same sense of duty.

It was a sombre, but uplifting sight to observe these decent, morally clean front-line soldiers enter into that Battle of Bastogne, with no one being able to foresee what sacrifices this battle would cost and what influence it would assume over war and peace.

A mobile command post had been organised: the division's operations officer (Ia) worked in a command car and with him were officer assistants and enlisted personnel. The entire motor vehicle pool of the division command staff was parked rather carelessly near the village church. No shot had fallen in the village since morning.

In the command car, the division commander found the commander of Reconnaissance Battalion 26 who was then just being briefed by the operations officer. The mission of the Reconnaissance Battalion 26 was briefly:

1. Pull out of the fighting elements, assembling in the area Benonchamps.
2. Move forward via Bras–Doncols–Lutremange–Clochimont into the area of Senonchamps.
3. Attack from Senonchamps area to the east. Objective: Thrust into Bastogne from the west.

It was clear that it would be possible only after complete darkness for Reconnaissance Battalion 26 to cross the north-south highway Bastogne–Martlelange and to move to the northwest. But it had been said 'The night is the tanks' – or motorised units' – friend!' Besides, any possible difficulties were not even to be mentioned. To top all this, Reconnaissance Battalion 26 with its choice personnel was led by a particularly capable and outstanding commander who, at other times, had been able to make possible 'what had appeared impossible'.

The commander of Reconnaissance Battalion 26 had left the command post about 15 minutes earlier and the division commander was getting ready for his drive ahead via Doncols–Lutremange to Remoifosse, when an artillery salvo – about 12 shots – landed straight in the centre of Wardin. This was not particularly alarming until there was, shortly thereafter, another battalion salvo, this time at the western edge of the village, which broke the windows of the command car. Orders had just been issued to disperse the motor vehicles further and all the drivers were busy with their machines and motors when, for the third time, the dull drumming of fire became audible and already the impact of the batteries was hitting – this time straight into the assembled motor vehicles; this was immediately followed for several minutes by a fire concentration with devastating effects on this assembly of men and machines.

The fire ceased. The enemy observers – and this can only have been an observed fire – appeared to be satisfied with their success. And they had reason to be satisfied; the command staff was considerably paralysed. The vehicles, including the command car, were damaged or had been knocked out of commission, a great number of men and almost all the officers had either been killed or wounded, among them the first liaison officer, the division intelligence officer (Ic), the two officers of the Signal Battalion, one

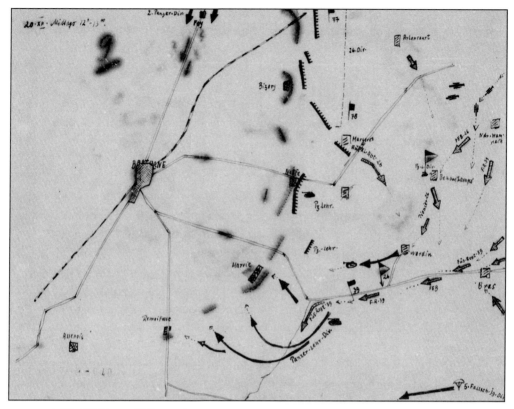

1200–1300 hrs – 20 December.

engineer officer and one liaison officer. The Ia (operations officer) and IIa (officer personnel officer) – the same as the division commander – had only been slightly wounded. This occurred towards 1300 hours.

It was fortunate that all the necessary orders had been given before and that all the movements had already been started. The dead were laid out, the wounded were bandaged. From the command post of Artillery Regiment 26 – located in a house – the command of the battle was taken over again and the command staff was somewhat restored.

Irregular fire concentrations had been placed on Wardin by the enemy artillery in the meantime, but they had not caused any additional major losses. Towards 1430 hours a message arrived from Rifle Regiment 39 to the effect that 'the forward elements of the regiment, after having crossed the north-south highway (Bastogne–Martelange) had become engaged with enemy forces'.

The division commander, together with the artillery commander, some time later drove forward via Bras–Doncols, accompanied, as usual, by a radio car. From Doncols on the road became poor, muddy, at some parts very narrow and there were many slopes. This, however, was the least concern. A lot more disagreeable was the fact that – in contrast to the exemplary traffic movements in the morning – a picture of considerable confusion now presented itself, everything was crowding onto this road: tanks of Panzer Lehr Division, so broad that they could barely squeeze through defiles and villages; trucks which had skidded off or had become stuck; motorised vehicles of an advance section of the 5th Parachute Infantry Division, supply vehicles, motorcycles; in between or pushed to the side or at a standstill due to exhaustion, were the horse-drawn vehicles of the 26th Division which again had been overtaken by the companies on foot of the 5th Parachute Infantry Division, with the men themselves pulling their vehicles. In addition, ambulances, damaged tanks and captured tanks were driving back from the west. In every village, at every narrow bridge site, at every turn of the road and wherever the road became steep, the stream of the traffic came to a standstill and became almost hopelessly entangled.

Worn-out motor vehicles, insufficiently trained driver personnel and inadequate knowledge of traffic regulations were, of course, other contributing factors. All the more regrettable is the fact that this state of affairs, which continued to exist all through the engagement around Bastogne and later during the withdrawal movements was not duly taken into consideration on the part of Army Headquarters.

US FORCES: Colonel Ewell's own infantry losses were almost nothing, but two tank destroyers were out of action for the time being and the defence had also lost two tanks. So ended the first, though not the most ruinous, of the piecemeal efforts which on this day presaged the failure of the German battle. This particular fighting had lasted about two hours, the artillery barrage perhaps twenty minutes.

Prisoner-of-war letters captured from the 76th Regiment said that their losses had been terrible. There followed a day-long wait along Colonel Ewell's 501st Parachute Infantry front. About 1900 hours the Germans put a heavy shelling from tanks and self-propelling guns on sensitive points over the ground held by the 501st – Bizory, Mont and the road junctions. The bombardment severed all the telephone wires connecting the battalions with the rear. As the German artillery slacked off, the 1st Battalion of the 501st radioed to Ewell that the enemy was charging straight down the road from Neffe.

Major Raymond V. Bottomly's 1st Battalion could hear the tanks coming on but it was so dark that they could tell little else. All the guns from the eleven artillery battalions in Bastogne dropped a dam of fire across the road 100 or 200 yards west of Neffe, the heaviest and most effective American defensive fire during the siege. Three German tanks, two of them Panthers and one a Tiger Royal, were hit and destroyed just as they drew past the last houses in the village. Some German infantry, which had moved down the Bastogne road before the barrage dropped, met their fate from machine guns Company B had posted in a house by the side of the road. That company took the shock without having to yield one yard of ground. Their strongpoint controlled the terrain so well that not one German drew near enough to close on the infantry line. They were killed to the last man, and for weeks later, their grotesque forms along the roadside, heaped over by the Ardennes snows, showed where the German death march ended. The most forward of these bodies was 300 yards ahead of the shattered tanks.

ZERBEL: 20 Dec. 2nd Panzer Division: At 1400 hours the division took Noville. The main reason why it was captured was probably because parts of the division had utilised the road past Rachamps. During the course of the morning the division had repulsed an attack from the direction of Foy. The reconnaissance detachment took, at about midnight, the undamaged bridge across the Ourthe at Ortheuville. During the advance on Ortheuville an enemy attack from Flamierge was repulsed.

Panzer Lehr Division: The division did not succeed in capturing Bastogne. But the reconnaissance detachment succeeded in capturing Wardin. An attack of the division against Marvie was repulsed.

26th Volksgrenadier Division: The 77 Regiment took Bizory and reached the railroad. The 78 Regiment crossed the railroad during an attack near the hill 540, but in the evening is pushed back to the railroad. The reconnaissance detachment of 39 Regiment are ordered by the Corps to advance past Remoifosse and to attack Bastogne from the south. The reconnaissance detachment takes Sibret at 2100 hours, the 39 Regiment reaches the line: 1km north of Remoifosse–Assenois.

US FORCES: In Noville they were running short of armour-piercing shell as the morning of 20 December dawned. In Bastogne, General McAuliffe was wondering whether Noville was worth what he might have to pay to hold it and was about to reach a decision. Deprived of any support from the commanding ridges, Noville is not a military position, but just another village on low ground and a perfect sinkhole for fog. The issue was already hanging in the balance because of the ammunition situation and the miscarriage of the American attack on December 19; only a little more pressure would tip it.

Sometime on the morning of 20 December, after the Germans had attacked at Bizory and then side-slipped northward, Company A of the 501st was attached to the 2nd Battalion with the mission of occupying the woods south of the railroad and making contact with the 506th Parachute Infantry. However, it did not proceed immediately on this assignment and during most of that day the effort to join with the 506th was limited to patrol actions out of Company D, 501st, which was in reserve in the 2nd Battalion. Four times during the day patrols from Company D tried to move north along the general line of the road running to Foy. But they were always turned back from the vicinity of Halt, where the enemy had taken up fire positions.

At the same time Company D, 506th Parachute Infantry, was pushing right toward the railroad station at Halt against stubborn resistance. When evening of the 20th came the company had reached the Foy-Bizory road. It stayed there with its right flank some hundreds of yards distant from the railroad station at Halt, which was held by an enemy force. There had been no contact with the 501st. Colonel Sink, commander of the 506th, called both Headquarters 501st Parachute Infantry and Headquarters 101st Division and urged that the 501st swing left to meet him. He said that his force was standing on the railroad line which was supposed to be the regimental boundary – but this overstated the case.

The first three patrols which had gone out from Company D of the 501st to search for the 506th's flank had been turned back by fire from the Bois Jacques. They got no idea of the enemy strength in the forest area for they were beaten back by a scattering small-arms fire at long range whenever they moved to right of the Foy-Bizory road in an attempt to gain the railroad.

Corporal Frank Lasik of Company D, 501st, led out his fourth patrol of the day just as the evening twilight of the 20th came on. There were eight men with him, and instead of beating over the same ground as the earlier patrols they swung around to the west of the Bizory-Foy road, when within a short distance of the railroad, Lasik dropped six of his men and continued on with two others. They reached the rail line and moved east along it to within 100 yards of the Halt station. At that point they saw a force of seven German tanks supported by a body of infantry moving straight toward them down the railroad track, and only 75 yards away. Private Manzi fired one shot toward the enemy force and then the three men withdrew as rapidly as they could. Lasik knew that Company A had been given an assignment and was supposed to be moving toward the same ground which the Germans were approaching. He rushed to the battalion command post and told them to get word to Company A, 501st, that tanks were coming down the railway track.

KOKOTT: On 20 December towards 1600 hours the division commander realised that, above all, it would be necessary to establish order on the road from Doncols to Lutrebois, so that it would be possible for the combat team to stream from there into the area south of Bastogne. With the aid of military police detachments called by radio and signal communications detachments taken from any unit available, the congestion was loosened, torn apart and gradually directed into orderly channels; a traffic regulation system was installed at all narrow points and blocking sites.

Thus it was possible – though only by early evening – to organise a fluid march movement to the west with elements of Artillery Battalion 26, Reconnaissance Battalion 26, which meanwhile had begun its movement, and the horse-drawn heavy infantry weapons and supply vehicles of the 26th Division together with those elements which were vitally important for the Panzer Lehr and the 5th Parachute Infantry Divisions.

US FORCES: Company A had moved out about 1600 hours on December 20 and was already engaged in clearing the woods that lay south of the railroad and west of the Foy-Bizory road. They found no enemy in the first wood and so they continued on to the next plantation lying south of the tracks, between them and the station at Halt. In the middle of this journey they met a patrol from the 506th Parachute Infantry. Until that meeting, they had believed that the 506th was already on the railroad track. But from the patrol they learned that the actual flank of the 506th was about 600 yards north of the railroad track and that Company D, 506th, had been having a running fight with small groups of the enemy for control of the station at Halt.

From the second woods, Sergeant Lyle B. Chamberlain of Company A, 501st, was sent with a four-man patrol eastward along the tracks to search for the enemy. This was at just about the time that Lasik was getting back to warn the battalion. Sergeant Chamberlain's patrol moved through the swampy ground that lay to the left of the tracks and had gone but a short distance when they sighted a German patrol coming toward them. It looked to Chamberlain like the point of a company. Darkness was already closing around them and the German group did not see Sergeant Chamberlain's patrol. The patrol fell back on the company and reported what they had seen. Hastily, the 3rd Platoon of Company A was deployed along the edge of the woods north of the railroad track to lay an ambush for the enemy group which Sergeant Chamberlain had sighted. While the platoon was deploying, thick fog closed in around the woods and this, coupled with the darkness, reduced visibility to almost nothing. The Germans were allowed to approach within 10 to 15 yards before Company A opened fire. The surprise volley wholly disorganized the leading German platoon and the men who were not cut down ran to the rear to the swampy ground.

The whole Company A front had by this time become engaged. The enemy had been advancing with two companies abreast astride the railway track. On Company A's right, the 1st and 2nd Platoons did not get the same chance to close with the enemy at short range, and after the dispersion of the German right, mortar, grenade and automatic fire from the German force south of the tracks beat heavily against the two platoons. Because of the darkness and the fog the men of the company could get no idea what losses they were taking themselves and could only judge the progress of the action by the build-up of the enemy fire. They saw little or nothing of the Germans they were engaging. The skirmish went on with both forces firing toward the flashes and sounds in the position of the opposite force.

Company A lost 15 men in the night engagements, 3 of whom were killed in action. But in the black darkness the men of the Company thought at the time that they were taking much heavier losses. The fog made more vivid their impressions of the opposing fire while keeping them from feeling their own strength. The murk was so thick by this time that it was only by the sounds of fire that a man could tell where his nearest comrade was fighting.

While the fire-fight on the south of the tracks continued, the Germans who had fallen back toward the swampy ground on the north of the track gradually collected themselves again. For half an hour or more there was a lull in the action on this side except that both forces tried to carry on at long range with hand grenades. Then the 3rd Platoon of Company A heard the enemy moving out through the woods around their left flank. Apprehensive that they would be outflanked if they maintained themselves in the forward ground, the 3rd Platoon pulled back its own left flank to the west so as to cover the rear of the company position.

This change in the form of the enemy attack was also indicated on the right flank. Private 1st Class William C. Michel, a German-speaking soldier who was with the company executive officer, Lieutenant Joseph B. Schweiker, could hear the enemy shouting commands and telling his men to move out around the left and right of the American force. The order may have been a ruse intended to cover a withdrawal, but as the fire fight began to build up again it seemed to Lieutenant Schweiker that the enemy was actively pushing out around the flanks of Company A and threatening his rear.

At about 2230 hours, 20 December, Lieutenant Schweiker ordered the company to fall back to the line of the second woods. Lieutenant James C. Murphy called all of the squad leaders together and told them that the signal for withdrawal would be a long burst of machine-gun fire and that all of the other machine guns were to be kept quiet until this signal came. The withdrawal was made in reasonably good order, the circumstances considered.

When Company A took up its position in the second wood it was deployed to the right of the railway line. The company was not pressed there at any time during the night. Apparently, the Germans had ordered a withdrawal at about the same time. After staying in the woods for somewhat more than an hour the company withdrew a little to the south and bivouacked in a third plantation.

The advance of the enemy down the railroad track had put them on the rear of Company D, 506th Parachute Infantry, but it was not until 0400 hours that Company D, which was somewhat engaged by small groups hitting directly at its front, discovered that its flank had been turned. Lieutenant Colonel Strayer reported to Colonel Sink that he believed an enemy force of about two platoons had penetrated between his battalion of the 506th and the 501st. But he did not know that Company D, 501st, was meeting this force frontally. Colonel Sink ordered Company D, 506th, to face some of its men toward the rear and hold their present ground. This, they did. The 1st Battalion, 506th, then in reserve at Luzery, was ordered to send Companies A and C forward to help contain the penetrating force. Both of these companies were badly depleted from their fight in Noville.

To the east where 506th stood guard, the boys who had prayed for morning soon wondered why. At 0730 hours two enemy tanks came hell-roaring through the field along the Houffalize road, swung in beside the first building of Noville, wheeled so as to protect each other, and then stopped. On their way in they had knocked out a jeep with one shell and had sprayed forward with their machine guns as they rushed. Unseeing, they came to a halt within 10 yards of a bazooka team and the first rocket fired set one of the tanks on fire. Staff Sergeant Michael Lesniak, a tank commander, had heard the German armour roaring along. He dismounted from his tank, walked up the main street for a look, then went back and swung his gun in the right direction and moved to the centre of the street. He fired before the enemy realized that he had gone into action and his first round finished the German tank. A third German tank that stayed just north along the road, but out of sight in the fog, threw a few loose shells into the town and one of them hit Sergeant Lesniak's tank, damaging the turret.

That was the beginning. Almost nothing that followed could be seen as clearly. During the next two hours the defensive perimeter was under constant attack from the German armour and infantry. But the enemy pressure developed quite unevenly as if their forces, too, were groping or were keeping active simply to conceal some larger design. It was battle with the bewildering shifts of a montage; there were momentary exposures and quick shiftings of scene. The enemy came on in groups of a few tanks supported by small parties of infantry and were held off by the armoured infantry and paratroopers with their own weapons just long enough to let a friendly tank or tank destroyer get into firing position. Fog mixed with smoke from the burning buildings again mantled the country between the village and the ridges, diffusing the efforts of both forces. It was all but impossible for anyone to get any impression of how the tide was moving; the combatants could tell only what went on right before their eyes.

Curiously enough the tank destroyer men of 2nd Platoon, Company C, 705th TD Battalion, who had taken position in the south of Noville, had the impression that in these early morning hours the infantry was standing off a full-fledged attack. They could see only 100 yards beyond their own guns and they could hear large numbers of enemy tracked vehicles moving toward them through the fog. Their imaginings were further stimulated by a direct hit on one tank destroyer at the outset which killed the gunner, Corporal Stephen Cook, and wounded several of the crew. For two hours they fired in the general direction of where they thought the German armour was massing; they could see no targets, but they thought their unobserved fire might have some deterring effect. At 1000 hours, 20 December the fog quite suddenly lifted and the sky became almost clear. In the field within view of the tank destroyer force were 15 German tanks; they were proceeding toward their own lines at about 1,000 yards range. Four of the tanks were hit and disabled and the tank destroyer men were confident that their own shells did it. They had seen their shots hit home and watched Private Steve E. Reed empty seven boxes of calibre .50 ammunition into the German crews as they tried to flee across the fields.

Just before the fog had cleared a Tiger tank had charged right into the heart of Noville. Visibility among the buildings was just about zero. The tank stopped in front of the command post of Company B, 20th Armoured Infantry Battalion. The tanker swung his gun uncertainly toward the door. Captain Omar Billett said a quick prayer. A joker beside him remarked, 'Don't look now, but there is an 88 pointing at you.'

Sergeant Lesniak's tank was within 20 yards but the German had failed to see him in the fog; by rotating his damaged turret just a short space to the right Lesniak had his gun dead on the Tiger. At 20 yards he fired three rounds of 75mm at the German tank without doing any apparent damage. The German quickly put his tank into reverse, but the left track ran up and over a jeep. The jeep was completely crushed but at the same time it fouled the track and beached the tank. The German kept on pushing back the jeep under him. He next collided with a half-track and the tank tipped dangerously over on its right side. That was enough for the German crew. They jumped from the tank and ran out of the town, going through the American lines without getting a shot fired at them, such was the thickness of the fog.

The radio inside the Tiger was on a busy channel, and talk flowed on inside the dead tank. It looked like a wide-open opportunity, but before the command post could round up anyone who could understand German, the channel went out. The tankers destroyed this Tiger with thermite and later on they caught hell from Colonel

Roberts for not bringing the tank back to Bastogne. But they had a good excuse. The losses among the tank drivers were already such that they did not have enough men to manoeuvre their own armour. Two tanks were without drivers and partly without crews, so the tankers asked the paratroopers if there were any men among them who could handle tanks and two of Major Harwick's men of the 1st Battalion, 506th Parachute Infantry, climbed aboard and started out with the Shermans. Later both men were killed in their tanks during the withdrawal.

They knew now that they would not be able to hold Noville much longer. The clearing of the fog revealed to Major Hustead (now commanding the 20th Armoured Infantry Battalion) and his staff a situation they had already suspected. During the night of the 19th the men on the outposts had heard enemy armour moving across their rear, particularly to the south-west. In the morning, patrols had gone out, and although they couldn't tell much because of the enveloping fog, they found enough to confirm the fact that enemy forces were between them and Bastogne. Hustead had lost radio contact with Combat Command B Headquarters during the night, so in the morning he sent First Lieutenant Herman C. Jacobs to Foy; he was to get to Headquarters, 3rd Battalion, 506th Parachute Infantry, in Foy and use their radio to inform Combat Command B of the situation and request that the Noville garrison either be withdrawn or reinforced.

He carried out the mission in a half-track and several times on the way to Foy he blundered into enemy parties and had to shoot his way through. But at Foy he found no one; by this time 3rd Battalion was engaging the enemy to the south of the village. Lieutenant Jacobs continued on to Bastogne and found Colonel Roberts who sent his only available reserve – an anti-aircraft platoon – forward. But the platoon was blocked by enemy forces before it could get to Foy. The Germans were coming across the road from both sides. When the fog rolled away the men in Noville could look southward and see the circling armour. To make their isolation more complete, they had lost all contact with the main body of 506th Parachute Infantry and they did not know whether the situation at Foy was developing for or against them.

The Germans had already made their attack against Colonel Sink's support position. In the early morning of 20 December, the 3rd Battalion of the 506th received light shelling and flat-trajectory fire along its lines at Foy. During the night and through the first hours of daylight the enemy had taken advantage of the heavy fog and moved in very close to the American outposts, though it seems probable that they knew very little about the location of the American lines and were only groping.

At 0800 hours on 20 December, a force of about two companies of infantry supported by three tanks attacked toward the ground defended by Companies I and H. By 0900 hours, they had driven in far enough to put direct fire on the American positions with their supporting weapons. The tank destroyers of 3rd Platoon, Reconnaissance Company of the 705th Tank Destroyer Battalion were not in position to give the infantry any direct fire support during the engagement. They were in the woods south of Foy when the attack came on, and in the later stages of the action they were established as roadblocks, but during that morning they did not fire on any enemy armour. Company G in Recogne was engaged by another company of German infantry supported by three tanks. The command post of the 3rd Battalion in Foy came under direct fire from an enemy tank. Until 1030 hours the battalion held its ground in Foy and then withdrew to the high ground south of the village. Here it reformed for the counterattack.

It was about mid-morning when 101st Airborne Division Headquarters called the 502nd Parachute Infantry and directed that its 3rd Battalion (under Lieutenant Colonel John P. Stopka) attack through Recogne and gain contact with the American force at Noville, thus re-establishing the left flank. The battalion crossed the line of departure at 1130 hours and then pushed right on, meeting little opposition. But when the 3rd Battalion, 502nd, reached Recogne a change in the order came. At somewhere around noon General McAuliffe had decided that Noville wasn't important enough to warrant a last-ditch stand on the inferior ground around the village. Colonel Stopka

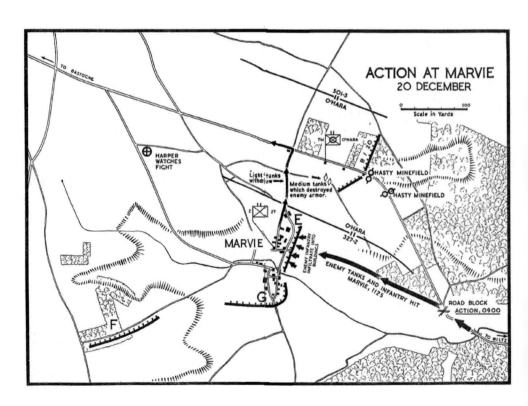

Three wrecked
vehicles.

Captain James R.
Lloyd, Lancaster P.A.,
a Ninth A.F. air liaison
officer stands by a
disabled tank.

Houffalize showing
extensive battle
damage.

Panther Tank and anti-tank gun destroyed on the Staumont–Stevelot road.

Ninth Airforce fighter-bombers in co-operation with ground artillery knocked out this King Tiger tank on the main road from Bastogne to Houffalize.

A German convoy wrecked by Ninth Air Force fighter-bombers in the Houffalize area. A dozen vehicles including a Sherman tank and half-track captured from the Americans are strewn along the highway near Viller-LaBonne-Eau.

German mobile artillery piece destroyed by a 9th Airforce P47 Thunderbolt.

A German half-track destroyed in Houffalize – object of repeated bombardments by 9th Air Force, before the Germans withdrew from their important communications centre.

A Douglas C-47 of the 9th Troop Carrier Command drop supplies over Bastogne on 23 December 1944.

Major Gen. E.R. Quesada (left) commanding the 9th Tactical Air Command, and his chief of combat operations Colonel Gilbert Meyers examine a disabled tank on a road north of St Vith. Fighter-bombers, co-operating with artillery units made the town untenable for the Germans. As the enemy withdrew, 9th TAC pilots destroyed or damaged hundreds of tanks, half-tracks and other motor transport.

Mine-detecting and meeting the locals in Houffalize.

A German convoy, including American tanks and half-tracks captured during the counter-offensive, attempting a withdrawal to Houffalize was caught in the centre of Noville by Ninth Air Force fighter bombers and ground artillery.

On Christmas afternoon more than 100 9th Air Force Martin B-26 Marauders dropped their bombloads on St Vith, the important road junctions and communications centre captured by the Germans in their counter-offensive. They bombed bridges, roads, towns and strongpoints as part of a systematic plan to isolate German troops from their supply sources.

US soldiers examining captured tracked German anti-aircraft guns

US officers make an inspection of a disabled German tank in St Vith. L–R – Major Albert Triers, Landsdown P.A.; Major William W. Abbot Jnr; 1st Lieutenant Richard Zinkowski, Norwood, Mass.

Members of the 101st Airborne Division walk past dead comrades, killed during the Christmas Eve bombing of Bastogne. This photo was taken on Christmas Day, 1944.

Photo taken by a U.S. Army Signal Corps photographer on 26 December 1944 in Bastogne, Belgium as troops of the 101st Airborne Division watch C-47s drop supplies to them. Jeeps and trucks are parked in a large field in the near distance.

Men of the 28th Division march down a street in Bastogne, December 1944. Some of these men lost their weapons during the German advance in this area.

Tanks of the 7th Armoured Division in St Vith.

was accordingly instructed to make a limited attack forward to cover the extrication of Major Harwick's men of the 3rd Battalion, 506th. That battalion was to fight the same kind of action on the other flank. It was figured that the Noville force could sideslip into the area of the 502nd once Stopka's battalion got up to it. However, his battalion had fought its way only a short distance past Recogne when the plan was again changed.

Colonel Sink, commanding the 506th, had looked the situation over and decided that the best way out was for Major Harwick's force to retire down the Bastogne road. Colonel Stopka's battalion remained in position on a line running through Recogne with its left flank extended westward to join the 2nd Battalion of the 502nd. Its advance had been made wholly without artillery support because of the dense fog.

Radio communication between Bastogne and Noville was not re-established until 1300 hours. The order then came through on the artillery radio network to Harwick and Hustead that their command would withdraw to the Bastogne perimeter of defence. They were told that an attack on Foy was being made immediately to relieve the pressure on Noville. When they saw that the attention of the enemy was diverted to the Foy attack, they were to make a break for the south.

A few local problems had to be solved in Noville preceding the withdrawal. A considerable amount of ammunition had to be destroyed. There were more than 50 wounded men awaiting evacuation. But the shrinkage of manpower in the Noville force through battlefield deaths and casualties already evacuated had totalled so many men that, despite a steady loss in vehicles, there were enough tanks, halftracks and trucks left to move back all the casualties and permit all the armoured units and most of the paratroopers to ride out of Noville.

Company C of the 506th was already south of Noville in a reserve position, and accordingly, it was nominated as the advance guard to move out on foot. Three tanks would support Company C. The halftracks and jeeps loaded with the wounded would come next in the column, then would follow the main body, the personnel carriers and armour. Those of the infantry who couldn't find a ride would move out in file on both sides of the road. Company B of the 506th was to be the rearguard, supported by four tank destroyers. One platoon from that company was detailed to destroy everything useful that could not be evacuated.

At 1315 hours, on 20 December, Company C took off. At 1325 hours the first vehicles quit Noville. Major Hustead and his engineer officer had prepared the ammunition dump for demolition; the dump was alongside a building and they were hopeful that the blast would lay the building low and block the highway. Hustead waited until the last vehicle had passed the ammunition point. He then gave the engineer the signal to set off the delayed charge. They heard the explosion as they moved on down the road.

The start was good. Until 1300 hours the air had been crystal clear for most of the noon hour. Then, as if Providence again chose to intervene in their favour, the fog closed around them and screened their departure from the enemy. They knew that they could be heard and they wondered whether the Germans would try to take them in the flank while they were on the move. But the fire which might have been turned against the road spared them and they moved along quite easily, except for an occasional flurry of bullets.

A little protecting belt of armour – one armoured M8, followed by four half-tracks, and five medium tanks – moved in front of the vehicles containing the wounded. Just beyond the village, one of the tanks broke down and had to be destroyed with thermite. The armoured car took off at full speed without waiting for the others and got to Bastogne without receiving any fire. The column continued on toward Foy and the half-tracks had come abreast of a farmhouse within 500 yards of the village when one of those chance things occurred, which may change the whole course of a battle despite their own intrinsic unimportance.

In the leading half-track the shutter dropped and the driver could not see. The driver raised up and moved his arm to adjust the shutter and Major James B. Duncan mistook the gesture and thought that the man had been wounded and was holding his eyes. So Duncan quickly pulled the handbrake. That stopped the entire column. The first half-track was rammed from behind by the second half-track which had lost its brakes. The third half-track pulled up close. At that moment bullets and grenades bit into the column from both sides of the road. The men could not see clearly what they were fighting but they knew that some Germans were deployed in the ditches and that they were also drawing fire from the house. Major Duncan figured that he had to fight it out on that ground. The machine gunners in the halftracks put heavy fire on the ditches; and the dismounted riflemen, after flattening themselves, blazed away with their tommy guns. In ten minutes the skirmish was over. Some of the enemy had been cut down, others had dispersed into the fog.

The fourth half-track had withdrawn a short distance to keep from jamming the column. Major Duncan had gone back that way. The amount of firing that he could hear from forward among the half-tracks, mingled with the noise of the firing of the 3rd Battalion, 506th, which was attacking north toward Foy, gave Duncan an exaggerated idea of the importance of the action. He asked for the tanks to get forward and fire on the house.

Meanwhile the three half-tracks had shoved on. Back through the column all men had dismounted and taken to the ditches. Major Hustead came forward to see what was blocking the road and he met Major Duncan near the head of the column. Both officers then tried to get the tanks moving again. The crew of the first tank told Major Hustead they had no ammunition. The second tank couldn't fire either; there was no ammunition for the big gun and the machine gun was jammed. Duncan prodded two of the tanks into carrying out the order and they shelled the house until it caught fire.

Thereupon, they backed away. Duncan was still worrying because he could hear small-arms fire, so he ordered them to go in.

As they moved away they were caught broadside by fire from three German tanks which had slipped through the fog from the east. The first American tank caught fire. In the second American tank the driver was hit and the tank came to a halt. Because of the murk, men who were only a few yards back in the column could get no true idea of what was happening. Captain William G. Schultz, the tank commander, was in the fifth tank. He walked up to the third tank, which was short of personnel, and drove it on down the road past the two disabled tanks. They were beyond his help and he thought that if he kept moving the rest of the column would follow. But in this he was mistaken. He drove through Foy alone and about a ¼ mile beyond the village his tank was hit by a shell from an enemy tank and disabled, but Captain Schultz and his men got out alive and walked on into Bastogne.

Meanwhile, Major Hustead and Captain Billett were striving to get the column moving. A tank destroyer of the 705th TD Battalion whipped up from the rear of the column to try to get a line on the yet unseen German tanks. A Sherman tank from the forward group backed straight toward the tank destroyer and the tank destroyer, reversing direction to save itself, backed over and crushed a jeep. Then the Sherman moved on up to have another go at the house and it was hit by a shell from a German tank and exploded in flames. The turret blew off into the road and blocked the passage. The driver of the fifth tank, who had been with Schultz, had moved up and taken over the second tank just before it was demolished. This left the fifth tank driverless. As the road was now blocked by the turret, Hustead and Billett moved back and forth among the tankers looking for a driver so they could start the column moving across the field to Foy. There was not a single response. Every tanker replied that he was qualified for some other kind of work but couldn't move a tank. The paratroopers and the armoured infantry jumped to the conclusion that the men were 'dogging it'. They walked among the tankers cursing them and calling them 'yellow bastards'; they threatened to beat up one man whom they suspected of being a driver. But they were all wrong about it. Most of these men were new replacements. Some were cooks, some were mechanics and some were riflemen. They were tankers only in that they belonged to a tank organization. The impasse at Foy could only be charged to the replacement system.

The paratroopers further back along the road had picked themselves up and moved out through the fields on both sides. The group on the right swept all the way to Foy, met no organized resistance but bagged a few Germans whom they found wandering around in the fog. The tank destroyer force at the rear also became restive and at 1430 hours First Lieutenant Tom E. Toms led his vehicles down a little stream line on the right of the road and by way of this defilade entered Foy from the west. He got there in ten minutes; the paratroopers who had swung out to the right reached the village at the same time.

The tank destroyers were not quite through for the day. The foot troops who had swung out to the east of the road were stopped by the line of fire which the unseen German tanks were throwing at the Shermans at the front of the column. They sent word back to the main body. However, the danger was removed by help from an unexpected quarter. Private 1st Class Thomas E. Gallagher was driving one of the tank destroyers which had gone into Foy and was on his way to an assembly area in a wood south of the village when he was stopped by an officer of the 3rd Battalion, 506th Parachute Infantry. He knew the location of the German tanks and told Gallagher to go after them. Gallagher said he had no crew and no one to work the gun. Two paratroopers climbed into the tank destroyer and took over the gun. Gallagher then moved forward and, with the infantrymen doing the firing, the tank destroyer engaged one tank at 200 yards range and destroyed it. The other German tank escaped over the hill.

Because of the fog Major Hustead and Captain Billett hadn't seen the infantry parties move out to right and left. Billett felt that he ought to clear a route for the tanks and vehicles to advance and he sent back for his outfit, Company B of the 20th Armoured Infantry Battalion. One platoon stayed back in the column with the vehicles and he started out with the other two platoons moving through the fields to the right.

Major Hustead had the same idea but didn't know that it had already been put into execution twice on this same flank. He gathered about 20 paratroopers together and made an additional hook to the right. The odd part of it was that although this party groped its way forward over the same ground as the others, they did so in time to reap part of the harvest. The enemy groups around Foy were now feeling the heat from both directions. Hustead's sweep toward Foy resulted in the capture of 43 Germans.

In the village Hustead met troops of the 3rd Battalion, 506th, who had advanced from the south and he asked them, 'Has our armour come through?' The men had seen the three half-tracks and Captain Schultz's tank go by and they thought this was the armour Major Hustead was talking about, so they reassured him. Hustead borrowed a jeep and drove to Bastogne to report to Colonel Roberts that he had completed his mission. But when he got to town, he learned that he was mistaken and could only tell Colonel Roberts that the column was on its way and should soon arrive.

Major Hustead in Bastogne and Captain Billett in Foy were both on the radio urging the column to come around to the right. But Major Duncan and Second Lieutenant Burleigh P. Oxford were already jockeying the column through the fields. The fifth tank was on its way. A crew of paratroopers had climbed aboard after telling the tankers, 'We'll learn how to run the son of a bitch.' When the column drew into Foy some of the vehicles got stuck in the soft ground. Lieutenant Oxford dismounted all of the men and got the winches and the manpower working first of all on extricating the vehicles that contained the wounded. At dusk on 20 December the column was finding its way through Foy and past the lines of the 3rd Battalion, 506th. The command in Bastogne had intended that the force would go into a defensive position on the high ground south of Foy. But Hustead told Colonel Roberts that the column was dead beat and had better be brought into Bastogne. The tank destroyers under Lieutenant Toms stayed in Foy supporting the 3rd Battalion.

Team Desobry had gone to Noville with 15 tanks; it limped back with only 4. The 1st Battalion of the 506th Parachute Infantry was in full strength when it went to Team Desobry's support. It lost 13 officers and 199 enlisted men at Noville. By their combined efforts they had destroyed or badly crippled somewhere between 20 and 30 known enemy tanks of all types including not less than 3 Mark VIs. They probably damaged or destroyed many more. Headquarters of the 506th estimated that the assaults of the German infantry had cost the enemy the equivalent of half a regiment.

Yet all of these material measurements of what had been achieved were mean and meagre weighed against the fact that the men of Noville had held their ground for a decisive 48 hours during which time the defence of Bastogne had the opportunity to organize and grow confident of its own strength.

First Action at Marvie
At 0645 hours on 20 December the enemy shelled Team O'Hara's roadblock on the Wiltz–Bastogne road about 1,300 yards east of Marvie.

The fog was thick and little could be seen of the enemy's movements out along the road. But as the light grew, the tankers could hear enemy armour moving somewhere in the fog up beyond the block. At around 0900 hours the fog lifted a little and they saw a dozen German soldiers trying to break up the block. A concentration from the 420th Field Artillery Battalion caught this group while they were, tugging away at the felled logs. Two were killed (they were later identified as part of an engineer working party) and the others fled the fire. The enemy then put smoke on the roadblock – enough to conceal the block and the terrain right around it. Figuring that an infantry attack might be coming, Team O'Hara covered the block with fire from mortars and assault guns. It is believed that this fire fended off the thrust toward Colonel O'Hara's front and deflected it toward Marvie, where five of O'Hara's light tanks had taken up position the night before.

In the meantime, Colonel Joseph H. Harper, commanding the 327th Glider Infantry, had been getting acquainted with Colonel O'Hara. The 327th had taken over the command post at Mande-St-Étienne at 1500 hours on 19 December, and at 1630 hours its 1st Battalion had been attached to Colonel Ewell's 501st Parachute Infantry to support his right flank. At 0400 hours on the 20th the 327th command post and the 2nd Battalion of that regiment were ordered into Bastogne and at 0600 hours they marched on into the town.

Without a pause, the 2nd Battalion, 327th, moved straight on to Marvie and took over that village from the 326th Engineers. The 3rd Battalion remained in Flamisoul (some 2,000 yards east of Flamierge) and established its command post in the woods at (494610).

The 2nd Battalion entered Marvie just about as the enemy first opened fire on Team O'Hara's roadblock. Colonel Harper had been told by division that the reconnaissance group of light tanks would be in support of his 2nd Battalion. Going straight away to see Colonel O'Hara, he said to him, 'I've been told to hold this sector. I understand from division that you are in support of me and I would like to go on a reconnaissance.'

O'Hara said, 'Let's get started.' With them when they went out was Lieutenant Colonel Roy L. Inman, commanding the 2nd Battalion, 327th Glider Infantry. The officers discussed the relationship of their respective forces as they made the reconnaissance. Under the existing arrangement, Colonel O'Hara's force was not under Colonel Harper's command, for the armoured force was still not attached to the 101st Division, but was in support only. Colonel Inman had moved his 2nd Battalion, 327th, in on the right flank of Colonel O'Hara's force, with his line so extended as to secure the village and then bending southwest to the main road just above Remoifosse. This was a distance of about 2,500 yards. The Engineers had three outposts distributed over this south-eastern facing arc and none of them had as yet been engaged. It was agreed that Colonel O'Hara would be responsible for the defence of his immediate front and that Colonel Inman, who would take over from the Engineers immediately, would be responsible for the sector to right of O'Hara's. Harper then left Inman and drove down the main road toward Remoifosse. He established the southwest extension of his line on the forward slope of the hill over which the main road passes a little more than half way from Bastogne to Remoifosse. The position thus chosen was a few hundred yards north of where the original Engineer outpost had been.

After looking over the situation and making sure that his men were where he wanted them, Colonel Harper drove back to Marvie. The jeep reached the road intersection just west of Marvie. There Harper stopped for a moment and debated with himself whether to go on into the village or take the west running road and have a quick look at the high ground above the village. He decided in favour of taking a look and the jeep moved on up the hill.

At 1125 hours on 20 December, Colonel Inman's command post in Marvie (2nd Battalion, 327th Glider Infantry) reported to Colonel O'Hara that they were receiving a great deal of shelling and that they could see enemy tanks coming toward them. This movement had already been observed from within O'Hara's sector. Yet Harper, driving up hill at the very moment of the attack, was unaware that anything untoward was breaking until he got to the crest of the hill. There he turned about and saw the enemy guns blazing from the edge of the woods directly southeast of Marvie and their point-blank fire hitting among the houses of the village. Harper could see that the fire came from tanks within the wood but he could not be certain how many.

The barrage was followed immediately by an advance out of the woods by four enemy tanks and six half-tracks. They were well spread out and they advanced slowly, firing as they came, apparently drawn on by the prospect of an easy success over the light tanks. These tanks kept dodging in and out among the buildings and the enemy fire appeared to follow their movements closely. The light tanks replied futilely with their 37mm guns and the enemy armour appeared to come on more boldly. Feeling that the presence of his unit, rather than helping Colonel Inman's men, was drawing more high-velocity fire into the town, the light tank commander asked Colonel O'Hara for permission to withdraw. It was granted.

By then, one of the light tanks had been set afire by a shell burst; a second had been hit in the suspension system but could make its escape by backing up the hill. Yet Colonel Harper did not know all of these things. He saw the tanks quit the village and concluded that they had been routed and were deserting his infantry.

Up on the hill behind Marvie, Colonel O'Hara's larger guns kept silent. In front of the oncoming armour a German self-propelled 75mm gun was pacing the advance. Its gunner spotted a half-track near O'Hara's command post and fired several quick rounds at it. The shells hit an Engineer jeep, demolished a one-ton trailer and blew through the lower portion of the command post, killing a cow. The command post was in the first floor of the house and this fire was hitting into the basement right under the headquarters.

The tanks were by now almost broadside to Team O'Hara at 700 yards range. Firing at right angles to their own front, two of Team O'Hara's medium tanks opened up on the line of Mark IVs and half-tracks. The Germans never saw what hit them for they were still shooting at the light tanks now pulling out through the end of the village. One Mark IV was blown up by a direct hit from one of the mediums. The other Sherman knocked out a second Mark IV and one of the half-tracks, the fire killing all of the tank crew and most of the men in the personnel carrier. One German tank fled to the rear. The fourth tank dashed for Marvie where the infantry destroyed it with bazooka fire. The self-propelled gun, having gotten almost into the village before the Sherman opened fire, tried to turn about. It was hit from all sides and went up like a torch.

In the last stage of the German advance, the half-tracks had sped forward and increased their interval so that they were almost closing on the first houses when the tank line was destroyed. They kept going. They got to the streets of the village and the infantry jumped down. With one small exception the glider troops stayed right where they were and met the German onslaught without flinching. The attack had come just as the relief of the Engineer units had been completed, and some of the Engineers were moving out of the north end of Marvie. Men from Inman's heavy mortar section, stationed in an apple orchard, saw the Engineer party leave as the fire began. They could not understand what the movement of troops was about and they thought that part of their own battalion was withdrawing, and so they followed.

Colonel Harper, watching all of these things from the hill, made the same mistake as his mortar section. He thought that his men had been stampeded and that the village was gone. He called General McAuliffe on the radio, told him what he had seen and said that he was on his way to gather the men and that he would make a counterattack. His car sped back over the route it had come and Harper started to rally his men. Then he learned that most of the party were Engineers and that only the mortar squad from among his command had displaced. He told that squad to get back into the battle and they moved at once. This error in judgment is the only instance during the siege of Bastogne when any American Infantryman is known to have left his position under fire and without orders.

Colonel Harper, still outside the village, called Colonel Inman on his radio. The executive officer of the 2nd Battalion, 327th Glider Infantry, Major R.B. Galbreaith, answered the call. He said that both Colonel Inman and Captain Hugh Evans, commanding officer of Company G, which was holding the village, had been hit by a tank shell while making a reconnaissance just as the German onslaught began. He did not know how badly they were wounded. Harper asked him, 'Are you still in the village?'

Galbreaith answered. 'Yes, but the Germans are here also. We expect to drive them out.'

The close-in fighting continued into the early afternoon. Inman's men stayed in their foxholes. Some died there, shot at 10 yards' range by machine guns as they tried to stop the half-tracks with their rifle and tommy gun fire, their bodies almost cut in half where the machine guns had ripped them through. Their comrades found them later sitting stiffly at their weapons. Colonel Harper himself inspected these positions. He noted that every one of his dead was still facing forward as if trying to engage the enemy.

The bazooka men had likewise met the attack head-on. Some of the German infantry, clearing away from the half-tracks, had ducked into the houses. The glider men went in after them and cleaned them out house by house. Within two hours 20 Germans were prisoners and 30 were dead in Marvie.

First Lieutenant Stanley A. Morrison of Company G, who had been captured when the Germans first came into the village, was recaptured by his own men. Colonel Inman had lost five men killed, each of them killed in a foxhole while resisting the half-tracks. Fifteen men of Company G were wounded in the action.

During all that time, Team O'Hara sat high and dry on the ridge, taking no part in the engagement except during the brief gun duel. On the right flank that force received some small-arms fire, but the enemy made no attempt to close on that side and the armoured infantry in Team O'Hara's position was too far away to lend any support to the men in Marvie. That village was again clear by about 1300 hours hours. At 1400 some of Colonel O'Hara's tankers saw an enemy half-track stuck in the mud about 150 yards southeast of Marvie. It had been with the striking force during the morning and had become bogged. In the previous excitement all hands had overlooked it. The tankers quickly knocked it out.

At 1420 hours the enemy put smoke down on Marvie. Some of the tanks made another sally from the woods but changed their minds. The situation began to ease and Colonel Inman's men went about improving their positions, digging their foxholes narrow and very deep right next to the foundations of the houses. The day ended fairly quietly but with a definite change in the weather. The Ardennes was cold and frozen. The ground had hardened enough for the tracked vehicles to get about over the hills in almost any direction. Still no snow had fallen. Now, as the first skirmish ended around Marvie, the first flurries fell. Soon the ridges were whitening and the snows thickened during the next few days. Increasing cold, light winds and deep drifts changed many of the characteristics of the battle. One of the problems that now pressed most heavily on the commanders was to get their men indoors and keep them from freezing. Villages became places of refuge not only from enemy fire but from the cold.

The Belgian villagers, clinging stubbornly to their homes even in the face of the German attack, had to be evacuated to provide shelter and cover for the infantry. In a world of white, the forest plantations were the only other areas of easy concealment for troops. The local actions swirled more and more around these two objectives to capture a few houses or to take a line of fir trees.

The first message from the 4th Armoured said, 'Hugh is coming.' When General McAuliffe had visited General Middleton (commander of VIII Corps) in Neufchâteau on the night of 20 December, he had been told that General Patton was attacking east of Bastogne. The two commanders then set up a simple code, each town along the route getting a letter. Bastogne was K. Others were designated A, B, C. Now the word was that 'Hugh' [Major General Hugh J. Gaffey, commanding the 4th Armoured Division] is on his way.'

On the heels of that assurance came another message, equally bright. VIII Corps radioed that pathfinders would arrive in Bastogne at 1600 hours and that resupply by air would start coming in at 2000 hours. Colonel Kohls, G-4, 101st Division, had waited all day long for that appointment, for on the day before VIII Corps had told him to prepare for 'resupply tomorrow if weather permits'.

Directly west of the houses of Bastogne are large, clear fields on a gentle hillside, close to where the 101st Division had made its command post. This was the designated spot. Under average operating conditions resupply bundles are recovered by Quartermaster and Ordnance companies and their items of *matériel* are then segregated in Class I, III and V dumps under Division control. At Bastogne, Colonel Kohls had no Division supply forces available either to pick up the resupply or manage the distribution. The regiments were therefore told to send at least five quarter-ton trucks to the field to handle the supplies directly and haul them to unit dumps. The units were told to report what supplies they had each recovered and then to distribute them according to orders which would be given by the G-4 Section.

ZERBEL: 20 Dec. 2nd Panzer Division: The situation of the Corps at the beginning of the night was as follows: the 2nd Panzer Division advanced well without meeting upon enemy resistance. If the gasoline and ammunition arrived in time – the bringing up of which was still as difficult as in the beginning because of the obstructed bridges – it could be expected that the division reached Marche in the afternoon of 21 December, chiefly because the right neighbour (116 Panzer Division) was already advancing on Laroche. Bastogne continued to worry the Corps more than all, but it was hoped that the 26th Volksgrenadier Division would succeed in taking the town.

The encirclement of this town was imminent, because the reconnaissance detachment of the 26th Volksgrenadier Division was fighting since dark at Sibret. If it was captured during the night, it was expected that the reconnaissance detachment would close the encirclement of Bastogne at Flamierge.

As the left neighbour reported progress in his advance, an attack on the south flank was expected next. It was ordered for 21 December that the Panzer Division were to thrust forward as far as possible. The Panzer Lehr Division was to leave an armoured group south of Bastogne, because the forces of the 26th Volksgrenadier Division were not strong enough to take Bastogne from three sides i.e. from the south, the north and the east.

Chapter 6

21 December: 'A Day of Bitter Fighting'

KOKOTT: The division commander reached the command post at Bras only after midnight, i.e. towards 0100 hours on 21 December. Based on incoming reports, the situation to him on that night appeared as follows:

- The 2nd Panzer Division had taken Foy during the course of the day. The enemy there had actually withdrawn in the direction of Bastogne. The 2nd Panzer Division had then, in accordance with instructions, turned in to the west and, with its bulk, was rolling in a westerly direction. Only weak security detachments had been left behind near Foy.
- The Grenadier Regiments 77 and 78, while fighting some very costly battles, had made but small progress. The heavily defended village of Bizory, however had been taken by Grenadier Regiment 78. The regiments were now located immediately west of the Foy–Bizory road. Enemy resistance there: strong.

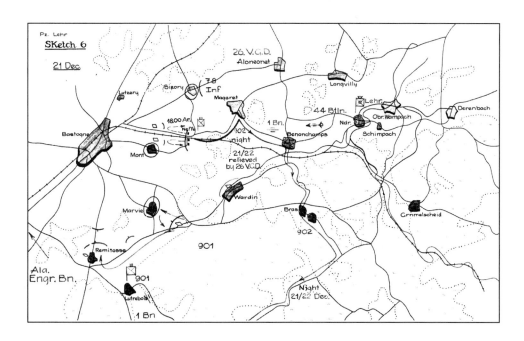

- The situation of the Panzer Lehr Division in the Neffe area was unchanged. Fighting there was stationery. The (left) Regiment 901 of the Panzer Lehr Division, however, had fought its way forward to the area immediately in front of Marvie. Marvie was still in enemy hands. The regiment fought approximately along a line extending from south of Marvie to Remoifosse. Enemy resistance: stubborn, but apparently becoming weaker.
- The reinforced Rifle Regiment 39 of the 26th Division had, as it came in, entered the battle west of the north-south highway since the late afternoon. With stubborn determination and excellent fighting spirits, the regiment carried on the attack without interruptions, had taken Salvacourt and the heights west thereof and was continuing the battle towards La Lune, direction of Assenois. The enemy forces opposite Rifle Regiment 39 fought stubbornly and were supported effectively by tank, artillery and, particularly, by strong mortar fire. Speaking without exaggeration, both leaders and men of the rifle regiment had given an outstanding performance.
- Reconnaissance Battalion 26, according to calculations by the division, should by that time (towards 0100 hours of 21 December) have been advancing somewhere between Lutrebois and Salvacourt. It was to be hoped that by the early morning hours of 21 December the battalion should have reached the area around Senonchamps.
- At about the same time, Rifle Regiment 39 should have captured Assenois as a base for the attack on Bastogne and it was therefore to be expected that the division could assemble at about the same time from the southwest and from the west. With the artillery and heavy weapons – insofar as they had not already reached Rifle Regiment 39 – then moving up smoothly, it could be anticipated with certainty that the necessary fire support would be available for the attack on the southwestern sector of Bastogne on the morning of 21 December.

As to the impression of the enemy, it appeared that – even if they would put up a stubborn and tough battle – they would be less strong and prepared in the southern sector than in the eastern sector. Here in the south – and maybe in the west – the success had to be aimed for and to be fought for with all the strength! Continuation of a tedious and costly drive toward the eastern sector, now known to be particularly well prepared for defence, had to be discarded. In that sector the enemy merely had to be tied down, while the last available man, the last gun, the last tank and the last machine-gun belonged into the southern or western sector! In that way, a precise and clear strongpoint position would have been established and that would, in all humanly possible estimation, have had to lead to the aspired speedy success.

It had been most regrettable when the 2nd Panzer Division had committed the undoubtedly tactical mistake of having failed to follow up the enemy's withdrawal via Foy towards Bastogne, and having instead contented itself with the capture of Foy, then turning the bulk of its forces in the westerly direction by-passing Bastogne in the north. Had the division been ordered ten times by the corps to push westwards after the capture of Foy, it should still have exploited this opportunity and should have followed on the heels of the withdrawing enemy forces, that would have paved the way for success. The mistake at Foy, regardless of whose responsibility it was, had been made. This could not be extenuated. The damage, however, could be repaired once more if a precise and clear decision could be reached regarding the question of Bastogne.

At this stage of the battle, now that enemy reinforcement inside Bastogne had been recognised and the enemy had established a strong switch line in the eastern sector, it was imperative for army and corps to lay their cards on the table and to state once and for all what was to be done. The decision to be reached was:

1. Is Bastogne to be captured? or
2. Is Bastogne merely to be encircled and the Maas River to be reached?

If Bastogne was to be captured, then all the forces would have to be committed at a single point, and concentrated at the 'soft' spot, i.e. the southern and western sectors. It would then be necessary for the 2nd Panzer Division to attack in the western sector, while Panzer Lehr Division and Rifle Regiment 39, together with Reconnaissance Battalion 26, would make their attack in the southwestern sector at the same time neutralising the western switch line. In that manner it would be possible to bring about quick the fall of this 'pus-filled boil'.

If, on the other hand, the Maas River should be the primary objective, then an encirclement, a siege of Bastogne without further attacks, by less numerous forces would be sufficient; to start with, one division, the 26th Division, would be enough and additional encirclement forces could possibly be brought up later. It would then be necessary and possible on 21 December for all mechanised and motorised units to stream past Bastogne to the west and not even a single tank would have to be left behind at the gates of Bastogne.

Regarding the strength of the enemy forces inside of Bastogne, about the following appraisal could be made as to the two possibilities:

- In the case of a weak enemy, a concentrated attack by three divisions at the 'soft' point could meet with an all the more rapid success.
- In the case of a strong enemy, it could presumably also be expected that, while neutralising the enemy forces in the east, a concentrated drive by three divisions from the west could not be repelled by these enemy forces inside of Bastogne.

In the case of a pure encirclement of Bastogne, it was, for the time being, of minor importance whether the forces encircled there would be numerically strong or weak. To start out with, in any case, a single division would have been entirely sufficient for the encirclement. No doubt, these deliberations also were borne in mind by the staffs of both army and corps.

Upon instructions by the Army Group Model and Army, Corps issued the following orders for 21 December:

1. 2nd Panzer Division, leaving behind security detachments in the northern and western sector of Bastogne, continues to push on to the west with all available elements;
2. Panzer Lehr Division leaves the elements located between the roads: Bras–Bastogne and Remoifosse–Bastogne in front of Bastogne (in other words: the entire reinforced Regiment 901), hands over the sector Neffe–road–Bras–Bastogne to the 26th Division and, by-passing Bastogne in the south, pushes on to the west on 21 December with all the elements thus released.
3. On 21 December the 26th Division takes over:
   A. From the 2nd Panzer Division the sector on both sides of Foy,
   B. From Panzer Lehr Division the Neffe sector and then continues the attack – particularly in the southern and western sector – with the objective of capturing Bastogne. Regiments 77 and 78, having been temporarily subordinated to the Panzer Lehr Division, return to the 26th Division.

This 'order for the battle on 21 December' had reached the division during the night of 20/21 December. This order therefore withdrew the two armoured divisions, with the exception of one regiment, from Bastogne, and the 26th Division was not only to encircle Bastogne all by itself, but also was supposed to smash the enemy troops in the Bastogne area by an attack!

The division dutifully expressed its doubts and considered the chances for success under existing circumstances unlikely. These doubts were eliminated, however, by the corps in its estimate of the enemy situation, which was about as follows: 'There are certain indications that the enemy had already become "softened"'. Furthermore, it could be assumed that there could 'not be much inside' Bastogne. Aside of parts of an airborne division, which, however, could not be very strong, it was reckoned that there would be the remnants of those enemy divisions, which had been badly battered at the Our River and which had taken refuge into Bastogne. On the strength of prisoner of war interviews, the fighting quality of the forces inside of Bastogne was estimated as 'not being very high.'

In addition, it was announced that progress was being made everywhere, both in the north and the south, where forward elements of the right wing of the Seventh Army (5th Parachute Infantry Division) were approaching the Bastogne–Neufchateau highway. The division – at first somewhat sceptical – was being placated by this news from higher headquarters and, towards 0400 hours, on its part gave out the orders for 21 December.

The previously given combat mission remained the same for the committed forces of the reinforced Rifle Regiment 39 and Reconnaissance Battalion 26. Grenadier Regiment 78 was ordered to relieve, by evening of 21 December, the elements of the Panzer Lehr Division located in the sector Neffe–Marvie (exclusive). Grenadier Regiment 77 was ordered to the north and to take over from the 2nd Panzer Division the sector via Oy as far as Recogne (inclusive).

By taking over the new sectors and by expanding their combat sectors, the two Grenadier regiments had been relieved of the mission to attack Bastogne in the north-eastern sector. Their mission was now to improve their position by a system of assault raids and exploiting every favourable combat opportunity and then – as far as possible – to move up closer to the edge of the town.

December 20 had been an eventful day. Despite some improvisations and many difficulties, the mounting obstacles had been mastered by the men with an admirable attitude. The troops had again justified all the confidence placed in them. The losses on that day for the division amounted to about: 8-10 officers and 300 men killed, wounded and missing. Most of this was suffered by Rifle Regiment 39 and Grenadier Regiment 78.

The orders had gone out to the regiments and battalions, when they arrived between 0500 and 0600 hours a message came from the Reconnaissance Battalion 26 with the information that Reconnaissance Battalion 26 'was having an engagement with the enemy outside of Sibret'. About half an hour later it was reported that 'Sibret was taken'. Shortly thereafter this message was retracted and it was then reported that 'heavy fighting for the strongly defended Sibret was in progress'. Inquiries were made by corps as to what was going on around Sibret. The 5th Parachute Infantry Division apparently had reported via the Seventh Army that it had captured Sibret at 0500 hours. Why, corps enquired, was Reconnaissance Battalion 26 then (about 0730/0800 hours) still hanging around outside Sibret?! Of our own artillery it was reported at the same time that it was engaged in 'heavy fighting immediately northwest of Sibret'.

Since it became apparent that a precise answer could not be received by means of radio, the operations office (Ia) of the division drove up towards the front, this time on a halftrack motorcycle, so that he could lift the veil of secrecy in person.

Towards 1000 hours the weather cleared up – for the first time since the start of the offensive. This had been dreaded by everybody for it was well-known what a clear day would mean! After barely two hours, the first enemy fighter-bombers appeared in the sky, through as yet not in great numbers. With that moment, the enemy was able to bring a dreaded and very effective weapon into the battle, and – on the basis of the assurances and promises which had been given by the highest command to both the combat leaders and men prior to the offensive – it could only be hoped that this time the German Air Force could knock the enemy out of the skies!

During the morning, even before the situation around Sibret had been cleared up, Rifle Regiment 39 reported a successful advance from the area Salvacourt–Clochimont towards Assenois as well as fierce, but slowly progressing, fighting in the wooded terrain between Assenois and Villeroux. Everywhere the enemy fought determinedly and also made some counterattacks but was forced back steadily.

Finally, towards noon, a clear report arrived from the operations officer on the events at Sibret. There, Reconnaissance Battalion 26 had accomplished a fine success and one that gave rise for further hopes: in a tough battle against a strong enemy, Reconnaissance Battalion 26 had taken Sibret already during the dark hours of the morning on 21 December. A group of the advance section of the 5th Parachute Infantry Division had come up on the Neufchâteau road during the night of 20/21 December. These elements had cut the road to Bastogne and also had reached the first groups of houses on the other side of the railroad line, but had then been thrown back again by an enemy counter thrust.

Towards 0500 hours on 21 December, the approaching Reconnaissance Battalion 26 met up with this group on the highway this side of the railroad line. The commander of the Reconnaissance Battalion 26, Major Kunkel, attached these elements to his unit – they may have amounted to something like a reinforced company – cleared up the situation and with his reinforced reconnaissance battalion – a wedge from south to north, two pincers from east and west – launched an incredibly powerful attack in the darkness.

Bitter fighting had taken place, particularly inside the town and around an anti-tank gun barricade in the southern part, and for a time the battle was fluctuating and dramatic. In the end, however, the brave defenders had succumbed to the incessant assault from all directions. Reconnaissance Battalion 26 – stimulated by its success and the personal example set by the battalion commander – kept at the heels of the withdrawing enemy and hammered the enemy artillery which was then just ready for displacement in the area north of Sibret. In addition to a sizeable number of prisoners, more than twenty guns of all types with ammunition were captured, as well as a great number of tanks and armoured vehicles with motors still running and also many trucks and jeeps. The enemy had suffered bloody losses. The reconnaissance battalion's losses had also been considerable. The enemy groups of forces had been smashed.

Without delay, the reconnaissance battalion after its success drove in the direction of Senonchamps with the bulk of its forces, while another group, for protection of the left flank, moved towards Chenogne.

In the course of the morning, corps had informed the division that, by orders of corps, a negotiator of the Panzer Lehr Division would be dispatched to Bastogne on 21 December who would ask the enemy forces there to surrender. The successful battles of the Rifle Regiment 39 in the Assenois sector and the continued thrust of Reconnaissance Battalion 26 after the capture of Sibret, together with the fact that the enemy was being asked to surrender greatly raised the morale of both leaders and men and justified the hope that the final objective, i.e. capture of Bastogne would be approached on that, or at least the following day.

The road via Doncols–Lutremange was this time more easily passable as there were only small groups who moved with great intervals. Most of the occasional enemy artillery fire was in the area around Lutrebois and on the north-south highway at the intersections with the roads leading up from Lutrebois and Villers-la-Bonne-Eau.

WAGENER: The LXVI Army Corps also spent this day, attacking St Vith fruitlessly. It had succeeded in taking a number of villages north of the city, but any penetration in the city itself was impossible. The 62nd Division gained slightly toward the west up to the line Galhausen–Grufflingen. The traffic situation within the Corps sector had degenerated to a catastrophic extent. The 2nd and 9th SS Panzer Divisions blocked the few available narrow roads and got themselves stuck again and again for hours at a time.

SCHRAMM: Thus, the turning point in the battle had arrived for LXXX Infantry Corps. On 21 December 44, the enemy attacks increased in ferocity to such an extent that it was no longer possible to doubt that in front of the centre and the right wing of the corps fresh enemy forces were being employed.

US FORCES: In the light of the morning, 21 December, they could see what had happened. The hillside between Neffe and Mont is crossed in both directions by barbed-wire fences spaced between 30 and 50 yards apart, with 5 or 6 strands in each fence. In ordinary times they were used, apparently, as feeder pens for cattle. With the tank fire behind them, the Germans tried to come right through this fenced area without first destroying the fences in any way or equipping infantry to cut them. On coming to the fences, they tried to climb through, but the spaces were small and their individual equipment was bulky. Griswold's men had perfectly clear fields of fire and so did the tank destroyer supporting them. The fences were as effective as any entanglement. The evenly spaced lines of dead told the story. They had charged right into a giant mantrap.

The 771st Field Artillery Battalion – a Negro unit – was commandeered on 21 December and their 155mm howitzers gave body to the artillery throughout the siege. Colonel Roberts also found in Bastogne eight new undelivered tanks, complete with their Ordnance crews, and he inducted them forthwith into his organization.

Colonel Ewell had the impression that night that the 901st Panzer Regiment had about expended itself and that it could no longer muster enough men to be an effective offensive force. They had been somewhat roughly handled before they got to Neffe and his own men furthered the good work. When the morning of December 21 came the situation was about as follows:

Company A, 501st, which had not been further disturbed during its bivouac, moved back up without opposition to exactly the same positions it had occupied during the night engagement.

Company D, 501st, which had bivouacked just to the south of Company A's bivouac area under the mistaken impression that it had moved into the woods lying south of the railroad tracks, discovered its error when the light came. It immediately moved further north, with one platoon going directly toward the objective woods and the others detouring east to clean out another small wood which they thought might contain enemy forces.

Through the accident of these shifts, the 501st Parachute Infantry thus had forces advancing from west, southwest and south as if to bring about a general envelopment of the German force at the Halt station. Coinciding with these movements from the south and west the two reserve companies (A and C) of the 506th reached the area to the north at about 0815 hours and were committed in companies abreast to beat through the forests lying south and west of Company D's position. The morning of the 21st was heavy with fog; none of these approaching forces moving in on them from northeast, north, west, southwest and south were visible to the Germans dug in around the Halt station and in some of the plantations westward of it. They were so completely misled as to their own position that when the platoons that had marched east for Company D, 501st, started their sweep north toward the Halt station, several of the enemy glimpsed them through the fog and came walking up to meet them, thinking they were friendly troops.

ZERBEL: 2nd Panzer Division: The shortage of gasoline prevented the division from enlarging its bridgehead till Tenneville (incl.) Moreover the division was forced to leave a combat team at the road crossing 2km southwest of Salle, in order to prevent an enemy attack from Bastogne against the important bridge of the Ourthe at Ourtheuville.

Panzer Lehr Division: The division was ordered – because Bastogne was encircled and the Army had announced that the occupants of the Schnee Eifel had surrendered – after having been summoned to send a negotiator to Bastogne. The division with the parts which were not engaged, started in the afternoon of 21 December towards the west and reached the area of Morhet. The 26th Volksgrenadier Division relieved in the evening the part of the division which occupied the castle of Neffe.

The 26th Volksgrenadier Division: The reconnaissance detachment takes Chenogne and blocks the road from the border of the forest south of Mande-Saint-Étienne by barrage fire. The 77th and 78th Regiment attempted in vain to cross the railroad. The 39th Regiment gains through an attack the borders of the forest northwest and north of Assenois. In the evening, parts of the Panzer Lehr Division situated near the castle of Neffe, were relieved by parts of the 2nd Panzer Division at Foy.

US FORCES: The line of the 506th came slowly but methodically on toward the railway tracks. Some of the Germans stayed to fight. Others gave up. Still others, in trying to get away, were forced back into the killing ground established by the semi-circular advance of the different forces of the 501st. By about 1100 hours, 21 December, the envelopment was complete and Companies A and C of the 506th had made full contact with units of the 501st along the railway line. The two companies were then ordered to return to Luzery, leaving Company D to solidify the front.

But in moving south and west through the forest, Companies A and C, 506th, discovered that the job was by no means completed. The morning advance had forced many of the enemy into the woods westward beyond the lines of Company A, 501st Parachute Infantry. The rat hunting continued throughout the day and it was almost dark before the 506th was convinced that the mop-up operation was complete. By that time it was realized that the original estimate of two platoons of enemy – these were troops of the 77th Volksgrenadier Regiment of the 26th Volksgrenadier Division – had far undershot the mark. The German force was more nearly the size of a battalion. About 100 of the enemy were captured and 55 killed by the units of the 506th Parachute

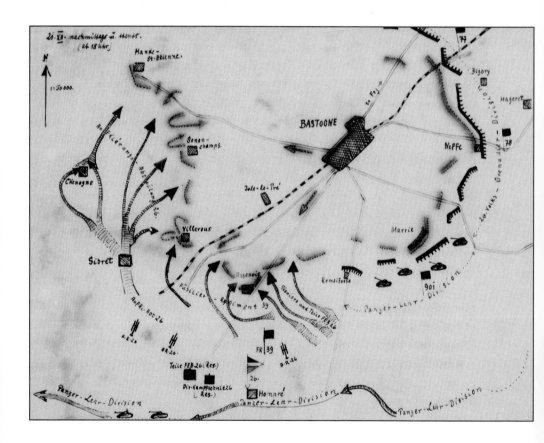

Infantry in an operation that cost them only 5 or 6 casualties. About 80 Germans were driven into 501st's sector, where they were either killed or captured. Later, when the whole battle could be reviewed clearly, the senior commanders of 101st reckoned that the enemy missed their finest opportunity on this ground and during these hours. A strongly-weighted attack straight down the railroad track could have carried through to Bastogne and turned the flanks of 501st and 506th Regiments.

With the end of this engagement on 21 December, sectors of both the 501st and 506th became relatively quiet until after 1 January. But there were other important consequences. Firm contact had been established between the two regiments, and it was never broken or weakened after that time. The Germans were served notice that the road to Bastogne from the east and north was not open.

Out of these things also developed a new feeling of confidence among the artillery in the Bastogne area. They were now fully covered on the north and east by a reasonably strong shield and they could more easily direct their attention to the other parts of the defensive circle, wherever the danger mounted.

From 21 December on, the Germans gave over their attack against the 501st Parachute Infantry's part of the Bastogne front. The road to Bastogne did not lie through Colonel Ewell and his 501st.

KOKOTT: On the afternoon of 21 December, the reinforced Rifle Regiment 39 fought its way up to Assenois against stubbornly fighting enemy forces and penetrated the southern part of the village. The Engineer Battalion and elements of the Replacement Training Battalion were advancing further to the right and fighting in the Bois Bechu Forest, or the southern part of the Bois Hazy Forest respectively, which resulted in loose contact with Regiment 901 of Panzer Lehr Division, located between Remoifosse and Marvie.

The enemy carried out several counter thrusts which, though at times leading to critical situations for the Engineer Battalion and Replacement Training Battalion, could in the long run always be checked.

Reconnaissance Battalion 26 in its continued advance came across stubborn enemy resistance outside Senonchamps and at the same time being attacked from the area north of Villeroux. The battalion was in quite a predicament, especially since those elements which had been committed for the protection of the left flank had failed to get past enemy-occupied Chenogne and were engaged in a battle for the village.

The enemy pressure between Assenois and Villeroux also became so great by late afternoon that the attack by the left-wing group of Rifle Regiment 39 towards Villeroux gained ground with little progress.

A noticeable relief for the fighting of Reconnaissance Battalion 26 arrived only by early evening of 21 December, after Chenogne had been captured by the left flank covering party and after elements of the left-wing group of Rifle Regiment 39 had at last pushed their way up between Assenois and Villeroux to about the highway south to and past the railroad line southwest of Villeroux.

Towards the evening the enemy gave up their attacks against the right flank of Reconnaissance Battalion 26 and began to concentrate for a stubborn defence inside Villeroux. Elements of Rifle Regiment 39 at first made futile attempts to attack these defences. Late in the evening, Reconnaissance Battalion 26 made several attempts – while neutralising the enemy forces near Senonchamps – to push up to the north, or northwest respectively, towards the Mande-Saint-Étienne road. Heavy fire from the north, however, as well as a number of furious enemy counter thrusts from the east, between Senonchamps and the highway, prevented these elements from reaching the road and from 'digging in' on both sides of the road.

Late in the evening, the division, prompted by the mounting losses of Reconnaissance Battalion 26, ordered these attacks against the road to be discontinued temporarily. The division could afford this after it had been found that the reconnaissance battalion had the northern and north-western edges of the Bois de Fragotte and Bois de Valet Forests well in hand and that it was in a position, to at least dominate the Bastogne–Ortheuville road with fire and at least to hinder traffic.

During the night of 21 December the position and the general situation of the division were as follows:

Rifle Regiment 39, reinforced by engineers and elements of the Replacement Training Battalion had reached the line: roadworks in the southeastern sector of Bois d'Hazy Forest – southern part of road Assenois–Villeroux as far as the intersection with the road Bastogne–Neufchateau, in salient bypassing Villeroux to the south extending to the halfway mark of the road Sibret–Villeroux.

Reconnaissance Battalion 26 had occupied the Hill 550 (1km south of Senonchamps), was located at the eastern edges of the Bois de Fragotte Forest in front of Senonchamps and in the small wooded sections north of the Bois de Valet Forest immediately in front of the Bastogne highway.

Division reserves (elements of the Replacement Training Battalion and Division Combat School) were in the area round Clochimont. The bulk of the division artillery was located in the area between Clochimont and Sibret, elements of the 1st Company of the Anti-tank Artillery Battalion near Salvacourt. The division Anti-tank Battalion was committed in the Assenois area and beyond Sibret for protection against enemy armoured penetrations.

In the northeastern sector, Grenadier Regiment 78 had relieved the elements of the Panzer Lehr Division which had been located in the area extending from Neffe to Marvie (exclusive). This regiment had not made any attacks and – linking up with Grenadier Regiment 77 – extended from about the railroad line Halte (1500 metres north-east of Bizory) to the cross-country road Mont-Wardin (1000 metres southeast of Neffe). There existed a loose contact to Regiment 901 of the Panzer Lehr Division to the left.

Regiment 77 had relieved security detachments of the 2nd Panzer Division in front of Foy and near Recogne and with its right wing had reached the forest edge 1000 metres northwest of Recogne. For artillery support of the two regiments there was merely a battalion of Artillery Regiment 26 whose two batteries were located beyond Arloncourt and northeast of Foy. Anti-tank and engineer platoons had been subordinated to the regiments.

Between Mont and Remoifosse was the reinforced Regiment 901 of Panzer Lehr Division. It had fought with great fortitude during the day but had gained only little ground.

The elements of the division surrounding Bastogne in a wide arc – from Recogne to almost Mande-Saint-Étienne – could be supplied only with difficulty. This was not only because the units were widely separated from each other – but especially due to the fact that, owing to enemy air activity, supply movements had to be confined to the hours of darkness. Movements by the horse-drawn supply columns, the regimental columns and the supply platoons of the battalions were carried out with untiring effort, and the loading space of the motorised columns was utilised to the limit of its capacity.

The entire southern sector, which now had become the point of main effort, could be supplied solely by way of the Doncols–Lutremange road. It had to be shared by: Panzer Lehr Division, 5th Parachute Infantry Division and the 26th Volksgrenadier Division. It can be well imagined what congestion this was to bring about, since the supply movements for three divisions could be carried out only during the hours of darkness, and this on a poor, rundown and narrow road. It was fortunate that at first there was only little enemy fire – and that only on certain points – directed against this artillery.

Losses for the day (21 December) amounted for the division to 300 to 350 men (including officers) killed, wounded and missing. The brunt of these losses was borne by Reconnaissance Battalion 26 as well as those elements of the Replacement Training Battalion which had been fighting together with Rifle Regiment 39.

December 21 had been a day of bitter fighting. It had brought successes in the southwestern sector. It had been possible to cut the roads leading to the west and southwest, or to block most of them. We were somewhat closer to the town of Bastogne. But to capture it, had not been possible. Our forces on that day – as fiercely as they had been fighting – had not been sufficient to accomplish this. The enemy had been fighting with utmost determination. They had been launching strong counter thrusts so frequently that one was inclined on the German side to interpret these attacks as desperate attempts to break out to the southwest. This viewpoint was further supported by the fact that in the other sectors the enemy remained altogether passive; in the east they merely defended with adequate forces (which the may have been willing to sacrifice?) and in the north and northwest they seemed to have only weak security detachments.

In view, however, of the withdrawal of the Panzer Lehr division and the 2nd Panzer Division, and the fact that Regiments 77 and 78, after having taken over the division's sectors, had become spread out over a vast sector, a German thrust from north or northwest into this thin line of protection was no longer feasible. There remained no alternative but to carry out once more on the following day the attack against Bastogne from the southwest, with all available forces in concentrated formation. It would be necessary to knock down the enemy (in his attempt to break out), to crush him and then to pave the way into the town.

Corps continued to maintain that the enemy forces inside Bastogne could not amount to a great number, in any event not strong enough to resist the attack by three reinforced battalions in a single sector.

In the late evening of 21 December, the orders for 22 December had arrived from corps. They stated:

'1. With 2nd Panzer Division and Panzer Lehr Division being successfully on the advance to the west, the overall command for the encirclement front around Bastogne is being passed on to the commander of the 26th Volksgrenadier Division.

2. For that purpose, Regiment 901 of Panzer Lehr Division and the 2nd Artillery Battalion of the Volks Artillery Corps are being subordinated to the 26th Division.

3. The (reinforced) 26th Division on 22 December relieved the security detachments of the 2nd Panzer Division which are still located between Recogne and Champs, closes the encirclement between Champs and Senonchamps and continues the attack for the capture of Bastogne.'

The 5th Parachute Division (left neighbour) had reported that it had formed the flank protection between Hollange and Remichampagne and that a sizeable advance section of the division had reached the Neufchâteau highway near Vaux-les-Rosières and had crossed the highway far to the west. No enemy resistance.

The division now was inclined to judge the situation in a more favourable light, based on the more than reassuring descriptions by corps, both with regard to the enemy strength inside Bastogne and also regarding the steady drive by the two Panzer divisions and the advance of the 5th Parachute Infantry Division.

Then the corps charged a single infantry division with the encirclement of Bastogne and at the same time with the capture of Bastogne – in other words it took the success of the attack for granted – such an order could only be based on the knowledge of the enemy's inferiority in numbers and his shattered morale. The corps therefore would have to have definite information regarding the strength and the spirit of resistance of the enemy who would be fighting with the advance of holding the 'inner line'. There was no other explanation for this mission of the division, unless higher headquarters had knowingly and thoughtlessly deviated from the most basic tactical rule which demands that the attacker – in order to be successful – has to be at least twice as strong as the defender.

A further thinning out, in favour, for instance, of a stronger attack wedge in the southwestern sector, could no longer be risked. Even then, the Regiments 77 and 78, in order to add to their forces had to bring up personnel from their supply and other rearward units (so-called 'emergency platoons').

The thrust from the southwest, required every possible reinforcement and local concentration. The losses of subordinate commanders and men of the Reconnaissance Battalion 26 and Rifle Regiment 39 had been considerable. The actual combat strength of the infantry companies had decreased to 40 men, at the most. By order of the division therefore, the Replacement Training Battalion had to transfer additional reinforcements to the Reconnaissance Battalion 26 and the Rifle Regiment 39, and in addition to the Division Combat School 26. The Replacement Training Battalion retained only two rifle companies and a heavy group with heavy machine-guns, 7.5cm heavy anti-tank artillery and medium mortars for disposal by the division. Further strengthening of the attacking troops by the division was at the time not possible.

For additional reinforcement of the attacking troops, a group of heavy infantry weapons of the Replacement Training Battalion was brought up and most of this group was committed opposite Mande-Saint-Étienne. In order to concentrate the attack wedge locally and to prevent the forces from becoming split up, the division disregarded a thrust by the Reconnaissance Battalion towards the north – i.e. in the direction of Mande-Saint-Étienne – for 22 December. Reconnaissance Battalion received orders to advance towards the immediate objective of Isle la Hesse, with main efforts along and south of the road Senonchamps–Isle la Hesse. Cover towards the road near Mande-Saint-Étienne was to be taken only by means of fire.

Rifle Regiment 39 had for its initial mission the capture of Villeroux. Then the immediate objective of Isle-le-Pré was to be aimed for, with main effort on both sides of the railroad line and road (Neufchâteau–Bastogne). The eastern section of the regiment, after capture of the northern part of Assenois, was to follow up, staggered rearwards to the right and to fight its way forward to the northern edges of the Bois d'Hazy Forest.

Regiment 901 was ordered to join with most of its forces to the left of the attack by the eastern section of Rifle Regiment 39. The division had to count with the possibility that the enemy might pull some of his forces out of the Foy–Neffe area, which was considered to be held by strong forces, and that he may throw them into the attack's southwestern sector. It would, in any case, have been desirable to neutralise these forces in some way. For this, however, the division no longer had the necessary requirements.

ZERBEL: At dusk the situation of the Corps was as follows: Bastogne was completely encircled. Would the 26th Volksgrenadier Division succeed in taking Bastogne? The Army did not permit the commitment of further forces for the attack against Bastogne, but it continued to worry the Corps a lot. Although the enemy was not expected to break through the encirclement around Bastogne, one had always to reckon with the possibility that the forces encircled at Bastogne – prisoners confirmed that it was the 101st Airborne Division – would attack the approach routes of the Corps from the rear and might even cut them off.

The Corps reckoned that on 22 December the two Panzer Divisions would advance far to the northwest. Reconnaissance squadrons had not met upon strong resistance. It seemed as if the enemy had not yet brought up stronger forces. The Corps did not believe that the troops situated at and near Bastogne would cease fighting, as long as there was no shortage of ammunition and supply.

BAYERLEIN: In the evening of 21 December, Panzer Grenadier 902 resumed its attack on Bastogne from Neffe, but failed again. The attacks of the two Infantry Regiments of 26th Volksgrenadier west of Bastogne on the whole were also unsuccessful.

The front of Panzer Grenadier 901 is being extended up to the road Bastogne–Arlon (Remoifosse). The attack of the other parts of 901 miscarried. In the night of 21-22 December Panzer Grenadier 902 at Neffe was relieved by Infantry Regiment 78 of 26th Volksgrenadier Division. Panzer Lehr was ordered to push, with all parts, towards Saint-Hubert. Panzer Grenadier 901, reinforced by Fifteenth Panzer and one Artillery Battalion, was to remain in the area of Marvie–Remoifosse. With that, the division lost its most precious and highly trained part.

US FORCES: On December 21 and 22 the opposing forces around the northeast sector simply sparred with one another. The enemy had been stopped cold at Neffe and Mont by Colonel Ewell's 501st Parachute Infantry and supporting units. The effort to slip through the ground held by the forces of Colonels O'Hara and Harper had been equally unsuccessful though less costly. After these futile passes, and following the shock action at Noville, the enemy seemed almost to abandon the effort to break through Bastogne and concerned themselves with extending the westward flow of their forces on both sides of it so as to complete the encirclement.

The road to Neufchâteau was cut by the Germans on the night of December 20, isolating Bastogne. General McAuliffe had gone that way just a few hours before to talk to the Corps commander. It was a pregnant conversation. General McAuliffe said that he was certain he could hold on for at least 48 hours and maybe longer. General Middleton replied that in view of the fact that the hour would probably come when communications could not be maintained, General McAuliffe would have to be prepared to act on his own. He pointed out that the 116th Panzer Division was coming in on General McAuliffe's flank – in addition to the three German divisions already fighting him. McAuliffe said, 'I think we can take care of them.' Middleton said that he certainly wanted to hold Bastogne but was not sure that it could be done in view of recent developments. It was important, General Middleton added, that the road to the south-west be kept open as long as possible.

As General McAuliffe walked out the door, Middleton's last comment was: 'Now, don't get yourself surrounded.'

McAuliffe noticed that he said it very lightly and felt that the Corps commander was simply having a little joke in a tense moment. General McAuliffe went on out, jumped in his car and told the driver to make for Bastogne as fast as he could get there. He figured he was already surrounded – or just about to be so. A half hour after he did come over the road, it was cut by the German armour.

That was not, however, an unmixed evil, for it brought an important change in the relationship of the forces in the defence. During its first two days the infantry and the armour had collaborated well, but they had not been a team. On the first night General McAuliffe had asked that the armour (Combat Command B, 10th Armoured Division) be attached to him and its commander Colonel Roberts had said, 'What do you know about armour?'

General McAuliffe had replied, 'Maybe you want the 101st Division attached to your Combat Command.'

It was partly because of this division in the command authority, and partly because the armour and the infantry were units strange and new to each other, that during the first stage there was a lack of cohesion. That lack was felt more as a morale than as a tactical thing. To one staff officer of the division the armour along the front seemed 'like a will o' the wisp'. The armour felt the same way about the infantry. Each force had the feeling those first few days that it was propping up the front pretty much un-helped. In general, neither force was feeling the presence of the other strongly nor having a clear idea how much support was being received from it. Liaison was fragmentary. Both tankers and infantrymen had to come out of their corners fighting and during the first crucial hours, they had no choice but to look straight ahead and slug.

But with the cutting of the Neufchâteau road and the isolating of the Bastogne garrison, General Middleton called General McAuliffe and told him that the armour (Combat Command B) and all other troops within the circle were now under his command.

General Middleton also called Colonel Roberts and told him, 'Your work has been quite satisfactory, but I have so many divisions that I can't take the time to study two sets of reports from the same area.'

Colonel Roberts reported in person to General McAuliffe to do command liaison and from that time on until the siege was lifted his post was almost exclusively at the 101st Division command post. The result was that the coordination was complete.

Roberts, a veteran tank commander, was particularly concerned that the armour be used properly, used to the maximum effect and not wasted. He strongly resisted the attempts of infantry commanders to use tanks as roadblocks. He worked specifically to get his armour quickly released after each engagement so that there would always be a maximum strength in General McAuliffe's mobile reserve for the next emergency. In the middle of the siege he published a mimeographed memorandum to the infantry officers on the right ways to use tanks.

The order to Combat Command B on 21 December from VIII Corps to 'hold the Bastogne line at all costs' gives a key to General Middleton's view of the situation during this period. On the evening before, he had talked with McAuliffe and had expressed a doubt whether the strength at Bastogne was sufficient for the task. All along he had been willing to take the gamble of an encircled force at Bastogne, and for a few hours he may have felt that the gamble was dubious. Now he had come to believe the gamble would succeed and that the battle must be fought out on that line. There was no longer any doubt or question anywhere in the camp. From this hour the action of all concerned, the VIII Corps commander, the 101st Division commander, and the armoured force commander of Combat Command B-Middleton, McAuliffe, and Roberts, became wholly consistent with the resolve that Bastogne could and would be held.

General McAuliffe now had the answer to all of his questions. No situation could have been more clearly defined. During the first two days he had entertained many doubts and had continued to wonder just what the situation was. He had heard about various groups from the 28th and 106th Divisions which were still out fighting somewhere and might fall back upon him. The 7th Armoured Division was supposed to be somewhere up around St Vith. He had also had to worry about the organization of stragglers. At the first, part of the 28th Division had been screening him on the south flank. Its commander, Major General Norman D. Cota, had called him on the morning of December 20 and said, 'I'd like to see you,' and McAuliffe had replied, 'I'm too damned busy.' Cota then said, 'I'll come up to see you.'

While the fog held, the first snow flurries came and the weather grew increasingly cold. On the night of 21 December came the first heavy snowfall, adding to the hardships of the front-line troops and the hazards of patrolling.

Now, (on the 21st) McAuliffe knew that General Cota would not be coming to see him, and that the only situation involving American troops about which he would have to worry for a while was the situation right within the 2½ mile circle of German forces closed around Bastogne. The only support he could expect for the time being was just what he had within ranging distance of his own 105mm batteries. It was a nice, clear-cut position and it had materialized in just about the way that he had expected upon first reaching Bastogne.

But what he had not foreseen, something that came like a gift from the gods, was that after the first hard collision, the enemy would give him a comparative respite in which to reflect on his situation and knit his armour and infantry close together, now that both were his to work with as he saw fit. The Germans had spent two days trying to break through Bastogne. They had failed to crush it; they would try to choke it. But while they were building up around the west and south, the pressure against the city relaxed.

The flow of bubbles on the G-2 overlays, showing the extension of the enemy to the south and westward, was moving along. Panzer Lehr Division had been the first to break upon the Bastogne rock, but the 26th Volksgrenadier Division had also come in from the east. A captured map showed that it had failed in one of its appointments, for the 26th Volksgrenadier was to have had the honour of capturing Bastogne.

The Germans were travelling light. Their commanders had told them that Bastogne was bursting with American food and that they could eat when they got there. Some had gone hungry for three days while trying to reach the American rations. Too, the enemy fire power manifested a certain weakness. While their heavy mortars and *nebelwerfers* were shaking down the store fronts in Bastogne and wounding a few soldiers and civilians, their artillery effort was largely limited to the covering fire given by the tanks and the fire of a relatively few self-propelled guns when their infantry charged forward. This, G-2 attributed to a critical shortage of ammunition.

The cutting of the Neufchâteau road, closing the German circle, appears in the 101st Division records as hardly more than an interesting incident. Up till then, the division's intelligence of the enemy's strength and movements was more notable for its blanks than for its specific detailed entries. The G-2 section had, of course, moved cold into an unknown situation and was having to build up its picture of the enemy and friendly forces piece by piece. There had been no pretty 'estimates of the situation' to take over and build upon. All that division could know for certain was what it learned from examining the enemy dead or questioning prisoners. That was enough for Lieutenant Colonel Paul A. Danahy's main purpose and enough also to satisfy his taste for melodramatic utterance.

Eleven dead men had been found on the ground where the hospital was captured. The corpses had civilian clothes and German military dogtags. Colonel Danahy went out to make the identifications. A few hours after this find, a message from 10th Armoured Division came through Combat Command B to 101st Division Headquarters saying, 'You can expect attacks from Sherman tanks, civilians and almost anything now.'

Reports came into the G-2 office throughout the first day of Germans killed while wearing American uniforms and of Sherman tanks pouring fire on our lines. Danahy checked up. He found that invariably, where the enemy used American dress, it was mixed with some of their own clothing, so that they could maintain they were in uniform. What he had seen gave him fresh inspiration for prophecy. 'Their equipment is augmented by captured U.S. equipment which they do not hesitate to use,' he wrote to the commander. 'Their morale is excellent but will disintegrate as they come in contact with American airborne troops. It is well known that the Germans dislike fighting. The false courage acquired during their recent successes has so far proved insufficient to prevent their becoming road-bound.'

While this message was going out to the regiments of the 101st, the enemy was crossing the Neufchâteau road and cutting the last line to the south, closing the

circle around Bastogne. Reconnaissance and combat patrols reported strong enemy infiltrations in the areas west and southwest of the town.

In the morning of 21 December, a patrol from Troop D of the 90th Reconnaissance Squadron went down the road to see what the Germans had there. The patrol, under 1st Lieutenant Arthur B. Arnsdorf, consisted of one tank destroyer and two squads of infantry. They met a group of 101st Division men near Isle-le-Pré (1½ miles southwest of Bastogne), then moved on some distance further until they encountered a well emplaced enemy force which made them turn about. Another armoured patrol under Captain Keith J. Anderson went to Clochimont where it observed a large enemy force riding in American vehicles and dressed in American uniforms.

Later in the morning of 21 December Team Pyle – 14 medium tanks and 200 infantry mostly from the 9th Armoured – moved to the vicinity of Senonchamps to assist the 420th Armoured Field Artillery. Lieutenant Colonel Barry D. Browne, in command of the 420th, had received reports that Sibret and Morhet had fallen into enemy hands. He figured that he was out on a limb and that the enemy might come upon him from either flank, so he turned one of his batteries to fire on Sibret and rushed a forward observer out to adjust on the village.

At that moment, he saw the motorized column of the 333rd Field Artillery Group as it came speeding up the road out of Sibret. Another column came driving hard behind the 333rd – men in American clothes and riding American vehicles. They got fairly close to Senonchamps, then stopped, deployed and opened fire with an M8 assault gun. Even as Colonel Browne realized they were Germans, they started side-slipping off into the Bois de Fragotte which lies just south of Senonchamps. Team Pyle got there in time to help Browne fill those woods with fire; one battery from the 420th Field Artillery Battalion and one from the 755th Field Artillery Battalion (155mms) also engaged in this action. The infantry and tanks moved west into the woods. Almost immediately, one of the tanks knocked out an enemy 75mm self-propelled gun. The force then advanced into a large clearing in the centre of the forest. While crossing the clearing, one of the tanks was disabled by a shell from a high-velocity gun somewhere in the woods. The tank lost a track. A smoke screen was laid in an attempt to cover its withdrawal, but the tank wouldn't budge and had to be destroyed.

The force then withdrew to a line further to the east, but within the forest. Additional support kept coming to it until by night Colonel Browne was commanding 300 infantry

and 19 tanks, in addition to running two battalions of artillery. His troops were covering a sector more than 4,000 yards long and running from south of Senonchamps to the Bastogne–Neufchâteau road. All of this had been built up during the day of December 21 as forces were shifted to meet the attack from the new direction.

But the heavy increase of fire on the left found Danahy ready to meet the emergency. 'The cutting of the roads,' he wrote in his periodic report to the commanders that evening, 'had had no effect upon our present situation except to make travel hazardous.'

LÜTTWITZ XLVII Pz Corps: On 21 December the reconnaissance group of 2 Panzer Division was located in Tenneville. Although I wanted their reconnaissance group to move fast through the Bois de Mande and reach Bande on that day, I could not order the movement because the weight of the division was too strung out to follow. It extended all the way back from Tenneville to Bourcy. The 2nd Panzer Division later reported to me that there was a roadblock held by strong enemy forces in front of Tenneville.

US FORCES: At 0700 hours on 21 December an enemy column was seen approaching from the direction of Salle. The men at the roadblock guessed it was an artillery battery for it contained nine half-tracks, seven 75mm guns and seven light vehicles. Captain McDonald's men were in a cut above the highway and their position was so well screened that the German column came to within 25 yards before the defenders opened fire. Then they let them have it with all weapons – their rifles, machine guns, a 57mm gun and the guns of the light tank. Only one light vehicle from the column managed to turn and get away. All of the enemy guns were captured intact but they could not be moved to town and they were therefore destroyed with the aid of the recaptured explosives.

Shortly thereafter, two tanks supported by a group of German infantry tried to flank the position from the northwest. Company B crippled one tank with a rocket and the other tank withdrew. The infantry group was driven back by small-arms fire from Company B's position, supported by artillery fire.

At 0730 hours on 21 December, the 1st Battalion, 502nd, moved to the area just east of Grosse-Hez (2 miles east of Champs) on division order, and with this shifting of the line, Company A was ordered back to its own battalion. (It had been attached to the 2nd Battalion to fill out the 2nd's long front.) One hour later, the 1st Battalion started up the road toward Recogne. Company G of the 506th Parachute Infantry had been hit at Foy and had pulled back its left flank to high ground. This manoeuvre exposed Colonel Stopka's (2nd Battalion) right flank which was anchored in the first few buildings at the north end of Recogne. Stopka had already swung his reserve, Company G, around to his right and faced it south so as to cover the open flank. He had been helped a little by one of the tank destroyers.

The morning was intensely foggy and enemy armour could be heard roaming around just beyond the murk. Sergeant Lazar Hovland got a clear sight of one enemy tank and set it afire in four rounds. A second German tank fired on Hovland and missed; Hovland crippled it with a quick shot, but it pulled back into the fog.

By the new order from 101st Division, the 1st Battalion was to clean out Recogne finally and then fill the gap between the 502nd and 506th regiments. The order was changed a few minutes later when Colonel Sink (506th commander) reported to General McAuliffe that despite Company G's difficulty the 506th's position was pretty sound. General McAuliffe decided that it made little difference whether he held Recogne. The 1st Battalion, 502nd, which had been sweeping forward with two companies abreast, was told to keep on moving but in column of companies. General McAuliffe asked Colonel Stopka if he could disengage, pull back of Recogne and stand on a line running southeast to where he could join Colonel Sink's flank. Inasmuch as Company G was already standing on this line which curved crescent-fashion around a reverse slope, Stopka said he would be glad to make the move. At noontime the 1st Battalion was moved back to Grosse-Hez and Company A was moved to the south of Longchamps to stop anything that might come that way.

The 377th Field Artillery Battalion had given support to the 502nd during the latter stage of this operation and had fired 60 rounds on the highway from Salle to Bertogne. The fire knocked out six vehicles of a German column which was turned back by these losses.

At noon the roadblock positions were put under fire by enemy tanks operating to the southward of Salle. The tank fire was silenced by two tank destroyers from the 705th Tank Destroyer Battalion which had just come forward to help Captain McDonald's company. However, by this time it had become clear that the roadblock had little importance. Patrols had been sent out to the northwest and southwest and they returned with information that the highway bridges in both directions had been blown. Since the highway was of no further service as a supply route for the division, Company B was ordered to return to the battalion sector. It did so in the early evening.

There were two relatively quiet days on the Marvie part of the circular Bastogne front after the snows came – December 21 and 22. Bastogne was searched for enough bedsheets to camouflage the patrols.

Early in the afternoon of December 21 the Germans came across the main highway directly south of Bastogne and then began working north toward the battalion lines on the hill. Colonel Harper shifted the 2nd Platoon of Company G, 327th Glider Infantry, from the ground immediately west of Marvie to a place west of the highway. Three of Team O'Hara's tanks were already on the hill where Harper had placed them the day before. The armour and infantry together were able to turn this thrust back before it became any real threat.

The 1st Battalion, 327th Glider Infantry, was relieved from attachment to the 501st Airborne Infantry, reverting to direct division control. It was moved to the southwest of Bastogne in the vicinity of the woods there and ordered to establish a roadblock along the main highway, and from this point to patrol westward to make contact with the 326th Engineer Battalion. They were also instructed to patrol to Villeroux and Chenogne and make contact with 'friendly troops', but before they could do it the enemy had moved through these positions and driven back the 333rd Field Artillery Group. The Engineers then set up as small combat groups and covered the ground between Colonel Hartford F. Salee's 1st Battalion, 327th Glider Infantry, which was over the Neufchâteau road and the platoon from Company G, 327th, which was west of the highway leading south from Bastogne.

In Team O'Hara's part of the sector, too, there was a lull. Sometime during the night of 20 December the Germans removed the trees from Team O'Hara's roadblock. At 1100 hours on the next day a combat patrol went forward to investigate. But on approaching the point where the block had been, they found that the enemy now had it covered with crossing bands of machine-gun fire. They were able to withdraw without casualties and mortar fire was then put all around the road junction.

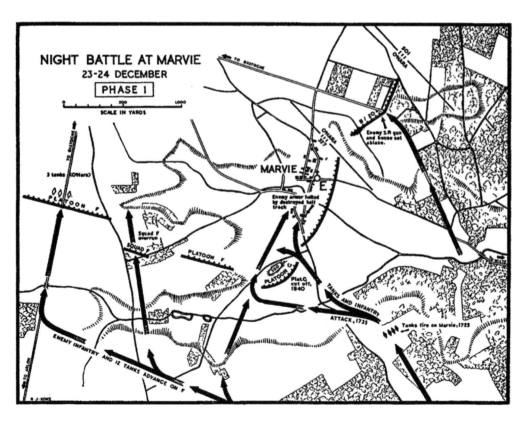

Chapter 7

22–23 December: 'Aw, Nuts!'

METZ: On 22 December, there occurred a decisive change in the entire situation, which had a lasting and damaging effect on the Ardennes front, as well as on the encircled sector near Bastogne.

Although until 21 December poor visibility and often foggy weather with low hanging clouds prevailed, measurably contributing to the German successes thus far, the morning of the 22 December brought clear and nearly cloudless weather, which continued to be clear during the next few days, bringing the most active sort of enemy reconnaissance and air bombardment. Supply units and troops lost many ammunition and fuel trucks through bombs and aircraft weapons; traffic on the roads in villages and narrow passes was seriously crippled; supplies, even those carried on the railroads, were greatly diminished (fuel for a few days) taking more time to arrive and, on the whole, the available transport area was from now on measurably smaller.

The attacks from the air by the opponent were so powerful, that even single vehicles for the transport of personnel and motorcycles could only get through by going from cover to cover. No attempt was made to drive the American Air Force out of the air above. The army received no results by its own reconnaissance, which was operationally, tactically and artillery-wise of the most decisive and weightiest disadvantage.

On the other hand, an attack by strong American forces from the south against the line of encirclement had to be taken into account because of the ground situation of the Seventh Army and our own ground reconnaissance. At this time we also received the first news of the arrival of the American 4th Armoured Division in the area east of Libremont.

WAGENER: The LXVI Army Crops captured St Vith on this day. The area around this city had been so thoroughly cleared of enemy troops, that it was impossible for the garrison in the city to hold out any longer. The Seventh Army reported that the most advanced battalions of the 5th Fallschirmjäger Division had reached Libramont with advance parties, the Army could turn its attention westward, without having to worry about Bastogne, a town which had retarded the entire operation on many occasions.

ZERBEL: 22 December: 2nd Panzer Division: The division in the early morning hours started for Marche, without making any contact with the enemy. A road demolition 300m northwest of the road crossing at Champion delayed the advance of the division for four hours. At about 1700 hours the division met upon strong enemy forces at the road crossing 2km southwest of Marche. On orders of the Corps, the division was veered past Hargimont. They could penetrate Hargimont, but take it completely only in the morning of 23 December. The advance detachment advanced on Dinant.

Parts of the division were covered on the line: Road crossing 2km southeast of Marche–Marloie by the right flank.

26th Volksgrenadier Division: The division relieved parts of the 2nd Panzer Division at Longchamps. The reconnaissance detachment reinforced by parts of the 39th Regiment attacked Mande-Saint-Étienne but could only reach the road.

US FORCES: In the early hours of December 22 one of Team O'Hara's patrols going forward saw an 11-man patrol enter their own lines. The night was clear and crisp. The small group from the 54th Armoured Infantry first heard the crunching of the snow as the other patrol came toward them. They lay quiet, not firing because they were outnumbered. Too, the strangers were moving as if they were wholly familiar with the ground. They had no visible weapons and they did not carry themselves stealthily. They went boldly over the fences and entered the American lines along the ground that lay between the 327th and the 54th. They walked right by the sentries, moved to within 100 yards of the command post of the 327th Glider Infantry and within 200 yards of the command post of the 54th Armoured Infantry.

Four different groups reported the patrol later and all four said they had seen eleven men. Yet the patrol was not challenged anywhere simply because it had moved so confidently. They got in and out without provoking any fire or interest. When Headquarters heard casually how this group had been drifting about, they checked to see whether any nearby unit had put out such a patrol and found that none had done so. Whether the eleven were friend or enemy was never learned. The visitation and its mystery became one of the legends of Bastogne.

A 1130 hours on 22 December four Germans, a major, a captain and two enlisted men, came up the road to Bastogne from Remoifosse carrying a large white flag. They were met on the road by Technical Sergeant Oswald Y. Butler and Staff Sergeant Carl E. Dickinson of Company F, 327th Glider infantry, and Private 1st Class Ernest D. Premetz of the 327th Medical Detachment. Premetz could speak German. The captain could speak English. He said to Butler, 'We are *parliamentaires*.'

The men took the Germans to the house where Lieutenant Leslie E. Smith of Weapons Platoon, Company F, 327th Infantry, had his command post. Leaving the two German enlisted men at the command post, Smith blindfolded the two officers and led them over the hill to the command post of Captain James F. Adams, commanding officer of Company F. Adams called 2nd Battalion headquarters in Marvie, Battalion called Regiment in Bastogne, and the 327th Headquarters called the 101st Division, relaying the word that some Germans had come in with surrender terms. The rumour quickly spread around the front that the enemy had had enough and that a party had arrived to arrange a surrender.

Quiet held the front. Many of the American defenders crawled out of their cover and spent the noon hour shaving, washing and going to the straddle trenches.

Major Alvin Jones took the terms to General McAuliffe and Lieutenant Colonel Ned D. Moore who was acting Chief of Staff. The paper called for the surrender of the Bastogne garrison and threatened its complete destruction otherwise. It appealed to the 'well known American humanity' to save the people of Bastogne from further suffering. The Americans were to have two hours in which to consider. The two enemy officers would have to be released by 1400 hours but another hour would pass before the Germans would resume their attack.

Colonel Harper, commanding the 327th, went with Jones to Division Headquarters. The two German officers were left with Captain Adams. Members of the staff were grouped around General McAuliffe when Harper and Jones arrived. McAuliffe asked someone what the paper contained and was told that it requested a surrender.

He laughed and said, 'Aw, nuts!' It really seemed funny to him at the time. He figured he was giving the Germans 'one hell of a beating' and that all of his men knew it. The demand was all out of line with the existing situation. But McAuliffe realized that some kind of reply had to be made and he sat down to think it over. Pencil in hand, he sat there pondering for a few minutes and then he remarked, 'Well, I don't know what to tell them.' He asked the staff what they thought and Colonel Kinnard, his G-3 replied, 'That first remark of yours would be hard to beat.'

General McAuliffe didn't understand immediately what Kinnard was referring to. Kinnard reminded him, 'You said 'Nuts!'' That drew applause all around. All members of the staff agreed with much enthusiasm and because of their approval McAuliffe decided to send that message back to the Germans.

Then he called Colonel Harper in and asked

General McAuliffe.

him how he would reply to the message. Harper thought for a minute but before he could compose anything General McAuliffe gave him the paper on which he had written his one-word reply and asked, 'Will you see that it's delivered?'

'I will deliver it myself,' answered Harper. 'It will be a lot of fun.' McAuliffe told him not to go into the German lines.

Colonel Harper returned to the command post of Company F. The two Germans were standing in the wood blindfolded and under guard. Harper said, 'I have the American commander's reply.' The German captain asked, 'Is it written or verbal?'

'It is written,' said Harper. And then he said to the German major, 'I will stick it in your hand.'

The German captain translated the message. The major then asked, 'Is the reply negative or affirmative? If it is the latter I will negotiate further.'

All of this time the Germans were acting in an upstage and patronizing manner. Colonel Harper was beginning to lose his temper. He said, 'The reply is decidedly not affirmative.' Then he added, 'If you continue this foolish attack your losses will be tremendous.' The major nodded his head.

Harper put the two officers in the jeep and took them back to the main road where the German privates were waiting with the white flag. He then removed the blindfold and said to them, speaking through the German captain, 'If you don't understand what 'Nuts' means, in plain English it is the same as 'Go to hell.' And I will tell you something else – if you continue to attack we will kill every goddam German that tries to break into this city.'

The German major and captain saluted very stiffly. The captain said, 'We will kill many Americans. This is war.' It was then 1350 hours.

'On your way, Bud,' said Colonel Harper, 'and good luck to you.' The four Germans walked on down the road. Harper returned to the house, regretting that his tongue had slipped and that he had wished them good luck.

ZERBEL: Panzer-Lehr Division: The negotiator, who was sent out to Bastogne returned with the answer 'nuts'. The combat teams of the division after long fighting took Gerimont, Tillet and Remagen and until midnight advanced until Saint-Hubert. The capture of this place had to be expected during the night.

MANTEUFEL: Panzer Lehr Division sent a *parlementaire* to Bastogne without my authorisation. The demand to surrender was refused as was to be expected. I did not authorise the surrender demand which was made of the Bastogne garrison, and I am still not sure exactly who did authorise this ultimatum.

US FORCES: General McAuliffe's confidence thus far had been well founded. In manpower, he had been able to maintain a very favourable balance between his reserves and his deployments. His infantry losses had been light. The circle of defences had been scarcely dented. The German forces, which as a whole had been rapidly moving in the Bulge offensive elsewhere, had so signally failed to put on a coordinated attack against his all-around front that he had been able to beat down each of their separate thrusts by massing the fire of his artillery.

The gun pits of all the defending 105mm batteries were complete circles. At different times during the siege nearly all guns fired around the whole 6,400 mls of the compass. Most of the artillery fired in support of each infantry battalion against every major attack the Germans made. More than that, however, the artillery could not do. All day long the infantry commanders witnessed the enemy build-up opposite their sectors. Tanks and half-tracks loaded with German infantry moved freely and contemptuously along the lateral roads, making no effort at concealment although they were within easy range of the howitzers. It made the defenders frantic.

SCHRAMM: This day represented from a tactical and organisational point of view the turning point in the conduct of the offensive by Seventh Army. On this day, the last offensive successes occurred on the one hand; on the other, a striking change occurred in the enemy situation. The flank attack of Third American Army, under General Patton, began to make itself felt.

In the meantime, we had received no news of what was happening to the right wing of the army. Lack of air reconnaissance on our part meant that the advance of the American formations remained hidden from our eyes until their forward elements clashed with our own ground reconnaissance (23 December 44).

The regiment to the right of the division (14 A/B Infantry Regiment) assembled in the Hompré–Hollange area and at the same time blocked, mainly with anti-tank guns, the road from Bastogne to Martelunge between Librebois and Assenois, to the north.

US FORCES: By noon of 22 December the 463rd Field Artillery Battalion, which was supporting the 327th Glider Infantry, had only 200 rounds of ammunition left and the other battalions were in a similar plight. During the first three days there had been shells enough. Now, in the face of the enemy build-up, the pinch was really hurting and General McAuliffe was about at the point where he would have to ration his guns to ten rounds per day.

There was a delightfully ironic touch even to that restriction, for the supply had dropped very low indeed. Checking the battalions on that day, Colonel Sherburne, the artillery commander, found that with the exception of one battalion which had several hundred rounds of short-range 105mm ammunition which it alone was equipped to fire, the batteries were down to less than ten rounds total per gun. Still, he kept his own counsel, and when men and officers asked him how the general supply of artillery ammunition was faring, he lied cheerfully and skilfully. At times members of the staff became confused between the true figures and the figures which Sherburne was quoting publicly for the sake of morale.

The shell shortage continued to be General McAuliffe's worst, in fact, his only real worry. He told his batteries not to fire 'until you see the whites of their eyes'. The infantry commanders and the few remaining artillery observers screamed their heads off about it. One commander phoned General McAuliffe, 'We are about to be attacked by two regiments. We can see them out there. Please let us fire at least two rounds per gun.'

Colonel Kinnard listened to this plea and later recalled General McAuliffe's reply, 'If you see 400 Germans in a 100-yard area, and they have their heads up, you can fire artillery at them, but not more than two rounds.'

At the same time, the Bastogne defenders were running low on small-arms ammunition. So, with somewhat mixed feelings, the word was received among the regiments at 1530 hours on that evening that a column from the 4th Armoured Division was coming up from the southwest to support the 101st Airborne Division and would be able to give the 101st relief in time.

It was still a neat question whether that relief would come before the ammunition ran out. In the smaller units which were attachments to the 101st perhaps the strain was even greater. Confidence can come of numbers around the headquarters of a large organization. Talking with his staff, General McAuliffe gained the impression that none doubted the outcome. But out on the fire line, friends shook hands as the darkness came, figuring that all might be overwhelmed before morning. They could take no measure of the reserve strength of the position. What they saw was how few rounds per gun they had left and how large were the numbers of the enemy. The paratroopers were somewhat accustomed to being surrounded by enemy, but it was a new experience for the units who stood with them, unwavering.

LÜTTWITZ XLVII Pz Corps: On 22 December I installed my headquarters in Chateau Roumont. Christmas time was coming on and although under the circumstances we had to take over this installation, I saw to it that the people were not moved out.

US FORCES: The rest of the day was comparatively quiet. The wholesale destruction by artillery that the Germans had promised did not materialize. But, at 1555 hours there was an attack by some 50 of the enemy against Company F, 327th Glider Infantry, over precisely the same ground where the German mediators had come into our lines. The attack was broken up by small-arms and artillery fire. At 1700 hours another small attack was again pressed to within 200 yards of Company F's lines but was beaten back by fire. The terrain at this spot formed a kind of bowl. The Germans came with their tanks into the bottom of the bowl and fired up against the foxholes along the slope.

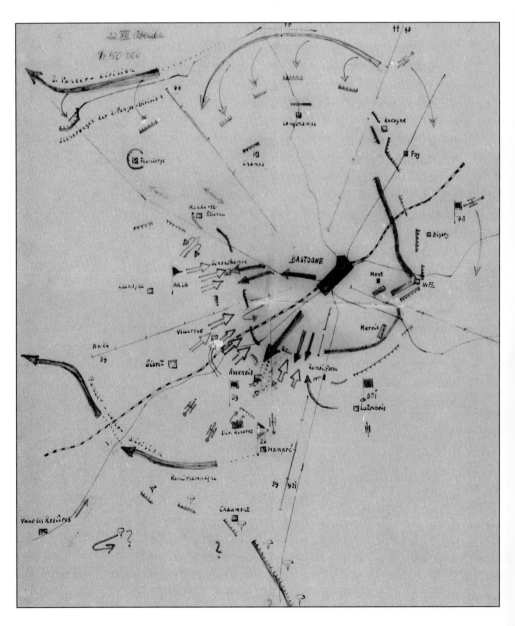

The men under Sergeant Butler, who had the rifle platoon, and Lieutenant Smith, who had the weapons platoon, held their ground and drove the attackers off with infantry fire alone.

The main event for that day was summed up, though not too neatly, in the G-2 Periodic Report No.4:

> 'The Commanding General's answer was, with a sarcastic air of humorous tolerance, emphatically negative. The catastrophic carnage of human lives resulting from the artillery barrage of astronomic proportions which was to be the fate of the defending troops failed to materialize. The well-known American humanity was considerate of the threatened possible civilian losses by firing artillery concentrations directed at the enemy's impudence.'

It was a victory for eloquence at some expense to grammar, but in keeping with the other grim humours of the day.

On 22 December the enemy build-up along the Salle–Bertogne road continued at such a pace that at noontime Colonel Chappuis, the 502's commander, moved Company A to Champs and the rest of the 1st Battalion to Hemroulle (2 miles west of Bastogne), which faced them to the west. A platoon from Company B was set up as a roadblock, where Company A had been, along the Longchamps–Bastogne road.

KOKOTT: The regiments had finished their preparations and arrangements – as per orders issued – by the morning hours of 22 December. Rations and ammunitions were carted up, the reinforcements were assigned to their units. Heavy infantry weapons came up, were assigned to their locations and went into position. It was a bitter, cold day. There was every indication that the weather would be clear – i.e. fit for commitment of the Air Force. The ground was frozen solidly. An icy wind was blowing over the snow-covered countryside.

Between 0700 and 0800 hours, the reinforced Rifle Regiment 39 and Reconnaissance Battalion 26 began the attack. Heavy fighting for the village of Villeroux flared up. Despite the fact that the village was being covered intensively by fire, thus causing considerable losses to the defender, almost every house and every cellar had to be fought for.

US FORCES: At 0730 hours on December 22, the task of recovering the aerial resupply was given to Major William H. Butler, S-4 of the 501st Parachute Infantry, and Captain Matheson, S-4 of the 506th. They went to the drop zone, got the crews and vehicles alerted, put out the panels to guide the plane and then waited.

At 0900 hours on 22 December, one German group cut the road to Mont southeast of Flamisoul near Mande-Saint-Étienne. The outpost which sighted it said that it had set up a roadblock with 'two halftracks, one jeep and a trailer'. Just before noon, Colonel Allen put on an attack directly south to clear the road. He took 25 prisoners and drove the rest off. The motor vehicles turned out to be ordinary farm carts which the Germans had hooked together for use as a block. A platoon of Colonel Templeton's tank destroyers then reconnoitred the road, the sections covering one another alternately from one terrain feature to the next. They reported to Colonel Allen that the road was open.

KOKOTT: After 0900 hours the day had become clear and the first fighter-bombers of the day appeared; they were more numerous than on the previous day. While not intervening in the closely-knit battles in the village, they all the more swooped down on the villages immediately behind the firing line, where the reserves, staffs, supply dumps, advanced message centres and similar installations were located, with the result that all movements from rear to front were, at least, greatly handicapped.

Similar to those at Villeroux, there were fierce engagements in Assenois (north) and the wooded section northwest of Assenois. Everywhere the enemy fought with great tenacity, stubbornness and skill against Rifle Regiment 39. Reconnaissance Battalion 26 had been attacking since 0800 hours from the Bois de Fragotte Forest towards Senonchamps. There also the enemy opposed the assault with all their strength. The battles between Assenois–Villeroux–Senonchamps were fluctuating all through the morning; it was a case of mutual attrition as always happens in a serious battle between equal opponents. Time and again there was the surprise fire – concentrated by battalions – of our own artillery which hit the enemy with deadly effectiveness. The heavy infantry weapons, also heavily concentrated, fired huge amounts of ammunition and paved the way for the riflemen metre by metre. Time and again the groups, detachments and platoons moved forward protected by our own fire, penetrated pockets and fought for farmyards, village roads and portions of woods.

The enemy's defence was strong. Everywhere the attacker was met by furious, well directed and sharply concentrated fire. The enemy artillery fire always lay at the decisive points in dense concentrations. As always, the enemy did not spare ammunition. In any case, a lack of ammunition on the enemy side could not be diverted by the attacker. The attacking infantry suffered heavily by the fire of numbers anti-tank and tank guns and the wide-angle salvos of the numerous enemy mortars. To judge by the messages coming in from the front, the enemy had a great number of tanks at his disposal for, in addition to the unmistakeable fire of tank guns, all the messages reported 'the noise of tank motors'.

All in all, however, there evolved on the German side in the course of the morning the overall picture that the attack, though slowly, was making steady progress towards Bastogne.

In the course of the morning, news arrived from corps to the effect that the commander in charge of the Bastogne forces had declined a surrender with remarkable brevity. This response was fully in accord with the stubborn tenacity displayed by the defending forces. During the morning, the reconnaissance battalion reported that 'it had penetrated Senonchamps had put several tanks out of commission and made prisoners. Fierce fighting in the village.'

At Villeroux enemy resistance had also been broken through Rifle Regiment 39 and towards noon Assenois (north) was taken as well. Rifle Regiment 39 also reported the capture of prisoners and the destruction of tanks. The first visible success of the day had arrived!

US FORCES: In the northwest sector, the 502nd Parachute Infantry engaged directly without any long-range sparring with the enemy. That came of the order which initially took Colonel Stopka's 3rd Battalion, 502nd, to Recogne to help extricate the Noville force. Four tank destroyers accompanied the battalion to Recogne and stayed there, backing up the line. They got no action the first day though two men and a jeep from the 705th's Reconnaissance Company set up as an evacuation team and shuttled the wounded out of the 502nd area after a heavy shelling by the German tank artillery.

The 3rd Battalion received German probing attacks all day long, but on a limited scale. Two of the tank destroyers which had been with Colonel Stopka's 3rd Battalion were switched over to support Company A in Champs. A patrol was sent to Rouette, a mile north of Champs, to check on enemy activities. It encountered a small detachment of Germans in the village, engaged 14 of them in a 20-minute fight, drove them off with machine-gun and rifle fire and withdrew under cover of fire from the 377th Parachute FA Battalion.

Air supply: Nothing happened during the day. In the late afternoon came the message from VIII Corps. At 1605 hours Corps said that the pathfinders would be dropped at 1723 hours and that the flight would be two planes with ten men each. Captain John M. Huffman, Assistant to G-4, went at once to the drop zone to notify Major Butler. However, at 1641 the operation was cancelled because of ice conditions. Then the division rear base radioed at 1700 hours that 60 C-47s would drop supplies on the first flyable day. However, VIII Corps had not yet given up. At 2115 hours, it radioed that an attempt will be made to drop a portion of the supplies.

Colonel Kohls again alerted Butler who went to the drop zone and put out the fluorescent panels. Nothing happened. Out of great expectation came only great disappointment.

KOKOTT: The reconnaissance battalion and rifle regiment continued their slowly advancing attack. There were sizeable losses on our side. It was also apparent that the enemy had suffered heavy losses.

Shortly after mid-day arrived the announcement: 'Attention! Strong enemy wing formation flying up from west!' and it did not take long until there arrived – flying in low altitude and accompanied by fighters and fighter-bombers – 50, 70, 80 large planes. Everybody expected the laying of bomb-blankets. The light and heavy anti-aircraft defences near Sibret, Cochimont and Salvacourt fired furiously, and the 3.7cm division anti-aircraft artillery, which was securing the artillery area, fired round after round in order to dispel and destroy the allied bomber formation. Some planes were shot down, some came gliding down – the bulk turned off as they approached Bastogne in low altitude. Only then it was realised what all of this meant. Larger supply planes were landing in Bastogne. Just what they were bringing in, whether men, rations or ammunition was at first uncertain. In any case, it meant that the defending forces would be strengthened.

The crews bailed out of several of the planes which had been shot down. Some of these men were captured east of Chenogne, while others escaped either to their own lines or disappeared in the woods east of Hompré and were captured only after they had been wandering around for several days. The planes which had been shot down in the area between Hompré and Chenogne had been – as we found out later – loaded almost entirely with artillery ammunition and medical supplies.

The supply by air had not caused any interruption in the ground fighting. The battle continued without pause and the attack made progress. With greater economy, though still with concentration and directed toward the crucial area, the German batteries continued to fire. The heavy mortars began to fire more slowly. Ammunition had become scarce. Transportation of supplies was barely possible during the day.

All major vehicle columns on the open road were attacked by fighter-bombers, brought to a standstill or set on fire. Only the ambulance vehicles, marked with a Red Cross, were free to move and carried their bitter load slowly to the aid stations. Not a single German plane could be seen in the skies.

Rifle Regiment 39 by afternoon reached the area Halte (2km northeast of Villeroux) and the road crossing 1100 metres northeast of Assenois, when the enemy began to stage powerful counter thrusts between the Bastogne–Mortelange road and the railroad line to Neufchâteau. The attacks were supported by heavy fire and accompanied by tanks.

While the left wing of Regiment 39 stalled, the enemy thrust between the crossroads and Halte and lost only little groups. The enemy thrust west of the Bastogne–Assenois road and split up the front of the Replacement Training and the Engineer Battalions (subordinated to Regiment 39) located there. The German combat groups were forced back to the southern edge of the Bois Bechu Forest. Enemy assault troops penetrated the German artillery position near Salvacourt. The situation was critical. The guns were firing from open firing positions, with direct fire; with machine-guns and assault rifles the artillerymen of the first Anti-tank Battalion or Artillery Regiment 26 were defending their firing positions. Located immediately in the range of the enemy fire, a battery had to change positions. It lost two or three guns through direct hits from tanks but had finished the change of positions cold-bloodedly.

Several enemy tanks near La Lune were put out of action. The enemy thrust came to a standstill in the last minute. Although itself gravely endangered, the western wing of Rifle Regiment 39 had branched off to the east all the forces it could spare and with these elements conducted a thrust from the northwest of Assenois and into the Bois Bechu Forest. The division had brought up its last reserves and committed them for the defence along the heights west of Salvacourt. An armoured group of Regiment 901 was ordered for commitment from south of Remoifosse towards the Bois d'Hazy Forest.

Disregarding the scarcity of ammunition and the blocked reserves of ammunition, the artillery was committed in the area Bois Bechu Forest–Assenois–La Lune from where it would smash the enemy's attack wedge. Assenois was recaptured and the forward enemy assault group was forced back into the Bois Bechu Forest. An improvised coherent line was formed in the southern third of the Bois Bechu Forest and Bois d'Hazy Forest.

It was beginning to get dark. To continue our own attack with the Rifle Regiment 39 was, for the time being, out of the question. The unit's front had to be reorganised, a new line had to be formed and, above all, ammunition had to be brought up. The enemy fire also died down, enemy pressure decreased. At some points friend and foe were facing each other closely.

Reconnaissance Battalion 26 had taken Senonchamps, but had, during its further advance towards Isle la Hesse in the afternoon, also run into strong enemy armoured attacks; it had withdrawn into the village of Senonchamps where now – towards evening – it put up a successful defence against enemy attacks.

In the course of these fluctuating battles and crises during the afternoon, when groups of the Panzer Lehr Division were rolling through Hompré via Remi-Champagne towards the northwest, some individual vehicles, when crossing the road junction 3km northwest of Remi-Champagne, were set aflame by fire from an anti-tank gun or tank gun coming from the south. There was no explanation for this and it was at first assumed that this was due to a mishap on the part of an anti-tank gun of the 5th Parachute Infantry, but then it turned out that a small group of enemy tanks had actually come up to the road fork 2km northwest of Cobreville and were keeping the road junction under fire. Some tanks of the Panzer Lehr Division, which were passing by, returned fire and shortly thereafter the enemy disappeared to the south.

During the late evening of 22 December the situation was as follows:

Regiment 78 had taken over its sector from Recogny (inclusive) to the road bridge (800m southeast of Mont).

Regiment 77 was in the process of relieving the security detachments of the 2nd Panzer Division near Longchamps and Champs. The regiment reported that it would have completed the movement by morning of 23 December.

The battalions of the Volks Artillery Corps, announced by the XXXXVII Panzer Corps, had come up; the two batteries of Artillery Regiment 26 were in the process of moving their positions from the Foy and Arloncourt areas to the southwestern sector.

Panzer Grenadier Regiment 901 continued to remain in its old position extending from the bridge (800m southeast of Mont) past Marvie via Remifosse as far as the country road leading from Salvacourt through the Bois d'Hazy Forest to the northeast towards Bastogne.

Through the day the enemy forces in the northern and eastern sectors had again been entirely passive. To judge, however, by the fire concentration of mortar and artillery as well as the machine-gun and rifle fire which had been encountered by advancing German reconnaissance detachments, no noticeable shifting of forces had taken place there. Only Panzer Grenadier

Regiment 901 in its report expressed the opinion that the enemy in the southeastern sector, i.e. in the Marvie sector, apparently could not be considered as being particularly strong.

Largely worn-out and fatigued, the reinforced Rifle Regiment 39 was located in the southern part of the Bois Bechu Forest via the northern edge of Assenois–Halte along the country road 1000m east of Villeroux. The enemy was, roughly speaking, facing the regiment more or less closely about the south and southwest of the Remioforce–Isle la Hesse road. The changeable and fluctuating battles of the day had brought considerable suffering to the enemy as well.

Even though heavy fighting as well as enemy counter-thrusts had been anticipated, such enemy pressure had not been expected. Could it have been the desperate attempt of the enemy to break out of the encirclement at all costs? There were indications which seemed to confirm such an assumption. Civilian refugees from Bastogne mentioned excitement, unrest and signs of excessive haste among the occupying forces inside Bastogne. Billets were evacuated, vehicles were loaded with equipment, motor vehicles drove off towards the west and congested the streets as well as a bridge at the western entrance. The population was in a state of panic.

At corps headquarters it was noted that interviews with prisoners revealed a discouraged outlook. The flying in of supplies led to the conclusion that certain things were lacking. The fact that the enemy was using the highways and roads to the west which, after all, were under fire, could possibly be interpreted as an attempt to save all that could be saved.

The curt and terse rejection of the American commander in Bastogne of the surrender proposal also did not exclude the possibility that the enemy was trying his utmost to break out of the encirclement. Unpleasant, in any event, was for the men facing Bastogne the knowledge that enemy groups had been able at all to move into the area of Vaux les Rosiers in their rear.

US FORCES: That night, December 22, the Luftwaffe began its bombing attack which was repeated on the next four nights. Despite the deceptively inactive appearance of the front, the defenders of Bastogne had actually reached the lowest ebb of their fortune by the night of December 22. The crisis was a matter of supply.

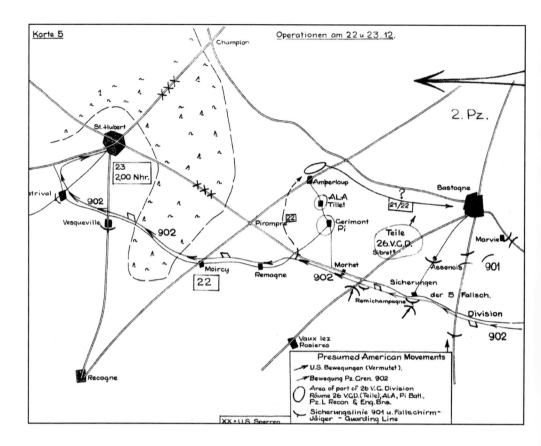

BAYERLEIN: CC902 drives forward through Remichampagne and Morchet. CC901 with two companies of tanks and one battalion of artillery still engaged southwest of Bastogne and attach to 26th Volksgrenadier Division. Advance of the 903 harassed near Remichampagne and Morchet by enemy tank fire from the south. Weak resistance broken near Remagen.

BUECH: Hitler sent Major Johann to Manteuffel about 22–23 December in order to observe the situation at Bastogne. Hitler was not satisfied with Manteuffel's report that he could not take Bastogne with the forces he had; however, he agreed with Manteuffel. This action was taken when Hitler realised it would not be possible to secure bridgeheads across the Meuse, and that we would have to fight east of the river. If we had to fight east of the Meuse, and if you maintained your forces in Bastogne, your troops coming from south and north would be a great danger to us. In this offensive, Bastogne was the key point of communications behind our own front lines, which we needed to be able to bring in supplies for the divisions.

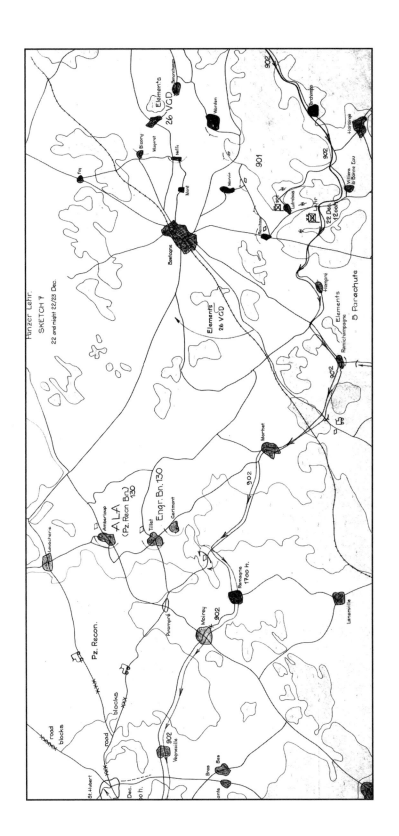

Panzer Lehr.
SKETCH 7
22 and night 22/23 Dec.

Elements
26 VGD

Elements
26 VGD

Elements
26 VGD

5 Parachute

A.L.A.
(Pz. Recn Bn.)
130

Engr. Bn. 130

Pz. Recon.

road
blocks

road
blocks

St. Hubert
Dec.
00 h.

901

902

902

902

902

902

902

902

Bastogne

Foy

Mont

Marvie

Neffe

Mageret

Bizory

Benonchamps

Wardin

Orteuville

Hompre

Remichampagne

Villers
la Bonne Eau

Harlange

22 Dec
(2 col)

Morhet

Remagne
1700 h.

Lamerville

Gerimont

Tillet

Moircy

Pirompré

Vesqueville

Brea

Sse

Amberloup

Lavacherie

22 Dec
(2 col)

We tried to capture Bastogne with other divisions, elements of the first, second, and third waves of Fifth Panzer Army, but we had no artillery there. They bypassed Bastogne, and each division that went by on the way to the west dropped off a small force. The 560 and 340 Volksgrenadier Divisions and elements of 2nd Panzer and Panzer Lehr Divisions remained there in order to keep the ring around Bastogne closed. When the infantry divisions of the second and third waves came through, they followed their own panzer divisions toward the Meuse. This was one of the reasons that Mayer was sent there – to find out why it was not possible to capture Bastogne with all these units. I remember that at the time, elements of these three/four divisions were not enough to capture Bastogne, and then came the decision from Hitler to move from the north one, and then two more, panzer divisions.

It was attempted, but not with strong enough infantry, artillery, heavy weapons, etc. From the rear came elements of other divisions, but they didn't succeed either. There was great difficulty in bringing up ammunition. I remember that the flak regiment from Hitler's headquarters (II Bn, Hermann Goering Flak Regiment) went to Bastogne, and it had to bring ammunition by car from the area near Koblenz. Mayer reported these difficulties to Manteuffel and stated that it wasn't possible to take Bastogne with such small means. Because he saw we had to fight east of the Meuse, Hitler then decided that we must take Bastogne and would need at least a panzer division in order to succeed.

26th Volksgrenadier Division: At nightfall the situation of the Corps was as follows:

The general situation of the Corps had not changed. As in the beginning it had to be expected that the Meuse would not be attained later than the 24 December. However, the Corps already feared for its right flank. If the elements on the right flank, in particular the 116th Panzer Division would not keep pace with the Corps, the parts which were advancing in the direction of the Meuse would get into a critical situation. But the Army believed that the adjoining units would succeed in crossing the road Hotton–Marche and advance past Sinsin toward the Meuse.

23 December

KOKOTT: The intention of the division for 23 December was to close the belt surrounding Bastogne between Senonchamps and Champs. To accomplish this, Reconnaissance Battalion 26 was to attack via Mande-Saint-Étienne towards the north and Grenadier Regiment 77 from the area west of Champs towards the south. The corps approved of this plan and promised the assistance of an armoured group of the 2nd Panzer Division for the attack against Flamierge from the west. The Corps still seemed to be of the opinion that the enemy inside Bastogne could not be very strong. The division was inclined to be of the same opinion.

After the failure of the breakout attempts on 22 December, the enemy was expected again to try on the following day to fight their way out of the encirclement in a general southwestern direction. It was quite possible that they would choose the weakest point of the ring – i.e. via Mande-Saint-Étienne – for that attempt. As a precautionary measure it was therefore necessary for the division to seal off the western sector as soon as possible, to close the existing gap and also to move the ring between Senonchamps and Champs as close as possible towards Bastogne. While this closing of the ring was to be of immediate primary importance, the division did not give up its plan for the attack on Bastogne.

In view of the hard fighting and the losses which had been suffered on 22 December, it appeared not only advisable, but even could be advocated, to grant to the reinforced Rifle Regiment 39 a certain breathing spell and to relieve it temporarily on 23 December of the continuation of a thrust on Bastogne. The attack should instead be carried out by Panzer Grenadier Regiment 901, however according to our own reconnaissance and opinion, the regiment was apparently not faced by a strong enemy. Furthermore, it had, with the exception of an armoured group, not been committed for the attack during 22 December. The attack was to originate in the eastern sector – between Marvie and Remoifosse. The dark hours of the afternoon on 23 December were earmarked for the time of attack. Reason:

A. Because of the additional difficulties of a daylight attack, during which the enemy fighter-bombers would possess unrestricted air superiority.
B. Because of the calculation that by the fall of darkness, at the latest, the encirclement between Senonchamps and Champs would be completed. By that time the front of all the units would again be facing towards Bastogne and it would be possible at any time – depending on the

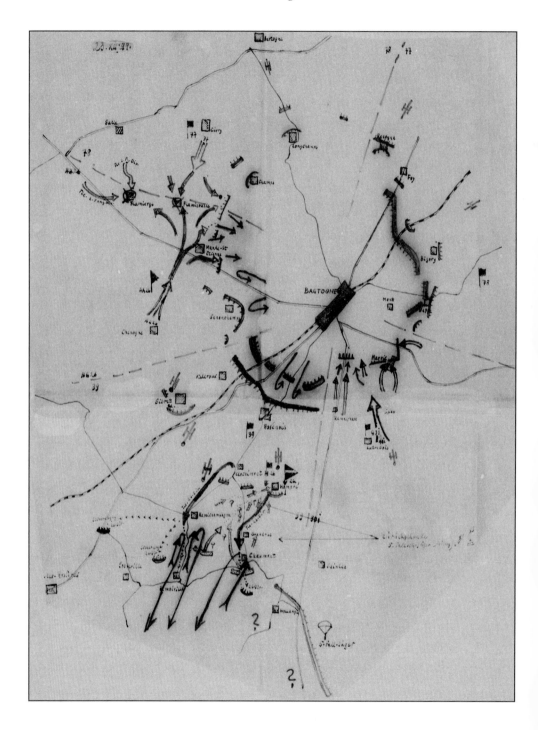

progress of the attack by Regiment 901, to assemble them for an attack on Bastogne as well. This would, above all, mean a state of readiness for Regiment 39 which was adjacent to the left of Regiment 901, and which would have to follow up the latter's attack in the darkness. For that purpose, Regiment 39 should organise and adjust its units during the daylight hours and, by means of limited assault troop action, should create for itself more favourable starting positions, provided the tactical situation should permit it.

Should the attacks for the closing of the gap in the west, as well as the pin-point type assault battles in the southwest, induce the enemy to pull some forces out of the eastern and southeastern sector, that could only be of advantage to the German intentions. If the enemy, in their tenacity, would again try on 23 December to breakout via Assenois–Villeroux – which, of course, had to be reckoned with – then the lines of Rifle Regiment 39 would have to be held in all events, even if they would be taxed to the utmost limit. The troops knew what was at stake.

The division therefore ordered for 23 December:

1) Reconnaissance Battalion 26, while screening off to the east and holding on to the territory gained on 22 December, will assemble the bulk of its forces for the attack in the Bois de Valet Forest and attacks over the highway to the north early on 23 December. Objective: Capture of Mande-Saint-Étienne and Flamisoul, link up in the wooded sections east of Flamisoul with Grenadier Regiment 77 attacking to the south. After the link up, Reconnaissance Battalion 26 will take over the sector of the encirclement front extending from height 500 (1000m north of Villeroux) to the country road Hemroulle–Flamisoul, inclusive.

2) Grenadier Regiment 77, while holding on to its present encirclement belt, will attack early on 23 December from the area south of Givry to the south and captures – in a thrust towards Reconnaissance Battalion 26 – Flamisoul and the wooded sections located to the east thereof. After the link up with Reconnaissance Battalion 26, Grenadier Regiment 77 will take over the previous sector of the encirclement front, with its right wing the country road Hemroulle–Flamisoul, exclusive. Adjacent to the right: Reconnaissance Battalion 26.

3) An armoured group of the 2nd Panzer Division, together with Reconnaissance Battalion 26 and Grenadier Regiment 77 attack early on 23 December from the area Macravivier–Tronle, take Flamierge and drive

through to the road Hubermont–Flamisoul. After linking up between the Reconnaissance Battalion 26 and Grenadier Regiment 77, the armoured groups and all other security forces of the 2nd Panzer Division return to their divisions and withdraw from the encirclement front.

4) Reinforced Rifle Regiment 39 on 23 December to hold all of its positions against enemy attacks. It improves its positions during the day by means of limited assault troop operations, depending on the tactical situation. In later afternoon the regiment will be prepared to attack Bastogne, with main effort between the road Assenois–Bastogne and the railroad line Neufchâteau–Bastogne, as soon as the night attack of Panzer Grenadier Regiment 901 in the Marvie–Remoifosse area will have gained ground.

5) Panzer Grenadier Regiment 901 to hold and improve its position during daylight hours on 23 December and to make all necessary preparations for the night attack. Objective: capture of Marvie and breakthrough to the southeastern edge of Bastogne. Time for the attack: after 1700 hours.

6) The division artillery supports the attack on Mande-Saint-Étienne and Flamisoul from the area on both sides of Sibret, keeps prepared to smash enemy attacks against Rifle Regiment 39 and makes all necessary preparations effective in support of the attack by Panzer Grenadier Regiment 901 and later by Rifle Regiment 39.

The losses of the division for 22 December amounted to about 400 men killed, wounded and missing. The losses of officers, subordinate commanders and forward observers were high. The losses of arms and equipment – destroyed through enemy fire – could, with the exception of guns, be replaced out of the division's reserves. There was a shortage of ammunition for heavy mortars and heavy howitzers. The high requirements for infantry ammunition could be covered.

The men suffered greatly from the cold weather. They had no winter clothing and on top of their uniforms wore only thin lined coats for camouflage in snow. The supply of bread had been handicapped for days. Up to ten men temporarily had to share a loaf of bread per day. To increase their combat strength, Regiment 39 and Reconnaissance Battalion 26 were compelled to fall back on their own resources by incorporating all possible administrative and supply personnel into the combat units.

In order to form a stronger division reserve, division ordered the organisation of three 'emergency companies' of about 40 men each, drawn from the division Supply Regiment, the Replacement Training Battalion and the Artillery Regiment.

LÜTTWITZ XLVII Pz Corps: On 23-24 December I personally drove up to the point of the division and discovered that the roadblock consisted only of thin barricades. I saw that there were no enemy forces. I then got the division moving, but we had proceeded northwest only a short distance when we came to a small river crossing. At that place, the whole road was blown up. It was an exceptionally good piece of work by the American engineers. We reconnoitred a bypass and the division then moved rapidly on to Marche. I had counted on the enemy building up a new defensive position on the line Rochefort–Marche; therefore, I tried to pass this line as quickly as possible.

In the later afternoon of 23 or 24 December, while still southeast of Marche, contact was made with the enemy. I ordered the division only to screen against Marche, while the bulk of the division was to make a breakthrough at Hargimont. I had had command of this division before I assumed command of XLVII Panzer Corps.

The XLVII Panzer Corps was responsible for the German effort to recapture Bastogne. The 26th Volksgrenadier Division was pressing against Bastogne from the south and had elements as far south as Sibret. The Corps boundary was between Assenois and Bastogne, which separated it from Seventh Army. Within that boundary, the troops of Volksgrenadier Division were facing Bastogne. Although it was recognised that the Americans were attacking from the south, it was the responsibility of 5th Fallschirmjäger Division of Seventh Army to contain this attack. The 5th FS Division was facing south from Clochimont, with elements in all the little towns, including Assenois.

ZERBEL: 23 December: 2nd Panzer Division: The advance detachment, without meeting strong enemy resistance, except at some points, where it had short fights with the enemy supply trains, could advance till Foy, Notre-Dame, On and Jemelle were taken.

Panzer-Lehr Division: The Division took St Hubert at 0100 hours and pushed forward till Forrières. They started from this place at 1600 hours and penetrated Rochfort at 1800 hours.

KOKOTT: During the daylight hours of 23 December, even before 0900 hours, the attack was launched for the closing of the ring.

Effectively supported by the fire of all arms, Reconnaissance Battalion 26 advanced from the Bois de Valet Forest towards the wooded section south of Flamisoul and the western part of Mande-Saint-Étienne.

As was to be expected, heavy fighting developed with the enemy who fought desperately for the road leading out to the west. Attacks and counter-thrusts were alternating. Relief attacks from the Isle-la-Hesse area towards Senonchamps and the Bois de Fragotte Forest were repelled with heavy fighting. Grenadier Regiment 77 had gone into the battle with a combat group towards Flamisoul and fought its way forward skilfully.

The situation at Flamierge was at first still uncertain. As usual, the first enemy fighters appeared towards 0900 hours, swooped down on communication roads and villages, and set vehicles and farmyards on fire. While fighting around Mande-Saint-Étienne, Flamisoul and Flamierge continued, there began in the course of the morning at first minor – but later increasing – combat action opposite the front of Rifle Regiment 39. The enemy repeatedly launched partial attacks which were frequently supported by tanks. Heavy fighting developed on both sides of the Bastogne–Neufchâteau road.

Towards noon, both in the area of Mande-Saint-Étienne–Flamisoul and opposite Rifle Regiment 39 the battle was in full swing, Regiment 77 (attacking from the north) radioed 'progressing attack'. Regiment 39 reported strong enemy pressure and high losses of its own due to heavy enemy fire.

At that time, when the fighting of the day noticeably approached its peak, the situation to the rear of the heavily engaged troops became unexpectedly critical: there appeared on the division command post at Hompré at first singly, but then in droves, men of the 5th Fallschirmjäger Infantry Division; they were coming from the lines and were moving on to the east. Barely an officer was in sight. When questioned, the men yelled: 'The enemy has broken through. He moved to the north with tanks and has captured Chaumont!' The parachute infantry battalion had been wiped out. They had great losses and they were the remaining men of the battalion. The enemy tanks would shortly appear in the village (Hompré)! From the west came at the same time vehicles in high speed; horse drawn vehicles were racing through Hompré. The vehicles became entangled with those coming from the east and blocked the road. Enemy fighter-bombers swooped down on Hompré and pushed their thrusts of fire into the fluctuating and congested mass. All rifle carriers inside the village and the anti-aircraft forces located close by were firing wildly at the planes.

Houses caught fire, vehicles were burning, wounded men were lying in the streets. Clochimont, Hompré, Salwâcourt were located in enemy artillery fire. In addition, there were suddenly heavy formations of planes which released masses of white and coloured parachutes in a wide circle surrounding Bastogne. In a short time, the sky was covered with a multitude of cargo chutes, dangling slowly to the ground.

Messages arrived, shouts were heard, 'Enemy parachutists are jumping and landing in our rear.' The division assumed that as well. It was an unpleasant state of affairs. The noise of our own and the enemy's fire, and the droning of the motors and whining of the fighter-bombers and accompanying fighters made a considerable humdrum!

The retreating men of the 5th Parachute Infantry Division were stopped by the division. The roads were cleared. Officers and men of the division staff occupied Hompré for the defence. The batteries near Hompré made an 'about face' to open fire to the south. Some of the anti-aircraft installations north of Hompré were being prepared for ground operations. The division reserves were being altered, moving anti-aircraft guns into positions, occupying a sector between Hompré–Clochimont for the defence. The elements located inside Sibret moved into positions for the defence of the village.

The division commander appropriated four tanks which happened to be located at Hompé, had them mounted by assault troops of the Division Combat School, added some artillery liaison detachments as well as a few groups of engineers with demolition equipment, then ordered these improvised 'combat groups' to drive forwards to secure and block the road. Everything happened very fast.

The young troops of the 5th Parachute Infantry Division after some time had got over their initial shock, which was entirely understandable. The situation became less tense after some time when the Reconnaissance Regiment reported 'Mande-Saint-Étienne taken, communication was established with Grenadier Regiment 77 in Flamisoul area!'

The ring had thus been closed in the western sector: Some individual enemy counterattacks did still take place in the afternoon, but their strength and force had noticeably weakened. In the area northeast of Assenois–Villeroux, Regiment 39 held on to its positions and even staged some limited partial thrusts, after the bulk of the division artillery had become available.

26th Volksgrenadier Division: Closer encirclement of Bastogne through relief of parts of the 2nd Panzer Division was accomplished. Mande and Saint-Étienne were captured. The 901st Panzer Grenadier Battalion attacked Marvie unsuccessfully. The 5th Para Division withdrew south of Clochmont. The division covered these parts in the prepared position on the line Clochmont-Hompré.

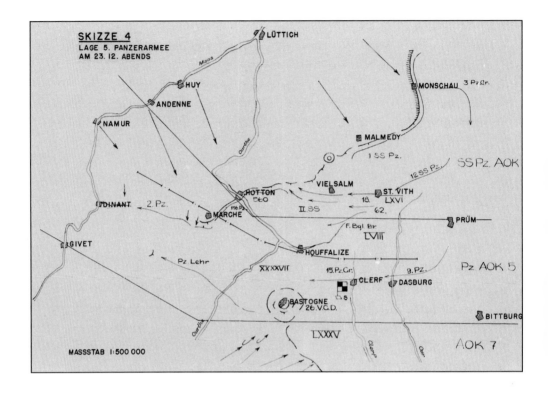

US FORCES: From daylight on December 23 all guards stood alerted for the first appearance of the C-47s. At 0935 hours a military policeman on duty at the entrance to the 101st Division command post carried the word to Colonel Kohls that several large planes were circling the area. A few minutes later, the pathfinders jumped in the area where the 2nd Battalion of Colonel Harper's 327th Glider Infantry was deployed. They were quickly rounded up by his men. One minute later, 1st Lieutenant Gordon O. Rothwell, commanding the pathfinder team, was on the telephone explaining to Colonel Kohls that the supply planes would arrive in about 90 minutes. Kohls told him how to get to the drop zone and where to put the radar set. Again, the regimental supply men were alerted; again, Major Butler displayed the panels. At 1150 hours on the 23rd, men all along the front saw the planes coming in; it was the most heartening spectacle of the entire siege.

Men and vehicles were all set for it. The pathfinder radar had given Captain Huffman and Lieutenant Colonel John T. Cooper, Jr. (Commanding Officer, 463nd Parachute Field Artillery Battalion) a half-hour advance warning that the planes were coming in and the supply parties reached the field ten minutes before the flight, in time for Huffman to assign zones of retrieving to each unit so that there would be a uniformly quick pick-up. There was very little enemy fire on any part of the field.

Sixteen planes arrived in the first flight, but these were just the beginning. By 1606 hours of that day, 241 planes had dropped 1446 bundles weighing 144 tons by parachute into the mile-square drop zone. The drop pattern was excellent and there was about a 95 per cent recovery of the dropped *matériel*.

Working against the approaching darkness, the supply crews threw whole bundles, parachute and all, into the jeeps and shuttled between the drop zone and their dumps as fast as they could tear over the ground. All supplies were in the unit dumps by 1700 hours, and even before that time ammunition had been rushed directly to the front lines and the battery positions. The artillery was firing part of the resupply ammunition at the enemy before the drop zone had been cleared.

By the time darkness came on, Colonel Kohls had at hand reports from all the unit supply officers telling what quantities of *matériel* had reached their unit dumps. It took only a brief checking on his part to see that his supply problem was far from being solved. The contents of the bundles were not in balance with the real needs of the troops. They still desperately lacked certain items and they had received others which they did not need or want. A great amount of calibre .50 ammunition had been sent up, but this was not much in demand. The new supply of calibre .30 for the M1, and of 76mm. APC and 75mm ammunition was insufficient. The division needed litters and penicillin badly and though it had collected all of the available bed clothing from the Belgian community, many of its men were still miserably cold at night and were asking for blankets.

At 1725 hours on 23 December, the 2nd Battalion, 327th, in Marvie was heavily shelled by enemy tanks concealed in a small plantation of firs within the hollow just above the village of Martaimont. From their position the tanks could shoot directly into Marvie. It was a characteristic enemy action for throughout the siege it was the German practice to use tanks as artillery, perhaps from fear of hitting their own troops if they used field guns from far back.

At about 1735 hours the 2nd Battalion, 327th, was attacked by tanks and infantry coming from the same general direction, though they had debouched from a larger wood lying a little further away from Marvie. The attack developed very slowly. The German infantry was clad in snow suits and a light snow was falling. They seemed to be waiting until the gloom deepened so they could make the most of their camouflage. The enemy barrage had ignored Team O'Hara's part of the sector, but the outposts of the 54th Armoured Infantry spotted two enemy machine guns that were firing into Marvie.

Flanking fire was placed on them and they were silenced. Heavy automatic fire then searched the position of the 54th. No enemy could be seen and the men of the 54th held their fire except for one heavy machine gun on the left. The enemy spotted that gun. A few minutes later a hand grenade dropped next to the gun killing the gunner and wounding one other man. The rest of the crew quit the position. Next morning a patrol returned to the gun and found the second man still alive, but so nearly frozen that he could only nod his head to them. Both he and the dead man had been searched and stripped of their possessions by Germans who had come in fast upon the position after the grenade fire.

Within half an hour the attack was fully developed and soon after 1840 hours, December 23, one platoon of Company G, 327th became surrounded on Hill 500 to the south of Marvie. The enemy had begun a gradual envelopment of the platoon's position by moving into and through houses and yards that were around the base of the hill on all sides. A few members of the platoon were able to withdraw along the flanks of the hill as the encirclement began. The others stayed in their positions and the time quickly came when they could not get out. Four tanks, which had accompanied the German infantry advance to Hill 500, turned their fire against Marvie, adding to the bombardment that was still coming in from the armoured guns in the big wood.

KOKOTT: During the afternoon of 23 December at last the situation to the rear of the division became somewhat less difficult. The four heavy German tanks had stopped the enemy's reconnaissance thrust near Chaumont by putting several enemy tanks out of action. After a short engagement, the enemy had retreated. Our own forward elements followed through and the improvised 'combat group' of the 26th Division now was blocking roads and crossings.

US FORCES: Colonel Harper had worried about this part of the perimeter. Earlier in the day he had asked Colonel O'Hara to put a tank on the hill. O'Hara agreed to station a 57mm gun on the lower slope of the hill where a 37mm gun had previously defended it. The half-track carrying the 57mm gun was just going into position when the German tanks and infantry closed in on Hill 500. The first few German rounds that came his way were enough for the driver; he turned the half-track around and sped north toward Marvie. The troops in the village saw the half-track coming toward them from out of the body of the German attack. They thought it was a German vehicle and they fired at it with everything they had, demolishing the vehicle and killing the crew.

Two German tanks that had followed along the same road crossed the stream south of Marvie and got into the village as far as the church. They saw then that the destroyed half-track blocked the road and that they could not advance any further, so they turned around and withdrew.

Having begun the attack in stealth, the German infantry now came on toward the houses in a frenzy, yelling and firing as they advanced and shooting many flares. To the men in Colonel O'Hara's position it looked as if the tracers were flying in all directions. Bullet fire began to envelop them from the southern edge of the village. A self-propelled gun came charging toward them up the Wiltz road. As it rounded the bend and came abreast of the farmhouse there, one of our medium tanks fired and the gun went up in flames. The fire lit the entire area. The enemy turned their artillery loose on the farmhouse. A loft filled with hay soon blazed like a torch. Because of the intense illumination from these fires, the tanks and infantry of Team O'Hara's line withdrew 100 yards to the west.

Counting an Engineer platoon on the right of Colonel Harper's 327th Glider Infantry, there were 98 men defending Hill 500. Already, a few had been killed or wounded. At the same time that a part of the German force pressed against Marvie from the south, 12 German tanks supported by infantry advanced north along the main road toward the position occupied by Company F, 327th. This body had debouched from the same woods from which the German tanks were firing. Instead of continuing along the Bastogne road, part of the German armour moved right toward Hill 500. The infantry were clad in white and were almost imperceptible.

On the slopes of Hill 500 Lieutenant Stanley Morrison and his men of Company G, 327th Glider Infantry, had dug in around the base of the houses. Colonel Harper in his command post got word that the enemy was attacking. He called Lieutenant Morrison and asked, 'What is your situation?'

'Now they are all around me,' Morrison replied. 'I see tanks just outside my window. We are continuing to fight them back but it looks like they have us.' To Colonel Harper's listening ear he seemed perfectly calm and he spoke in a level tone.

Harper called him back in about three minutes. Morrison replied but he said only these words, 'We're still holding on.' Then the line went dead. Lieutenant Colonel Thomas J. Rouzie, the executive officer of the 327th Glider Infantry, said to Harper, 'I guess that's the end of Morrison.'

The men of Hill 500 were never heard from again in the battle. They had been overwhelmed by troops of the 901st Panzergrenadier Regiment of the Panzer Lehr Division. The end came for Lieutenant Morrison's detachment sometime after 1900 hours on 23 December.

There had been no tanks or tank destroyers in support of Morrison. Force O'Hara had not fired either in defence of the hill positions or against the German front moving into Marvie from the south. Colonel Harper couldn't understand it. He called Colonel O'Hara who said, 'They are attacking me also and are trying to come around my north flank.' This flank had a patch of woods lying just north of the bend of the road, but not within the American position and the enemy was striking from out of those woods. Now the snow suits no longer helped them for they reflected the light of the blazing house. From 100 yards away O'Hara's men fired. Some of the figures pitched forward in the snow and others sought its concealment.

One of Colonel O'Hara's men had failed to withdraw in time. He played dead when the Germans came to his foxhole. They said, 'Hello, hello,' then kicked him, sat on him, took his BAR and rifled his pockets. But he kept absolutely still. Sometime later he heard them bring up two guns on the left, a large one and a small one. They fired the small gun indiscriminately, apparently with the expectation of getting return fire which would provide a target for the large gun. Yet during the night the large gun never did fire. The man in the foxhole also heard the German ambulances make numerous trips into the area for the purpose of taking out their dead and wounded.

Major Galbreaith (executive officer of the 2nd Battalion, 327th), reported to Colonel Harper at 2000 hours, December 23, that the German infantry were in the south end of Marvie and were working through the houses. The tanks which had been on Hill 500 and had shelled Marvie from there were now moving toward the houses. Galbreaith asked Harper, 'Can't I get tanks?' Harper replied, 'I'll try.' But the line to Team O'Hara had gone out. Colonel Harper tried the radio but could only hear Team O'Hara headquarters faintly.

Major Galbreaith called Colonel Harper again, and said, 'They are all around us now and I must have tanks.'

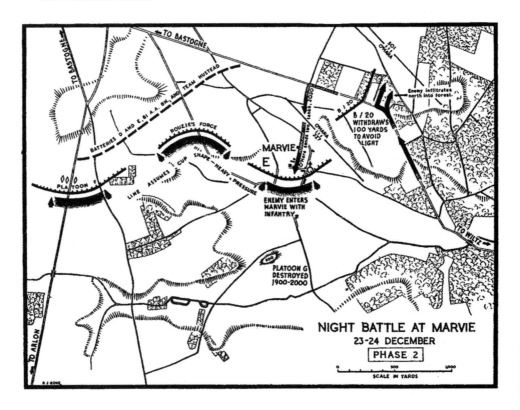

'You call O'Hara on your radio,' replied Harper, 'and say "It is the commanding general's order that two Sherman tanks move into Marvie at once and take up a defensive position."'

Colonel Harper had no authority for his action, but he figured this wasn't the time to stand on ceremony. A few minutes later the two Sherman tanks moved into Marvie on Colonel O'Hara's orders. The infantry of both sides were already locked in a fight for possession of the houses, but the destroyed half-track kept the enemy armour from entering the south of the village. Colonel Harper's force was now totally stripped of reserve. His line was buckled in and from Hill 500 the Germans were in good position to exploit the break in his centre, roll back the flanks of his position, and through this breach enter the heart of Bastogne. But once again in renewing their direct assault on the city the Germans had made the same error of engaging heavily only along one part of the front.

The front at Foy had cooled off and Colonel Ewell's forces along the Longvilly road could even doze a little. At 2145 hours a platoon of paratroopers from Company A of the 501st Parachute Infantry under Captain Stanfield A. Stach was sent to reinforce Company F of the 327th Glider Infantry. That company was already in a pretty bad way. One of its squads had been in the small patch of woods just to the southwest of Hill 500 and part of a platoon had been on higher ground to the squad's right rear. These positions had been overrun by the German armoured advance from out of the woods around Martaimont. A few of the men got away. Others had been killed or taken prisoner defending their ground.

The bulk of the company, in position along the crest of the hill commanding the main highway into Bastogne from the south, had held like a rock. The German assault had come on with its right closing around Marvie, its centre enveloping Hill 500 and its left lunging forward along the main highway. The armour that supported the advance of the German left could be stopped only by bazooka fire from Lieutenant Smith's platoon, for this was no place for tank destroyers. Anything that came over the skyline of the hill moving southward from Bastogne was immediately put under fire by German tanks or self-propelled guns firing from defilade. No tank destroyers could be risked at the position.

Three of Colonel O'Hara's tanks, known as Force Charley 16, were in support of our infantry line, but the night attack closed in in such manner that the fate of the line depended on the infantry weapons. There was a respite after Smith's fire beat back the first attack, but the enemy tanks withdrew only a short distance.

The ruptured line north of Hill 500 was quickly patched and strengthened before the enemy could exploit their opening success. One platoon of Company F, which had been astride the Bastogne road, was put in position to east of it. The 327th Glider

Infantry was also given Batteries D and E of the 81st Anti-aircraft Battalion and Major Hustead's part of Team Cherry. Twelve guns were put in an arc along the high ground in the road triangle just above Marvie.

Colonel Rouzie picked up 24 men of Company F and with the 40 men under Captain Stach proceeded through Lieutenant Smith's position and took up a defence line corresponding with the distribution of the 81st's anti-aircraft guns. These moves – made between 2400 and 0100 hours (24 December) – temporarily closed the breach. Colonel Rouzie took personal charge of the defence of the threatened area. Upon reaching the ground he had decided he was in no position to attack. He felt that he would simply waste his strength if he tried to drive the Germans away from Hill 500. The best course open was to establish a defensive line on the 'inner part of the cup'. Captain Adams reorganized the position of Company F so that the line bent back north-eastward to join with the position covering the 81st's guns.

SCHRAMM: LIII Inf. Corps – south and southeast of Bastogne – 23 December. The situation of the Army Right Wing on 22 December 44.

The more likely it became that Bastogne would not capitulate, the more clearly did the enemy comprehend that this area would totally become the main point of the battle of the Ardennes, and through here was the decisive point in its attempt to protect the flank of the Army Groups.

US FORCES: Twice again that night the German armour lashed at the left flank and always the fire fell heaviest, not on Colonel Rouzie's scratch force, but on the position held by the platoons of Lieutenant Smith and Technical Sergeant Butler. The regimental officers of the 327th Glider Infantry said later that Sergeant Butler's courage and energy were the mainstay of the defence. In one of the assaults a pair of German tanks got to within 50 yards of the foxholes held by Lieutenant Smith's men before they were turned back by bazooka fire. By then Smith's command post was blazing, for the tanks had fired 15 rounds into the house as they came on. Smith and his assistants had set up in the basement and they stayed there while the upper structure burned.

Rouzie's force patrolled southward to the small woods from where part of Company F had been driven and found that it was now held by an enemy outpost. A few Company F stragglers were trying to work their way out of the woods. The patrol mistook them for Germans and fired on them. They hit the ground. One member of the patrol, suspecting that they were Americans, crawled forward, identified them and brought them out. The enemy had captured a number of American mortars around Marvie and through the rest of the night American mortar shells dropped on the ground which Smith and Butler were defending.

In the early morning the Germans asked and received permission to remove their dead and wounded from in front of Smith's platoon. It was only when the Germans came forward to collect their dead that the pressure slackened and the mortar fire ceased.

Elsewhere along the sector the issue of the fight was still in balance. Two tanks which had ripped through Harper's forward line had gone right into Bastogne and shot up the houses around his command post, without doing any vital damage. In Marvie the arrival of the two Sherman tanks had stabilized the fighting.

KOKOTT: The 26th Volksgrenadier Division was surrounding Bastogne. The 78th Grenadier Regiment front extended from Foy to Marvie; 901 Panzer Grenadier Regiment, attached from Panzer Lehr Division, extended from Marvie to the Arlon–Bastogne road; 39 Grenadier Regiment extended from Senonchamps to Champs. There were also some reconnaissance elements here. An engineer battalion and a replacement training battalion were on the northern perimeter. There was also an outpost on the western boundary, facing west.

(Southern sector) The 39th Grenadier Regiment had two battalions, each having companies of 40 to 50 men and a battalion strength of 300 to 350 men. Regimental strength was about 800 to 900 men. The 901 Panzer Grenadier Regiment had two battalions of approximately the same strength, plus one company of the field ersatz battalion, four infantry cannon and eight machine guns attached.

I had my Command Post at Hompré on 23 December 44. Technically speaking, I was in the zone of 5th FS Division, Seventh Army, which was blocking to the south; however, this was no time to be concerned about boundary lines. The action of 5th FS Division was of vital concern to me. I was facing Bastogne. The American 4th Armoured Division drive north threatened my rear. It is an uncomfortable feeling to have someone launching a drive toward your rear; so, boundary or not, 5th FS Division was of constant concern to me. The situation was not aided by my knowledge that 5th FS Division was a very poor division. I feared 4th Armoured Division (US). I knew it was a 'crack' division. Furthermore, Genmajor Heilmann, Commander of 5th FS Division, was in Lutrebois. He had a very wide front and could not be everywhere. As it happened, I was nearer to this danger point than he; therefore, I gave orders to build a resistance line near Chaumont.

On 23 December 44, elements of 14th FS Regiment, 5th FS Division, began to fall back to Hompré. I ordered them to return south and gave them some of my officers. An unknown major in command of four Tiger tanks came into Hompré. I don't know where he came from, or where he was going, but I ordered him south to aid 5th FS Division at Remichampagne and Chaumont.

The attack plan called for a strong push from the west, while at the same time the enemy would be warded off and tied down through harassing attacks in the east and southeast.

The entire Panzer Grenadier Division was to carry out the main thrust in a narrow, deeply staggered formation. In the north i.e. between Foy and Longchamps nothing could be undertaken on the German side. The forces were lacking. The forces occupying that sector had decreased to a point where their effectiveness was most questionable. With a good deal of anxiety, the division had watched that area for quite some time and it appeared inevitable that any enemy thrust in platoon strength would be successful there. The enemy had fortunately abstained from such action up to that time.

The northwest sector – i.e. the area extending from Champs (inclusive) to Mande-Saint-Étienne – had been selected as the area for the main thrust. The terrain was most suitable for an armoured attack. The small gullies (now covered with snow) there did not present any hinderance. The terrain offered a clear view for observing effectiveness of artillery and supporting heavy infantry weapons. Between the highway and to the west and the road Hemroulle–Champs there were no villages and major wooded sections which, as experience had shown, always caused drawn-out engagements which took much time. There was, furthermore, reason to expect that in that sector of the front the enemy would be less strong and less ready for the defences that had proved to be in all the other sectors – the eastern, southeastern, southern and southwestern ones – where they had been attacked.

The individual missions were as follows:

The 15th Panzer Grenadier Division, located at the point of main effort, after having assembled in the area around Flamisoul, was to pierce the enemy front between Grande Fangne and the highway to the west. It was then to drive on to Bastogne between the highway to the west of Hemroulle. Initial objective: country road Hemroulle–Isle-la-Hesse.

Reconnaissance Battalion 26 – starting out from the area around Mande-Saint-Étienne – was to proceed along both sides of the highway to the west, was to protect the right flank of the main thrust and, for its initial objective, was to take the heights near Isle-la-Hesse.

Grenadier Regiment 77, staggered to the left, was to attack with its bulk from the area south of Rouette along the road Champs–Hemroulle, was to protect the left flank of the 15th Panzer Grenadier Division and, for its initial objective, was to capture Hemroulle.

Rifle Regiment 39 had the mission to link up with the attack by the northwestern group and, in its drive on Bastogne – with main effort on both sides of the railroad and road to Neufchâteau, to capture 'Isle-le-Pré as the first objective.

Panzer Grenadier Regiment 901, by means of assault troops operating between Marvie and the highway to the south, was to ward off and tie down the enemy.

Grenadier Regiment 76 was to conduct attacks with limited objective through sizeable assault detachments on both side of the Bizory–Bastogne railroad and also minor operations south of Neffe.

The entire artillery of the 15th Panzer Grenadier Division, the bulk of the artillery of the 26th Division and the attached reinforced artillery from several heavy batteries (10cm guns, 15cm howitzers and mortars) had been assembled to the rear of the attack wedge – particularly in the Flamierge–Givry area.

All other batteries in the area surrounding Bastogne were hooked up to the main fire control net and were able to enter the battle at the crucial points with observed fire. The division was trying its utmost to get to Bastogne between 0500 and 1000 hours or even to be inside Bastogne by that time. The group was familiar with that goal. Troops and leaders were aware of the fact that after 0500 and 1000 hours fighting would be entirely difficult and would bring many losses as by then the skies would be covered with the customary motors of fighter-bombers.

The strength of the 15th Panzer Grenadier Division, a unit of well-known quality, was disappointing. This Panzer Grenadier division has just been in combat, its losses had not been replaced and had been quickly pushed forward through the Army Group Model. The decision of Army Group Model to push this depleted 15th Panzer Grenadier Division for the large-scale attack on Bastogne, appeared incomprehensible. This measure could – as had been felt by the troops for some time – only be an indication that Army Group Model, at least, was in no way aware of the entire difficulty of the battle and the very high losses.

Changes could no longer be made regarding the attack itself, i,e. the time for the attack and the details of its execution. It had to be started and taken to a successful conclusion. The fortitude and combat experience of the troops, the inflexible determination of leaders and men, the fighting spirit of men and each and every individual, the clear and detailed preparation – those were factors with which the battle was entered.

US FORCES: Without fully realising it, the defenders of Bastogne passed their crisis on December 23. They could not measure the change, nor did they know how many elements were acting in their favour. But quite suddenly everything began to come their way. This was not a matter alone of successful local tactics against the enemy. Nor was it only that the measures taken by the VIII Corps and the larger forces concerned with the relief of the defenders were at last beginning to bear fruit, as evidenced by the arrival of the resupply missions. For one thing, such a vital matter as the weather continued to favour the defence. In the beginning there had been fog and acute dampness which appeared at first blush to doubly jeopardize the situation of a force that was having to feel its way to the enemy and was suffering from shortages of clothing and blankets.

Yet all that happened in the opening encounters during the first two days while Bastogne's fate was in the balance proved that the atmosphere served almost as a protecting screen for the defenders and wrought confusion among the oncoming forces. Had there not been fog, of course, there could have been air support. But it is a question whether that support could have been greatly effective during a period when it would have been difficult to distinguish between the retreating remnants of the broken American divisions and the advancing German columns. Again, an early intervention by the air power might have forestalled those concentrations of German armour and other vehicles which were to provide such inviting targets, when the opening at last came.

The overcast was still thick and the ground fog irregular. On the morning of December 23, for the first time since the Bastogne defenders were committed to action, a day dawned fair and clear, though with freezing temperatures. It looked like the hour of opportunity. By then the defences of Bastogne had become so closely knit, and there was such complete harmony and mutual confidence among the oddly assorted groups of the defence, that it seemed certain that all of the changes in the natural conditions of the battlefield would work only to the disadvantage of the enemy. The defensive lines were set. The crisp clear air ensured that if the Germans came on, their snow-suit camouflage would not be overly helpful; at least their features and their weapons could be seen.

The roads from Bastogne to all parts of the perimeter were like the spokes of a wheel. They were generally good roads. But particularly around the northern half of the defence they entered the perimeter over ground where a stout roadblock might well hold up an armoured regiment for hours. The German armour and its support had largely held to the roads during the period of build-up; and they were still out there, daring the lightning.

Wire communications from Bastogne command post to all parts of the perimeter were working as strongly on behalf of the defence as was the axial highway system. Only a few times had the wire gone out. The 101st's practice of emphasizing a net of lateral wires, which set up several ways of reaching the outfits on the perimeter, had saved a number of situations that might otherwise have been blacked out. And foresightedly, the Signal Company had brought in plenty of extra wire.

Now that there was the sure prospect of air resupply, the artillery situation was looking up. It had suffered thus far only from its fears that the ammunition wouldn't last. By the 22nd, General McAuliffe's supply had dropped down to twenty-odd rounds per gun and Colonel Roberts's about as low; some guns were down to ten rounds. But both commanders were certain that as long as the artillery ammunition lasted, Bastogne would hold.

The opening engagements had reaffirmed the power of an ample artillery properly directed, and by committing their forces piecemeal the Germans had played right into the hands of the defence which had staked its life on the massed fire of its guns.

The guns of Combat Command B, 10th Armoured Division, were capable of getting 11,000 yards out of their 105mm ammunition, while the same ammunition in the short 105 tubes of the Airborne Artillery units could only reach about 4,500 yards. The Armoured Artillery was therefore the real power of the defence together with the twenty 155mm howitzers of the Artillery battalions that had been caught in the town (the 755th and part of the 333rd Field Artillery Group).

During the first stage, the great natural strength of the position and the vast superiority of the American artillery had worked together for the salvation of Bastogne. The German artillery had been little more than a cipher, save for the fire from the tanks and self-propelled guns. At times it seemed to consist of single guns and their shoots were never very long. The town itself had not yet been given any steady shelling by the enemy guns and the command posts were able to maintain their liaison with little difficulty.

This lack of power in the German artillery and the inability of the German foot and armour to coordinate their assaults against different parts of the perimeter – probably because their communication system had broken under the pressures of the advance – minimized the moral strain which would normally afflict a body of troops that found itself surrounded. The command and staff of the defence were not feeling what they had expected to feel from the lessons they had learned at Leavenworth and Benning. They knew they were cut off. The G-2 reports and the incessant patrol activities against all portions of the defensive circle told them so. But they did not feel cut off. They remained mobile and mentally able to promote all of the tactical advantages of their interior position. The thought that there were Germans all around them brought no particular extra worry. They were confident that help from the outside was just around the corner.

However, the most decisive gains of the period had been in the work of the fighting men themselves and in their feelings about one another. In the beginning the different elements of the defence were almost out of communication one with the other. Things had happened so fast that they had been compelled to engage the enemy before giving a thought to their own liaison. But in the course of battle the infantry, the armoured force and the tank destroyer crews had taken full measure of each other and found the measure sufficient. The birth of mutual confidence and respect had produced not only tactical cohesion but comradeship in such a degree, that before the siege was over these units were to ask their higher commanders whether it wouldn't be possible for them to be joined permanently in one large force. They had come to believe that together they had become irresistible.

After their first tilt in which each had spoken bluntly and made his point, General McAuliffe and Colonel Roberts tabled their feelings and worked together to perfect the team play of their respective forces. As McAuliffe's advisor on armour, Roberts found himself among 'the best and keenest staff' he had ever seen. Not only did they radiate extreme confidence, but they proved to be 'great bird dogs' in detecting early enemy build-ups. As soon as the first signs of an enemy attack became apparent, Colonel Roberts would alert his division reserve and get it moving toward the likely area of eruption. He would then concern himself with building another division reserve. He never bothered General McAuliffe with these details. If it chanced that Colonel Cherry, the division reserve commander, got cut up, or if the 101st Division troops moved over during an action and drew parts of Team Cherry into the front line, there was always Team O'Hara with 14 tanks which he could get out of line quickly in case of necessity.

Colonel Roberts' force had more than paid for itself during the first two days. He had taken his greatest losses in tanks and men in the opening engagement, but that sacrifice had staved off the Germans and gained the exact amount of time needed for the 101st to establish itself solidly. After the first two days Colonel Roberts' two chopped-up teams were consolidated as one and this part of the force became his division reserve. The number of tanks available for it varied from day to day between 6 and 10.

Lieutenant Colonel Templeton, the Tank Destroyer commander (705th Battalion), took hold in the same strong way, even having his men fight as infantrymen when they could not be employed otherwise. On the other hand, he was never loath to make his point strongly any time he thought the higher commanders were planning to make an unwise employment of his forces. Colonel Templeton's command post was only 100 yards from the command post of the 101st Division, so coordination was simple. In turn he received from the battalion commanders of the 101st the kind of support that rewarded all of his effort. During relief periods the infantry platoons covering his tank destroyers made the security of Templeton's guns their first concern.

Colonel Roberts, too, was learning from Templeton as they went along. He had reached the conclusion that, properly employed in a defence like Bastogne, some tanks must be up with the infantry and some in reserve in the 'socker' role. But what bothered him was the discovery that while his tankers were actually having to work as tank destroyers about 98 per cent of the time, the tank destroyer men seemed so much better trained to get away with it. This was strongly reflected in the ratio of losses in the two forces when compared with the damage done to the enemy armour.

At 1000 hours on December 23 Captain Parker at his radio heard that supporting planes were on their way. Within a few minutes he was telling them where to strike. The strongest enemy build-ups at this time were west and northwest of the town, threatening the sectors held by the 502nd Parachute Infantry and the 327th Glider Infantry regiments. The infantry front lines had been hearing and seeing the arrival of these concentrations during the past two days. But because of the shortage of artillery ammunition, there had been no real check against them. The planes dropped low and came in fast against the enemy columns, gaining complete surprise. The German vehicles were on the road facing toward Bastogne when the first bombs fell among them. Such was the execution that one of the pilots later said to General McAuliffe, 'This was better hunting than the Falaise pocket and that was the best I ever expected to see.'

On that first day the Germans did not use their anti-aircraft guns against any of the dive bombers. If this reticence was due to a desire to cover up the positions of the guns, it was a view quickly changed because of the damage the Ninth Air Force planes had done during the first day. For thereafter the German flak was intense over the front at all times and the air units had no further hours of unopposed operation. They made the most of their opening opportunity. The snow was a great aid. Clearly visible tracks pointed to forest positions which were promptly bombed. The fir forests burst into flames from the fire bombs and before the day was out the smoke from these blazing plantations and from the brewed-up enemy columns made a complete circle around the besieged forces until it seemed almost as if the fog was closing in again. The air people hit every nearby town at least once with explosive and fire bombs. Noville was hit ten times.

The entire air operation was carefully systematized and then supervised in detail. As planes were assigned to the 101st Division by VIII Corps, they checked in with Captain Parker by radio. He put them on a clear landmark such as a railroad or highway as they came in toward Bastogne. Several checkpoints were then given to them from the map. When the approaching planes were definitely located, an approach direction was given that would bring them straight in over the target. This procedure eliminated all need for circling and searching and helped them surprise the enemy. When the bombs and gun ammunition were expended, the planes were ordered up to a safe altitude to patrol the perimeter of the defences or were given specific reconnaissance missions. Their reconnaissance reports were used as the basis for giving targets for succeeding flights and for giving the ground forces advance information on the build-up of enemy strength.

After the first flight there were always targets listed ahead. Captain Parker, carefully monitoring the air, also came across flights assigned to other ground forces battling in the Bulge which had no missions for their bombs. He would then call to them and he often succeeded in persuading them to drop their bombs in the Bastogne area. In a few minutes these planes would be back on their assigned missions.

During the first four days of their support, December 23 to 26, the planes averaged more than 250 sorties daily. After that there were two days of bad weather and then the weather came fair again. But it was on December 23 that the air support clanged the bell most loudly and thereby assured decision for the American forces. Colonel Roberts, watching the planes at work, said with enthusiasm that the effect was worth two or three infantry divisions. General McAuliffe bracketed their work with the overwhelming superiority of his artillery and the supreme courage of the men on the ground in his analysis of why Bastogne was saved. It was not unusual during the siege to have an infantryman call in that five tanks were coming at him and then see six P-47s diving at the tanks within twenty minutes.

For six days the enemy had made only a few swift passes at General McAuliffe's line facing toward the west. That was the way the command and staff had figured the battle was most likely to develop. Colonel Kinnard, who had worked out the tactical plan for the defence of Bastogne, felt that the forces could be spread thinnest toward the southwest. Between Colonel Harper, commanding the 327th, and Lieutenant Colonel Ray C. Allen, commanding the 3rd Battalion which held the attenuated lines covering toward Neufchâteau, there passed a jest typifying the situation. 'How are you doing on your left?' 'Good! We have two jeeps out there.'

In the northwest sector, the Germans accommodated General McAuliffe's plan of saving the 502nd Parachute Infantry for his Sunday punch and that regiment had relatively little fighting, though it went through a great many motions.

In the beginning Colonel Allen's 3rd Battalion, 327th, became engaged because of the enemy penetration, which on the night of December 19-20 reached the Bois de Herbaimont from the direction of Houffalize and overran and captured the 326th Medical Company near crossroads 'X'. Nine men from the 28th Division – remnant of a group of more than 100 men – got back to Colonel Allen's command post at 2030 hours and told him how this same German force had ambushed and destroyed their company. It was the first information that the Bastogne–Saint-Hubert road had been cut and it meant the probable end of any possibility that supplies could be brought in from the northwest.

The 101st Division Headquarters became alarmed. At 2200 hours Colonel Allen was told to move a company out against the roadblock which the enemy had established and destroy it. Company B under Captain Robert J. McDonald was two hours in preparing for the attack, but it moved out at midnight, December 20-21, and was approaching the roadblock after about a 90-minute march. The men moved down the ditches on either side of the Saint-Hubert road with two guides walking on the road to keep contact in the darkness. Ahead, they could see a number of vehicles burning and they could hear the enemy laughing and talking. The horns on several of the vehicles had become stuck, adding volume to the sounds which guided them toward their target. The company moved to a ridge within 75 yards of the roadblock and there deployed.

The din from the German position was such that they accomplished this movement without being detected. They formed up with the 2nd Platoon on the left, the 3rd Platoon on the right, and the 1st Platoon in the centre, supported by the heavier weapons. One squad of the 2nd Platoon moved to the Sprimont road and formed a block across it about 100 yards from crossroads 'X'. On the other flank a squad from the 3rd Platoon established a block for the same purpose about 100 yards outside the enemy outposts.

Captain McDonald had figured that the roadblock on the right would take longest to establish, so he directed the squad leader to fire two quick rifle shots when his men were in position. The plan worked perfectly. When the two shots were fired, the centre moved forward, the men shooting from the hip as they advanced. The Germans were taken wholly by surprise and most of them fled toward the Bois de Herbaimont just to the north whence they had come originally. So doing, they crossed the killing ground which was covered by the squad on the right under Technical Sergeant Mike Campano. They were in such numbers that Campano's men could hardly shoot fast enough. More than 50 Germans were killed. None were taken prisoner. Company B didn't lose a man.

When the last German had been cleared from the area roadblocks were organized in all directions, with an especially strong block being set up on the highway to Salle (31 miles southwest of Bertogne). In this general position, Company B became the furthest outpost of the division. In their search of the area the company found three Americans who had been prisoners of the Germans. One was a Negro truck driver and the other two were from the finance department of the 28th Division. They also found two dead paratroopers whose throats had been slashed; they guessed that these men had been patients when the hospital was overrun. A number of American trucks were recovered, some containing medical supplies, one carrying a load of mail and another loaded with explosives.

On finding an American light tank among the enemy booty, Company B incorporated it into their defences along with several calibre .50 machine guns from the recaptured trucks. The noise of the skirmish had drawn an artillery observer from the 333rd Field Artillery Group and he attached himself to Company B and stood ready to deliver supporting fire from the 155mm howitzers when it would be needed.

On December 23, the positions were unchanged. Another patrol went into Rouette under the leadership of 1st Lieutenant David E. White. They got close enough to see that the enemy was occupying a line of outposts on high ground which overlooked the roads to Champs and Givry (2 miles northwest of Champs). The enemy was feverishly at work setting up roadblocks of farm carts bound together. There was a great deal of digging going on next to the positions.

Further to the south the signs were becoming equally ominous. Colonel Allen's 3rd Battalion of the 327th Glider Infantry was situated in defence of the area of Flamierge, Flamisoul and the Saint-Hubert highway west of Mande-Saint-Étienne. This put it well to the west of any other unit, without friendly contact on either its right or left. Feeling that his battalion was overextended, Colonel Allen issued a withdrawal plan to his units on December 21 which was known as Plan A. By this plan, Company C would move through Company B in Flamisoul and Company B would then follow and go through Company A. It was the responsibility of Company A to hold off the enemy until the two other companies were situated on the high ground west of Champs and Grande-Fagne (1 mile to the south). Company A would then withdraw through Company B and Company C would go into a reserve position.

At noon on December 23, patrols reported enemy tanks approaching from the woods to the south of the Saint-Hubert road. On drawing nearer, this force revealed itself as 12 tanks accompanied by infantry in snow suits. About 1330 hours Colonel Allen's outposts began their withdrawal without trying to engage the German armour. Allen was fearful that the Germans would move to his right and cut him off from Bastogne. Instead, they moved to the left and halted on the ridge just south of the main road near Cochleval. From this ground they fired upon Company C's position, but upon trying to advance, were turned back by the American artillery. In one sortie they lost two tanks to artillery fire and the rest of the German armour then withdrew to turret defilade and continued to fire into Company C for the rest of the afternoon.

Six of Colonel Templeton's tank destroyers (of the 705th), along with the reconnaissance platoon, had been in position where with good fortune they might have supported Company C in the first stage of this action. But as they pulled out of the cut just beyond Mande-Saint-Étienne, enemy tanks shelled them from the woods off their flank and two tank destroyers were lost immediately. This caused a more cautious attitude on the part of the other tank destroyers and they withdrew slightly while the reconnaissance platoon went forward to screen them on the left flank. The other tank destroyers distributed themselves so as to block the roads leading into Mont and the Reconnaissance Platoon dug in along the same line.

As darkness came on, Colonel Allen got word that his roadblock at Flamierge had been overrun by an enemy infantry force wearing snow suits. This German column had come down the Saint-Hubert highway from out of the northwest. Allen's men had been under the mistaken impression that a friendly force – the 4th Armoured Division – would arrive by this same route. They mistook the identity of the group and let it come on until the time had passed for successful resistance. Four tanks moving along with the road column suddenly opened fire on Company C, hitting a number of men and destroying the company aid station, an anti-tank gun and a pile of mortar ammunition with the first few rounds. The four tanks pressed on against the company position. At the same time the 10 tanks to the south began coming over the ridge. Company C withdrew as best it could.

Colonel Allen figured that by now his whole battalion position was in jeopardy and he ordered Plan A put into effect, but Company C was in such confusion that it couldn't carry out the withdrawal exactly as planned. One platoon got out to the southeast by way of the main road to escape being cut off. The other platoons pulled back along the predetermined route. Company B came through Company A as planned and took position on the left flank of the high ground where Colonel Allen had determined to make his stand. Company A moved to the rear in reserve. However, Company C's losses were such that Company A had to come back forward again and take Company C's place in the line. Fortunately, the enemy did not press the attack.

Allen told his men, 'This is our last withdrawal. Live or die – this is it.' He had spoken correctly; the battalion was never pushed from that ground, though it was still to face its worst ordeal. The men cleaned their weapons and waited.

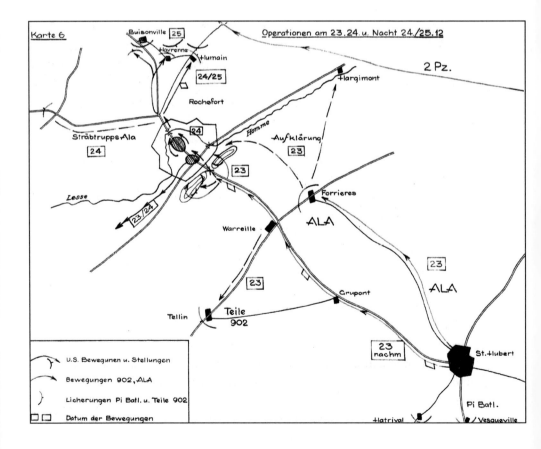

BAYERLEIN: 1600 hours. Continuation of the thrust from Saint-Hubert against Rochefort. The attack on Rochefort from the south breaks down at a road barrier. At the same time sudden fire from the heights surprised us and losses were suffered. Towards midnight CC 902 penetrated the town by an enveloping attack. Strong resistance in the centre of the town and severe German losses.

KOKOTT: Shortly after 2200 hours, the Panzer Grenadier regiment reported that 'the attack had been halted by increased enemy resistance and that there were no longer any reserves for continuance of the attack with any hope for success'.

Our own losses were quite considerable. There were also many men killed and wounded on the enemy side. The enemy had also lost a sizeable number of men through capture. The division ordered the attack to be stopped. It did not want to throw its last reserves into the battle since – in agreement with Regiment 901 and based on its own impressions as well as reports – it considered the battle as having become stalled. Had there been any indications that success would be possible, the division would undoubtedly have brought up and committed the last possible reserves. The division would then have gone into the battle during that very night with its last remaining man, despite an order which had arrived in the afternoon, after the attack by Regiment 901 had already stalled.

This order by army, having arrived in the afternoon, was as follows: '26th Division prepares large-scale attack on Bastogne. Objective: Capture of Bastogne.'

Late in the evening, the division commander, returning from the front, received a message from Reconnaissance Battalion 26. This message stated that two American officers who had appeared during the afternoon at a German post to discuss the possibility of evacuating a larger number of wounded (among them some German prisoners of war). A German officer located nearby took cognisance of the request and – not being authorised to make decision on his own – passed on the information through channels.

The American officers had returned to their lines but would return the following day. The division, of course, was in agreement with the evacuation of the wounded and gave assurance for safe transport. This assurance was announced during that very night to all the regiments. If negotiating groups would again appear – no matter, at what point of the encirclement front – the regiment would be authorised to announce this decision. Evacuation road: Bastogne–Noville; the transports to be taken over at Foy. Code work for cessation of fire on both sides of the road to Noville had been issued. Medical attention and transportation from Foy had been prepared. (The evacuation of the wounded, however, did not materialise. The American officers – probably because they were more familiar with developments south of Bastogne – did not reappear in the German lines).

Towards midnight of 23 December, the entire front around Bastogne was relatively quiet. Somewhat more lively than usual was the fire in the Marvie sector. Our own and the enemy batteries kept up the customary harassing fire on road crossings, village exits and certain sectors of the terrain.

It was self-evident that furthermore everything had to be done to reinforce the flank and rear protection at Seventh Army. There were hints to the effect that motorised reinforcements were moving up for that purpose. The 15th Panzer Grenadier Division, in any case, had been earmarked for the attack on Bastogne – subordinated to the 26th Division.

The losses on 23 December were at least 350 – 400 men.

All supply and other major movements possible only during the evening and night hours. The supply roads often were under artillery fire and were frequently jammed and blocked. Regarding the over-all situation, it was known on 24 December that the 2nd Panzer Division was engaged in heavy fighting south and west of Marche and that the Panzer Lehr Division was advancing via Rochefort. Everything possible was being done to detain the enemy in the south at least for the duration of the attack on Bastogne.

US FORCES: Near midnight, December 23, as the Shermans rolled south into the village, they could hear German armour coming north. They could not see the force nor tell its numbers, but the muzzle flashes told them they were engaged at very short range. Again, the dead half-track helped save the situation. The leading German tank got up to this accidental roadblock and then tried to turn around but was knocked out by the two Shermans before it could do so. This loss checked the rest of the enemy armour.

Colonel Harper's infantry in Marvie had dug themselves in very deep right next to the foundations of the houses and they stayed in their holes without flinching. They now had all the best of it because the village was blazing from many fires set by the artillery. Their foxholes were in heavy shadow while the snow-suited German infantry were highlighted as they came across the open spaces. The general assault was quickly checked by bullet fire, but enemy parties got a lodgement in the houses at the lower end of the village and pushed slowly northward.

Along Team O'Hara's front things had quieted well before midnight. The enemy advance into the firelit area was checked and then driven back by machine-gun and rifle fire. Later, after the scene had again darkened, an enemy tank was heard advancing along the road. The artillery forward observer fired the 75mm gun from his tank and a 105mm assault gun fired in the direction of the rumble. Second Lieutenant Sherwood D. Wishart, tank platoon leader, reported that night that he was certain his shells had bounced off and the tank had backed away. But he had scored a bull's-eye in the darkness and in the morning the tank – a Mark IV – was found sitting to the left of the road with a 75mm hole clear through it. Not a single body was found on the ground which had been held by the enemy infantry, though the snow bore many other marks of death and confusion. The German medical units had done their tasks well.

ZERBEL: At the beginning of the night the situation of the Corps was as follows: The two Panzer Divisions were advancing well, but they had not arrived as far as was expected on 22 December. The adjoining unit, the 116th Panzer Division, announced that it had met strong enemy resistance on the road Hotton–Marche. It was doubtful whether this division would succeed in crossing the road. Prisoners confirmed that the 84th American Infantry Division was situated in the line Hotton–Rochfort. It had arrived in the area of Marche on 21 December. Further enemy forces were not located at any other points, therefore it was important for the Corps to reach the Meuse rapidly before the enemy would succeed in bringing up more forces from the north.

The left flank adjoining unit was engaged in heavy fighting at Vaux-les-Rosières. Parts of these forces had even to be disengaged and withdrawn for the protection of the 26th Volksgrenadier Division situated at Clochimont. The Corps reported to the Army about the situation and expressed its great apprehension with regard to the right flank. The Army promised that on 24 December the 9th Panzer Division and the 15th Panzer Grenadier Division would be put under the command of the Corps and probably arrive at Noville. Moreover the 3rd Panzer Grenadier Division would be brought up later to the Corps.

If the 9th Panzer Division would arrive in time on 24 December, the situation of the endangered right flank was no longer critical.

von RUNDSTEDT: Heavy air attacks made impossible almost all daytime transport, either of troops or of their supplies. Even regrouping of troops in occupied positions was rendered extremely difficult by the bombardment. About 24 December it was deemed necessary to make preparations to defend the territory gained. The defence was not to be made in the March–Rochefort–Saint-Hubert salient, but at a strongpoint on the Houfflaze line east of Bastogne.

Chapter 8

24 December: Christmas Eve Attacks

KOKOTT: I was to participate in an attack on Bastogne on 25 December, and in preparation, I moved my command post to Givry on 24 December. Just before I departed, I left a few guards and directed the placing of some anti-aircraft guns on the heights around Hompré. There was only one good thing about 5th FS Division; it was heavily equipped with weapons. I assisted by giving instructions as to how some of these weapons could be used to the best advantage.

I made a trip around the perimeter defence of Bastogne and did not return to my Command Post until 2100 hours. I knew nothing more about the situation to the south, although my troops at Assenois had reported much artillery fire. I talked to General der Panzertruppe von Manteuffel on the telephone. I told him that I could not watch two fronts and that the southern situation was most dangerous. I did not think that 5th FS Division could hold, and I was in no position to prevent a breakthrough. He told me to forget about 4th Armoured Division (US), that it was quiet for the moment. The only solution to the problem was to attack Bastogne; he directed that I stop worrying and devote all my efforts to the attack from the northwest. I followed his advice, but the situation was most 'disagreeable'. It was this situation which precipitated our attack on Bastogne at 0300 hours on 25 December.

ZERBEL: 24 December: 2nd Panzer Division: On this day started the attacks of the American 2nd Armoured Division against the advance detachment, which had reached Foy-Notre-Dame. In the evening Foy-Notre-Dame was lost. The enemy succeeded in also taking Humain. During the night he penetrated into Buissonville. The line: Road crossing south of Marche–Marloie, was attacked and at several points pushed back.

Panzer-Lehr Division: the division mopped up Rochefort and built up a bridgehead at this place. One combat team reached Ciergnon. The division intended to advance with the bulk past Ciergnon–Celles, but the Corps gave the order not to continue, but to liberate Buissonville and Humain, because the 2nd Panzer Division had not the necessary forces for this operation. The road Buissonville–Humain was necessary for the bringing up of the supply for the troops situated there which were without gasoline.

<u>26 Volksgrenadier Division</u>: The advance parts of the arriving 15th Panzer Grenadier Division are put under the command of the division and take position for the attack in line Flamierge–Givry.

The situation at the beginning of the night was as follows: Unfortunately, the Corps had been blinkered, when worrying about the right flank. The right neighbour had not advanced further than the road Hotton–Marche and had even taken the defence. An ordinance officer dispatched to the 11th Panzer Division reported that the division would not be able to cross the road Hotton–Marche. The advance route of the 2nd Panzer Division was interrupted. The main danger at this moment was the possibility that the enemy would succeed in approaching the road Harsin–Hargimont.

The 9th Panzer Division, which could have altered the situation had not yet arrived. In spite of the doubts of the Corps, the Army ordered that the bridge of Dinant was to be held and promised again that the 9th Panzer Division would arrive in the evening of the 24 December.

The advance detachment of the 2nd Panzer Division had no gasoline. Supply could have been brought up past Rochfort–Ciergnon, but between Hargimont and Conneux were some isolated groups of the 2nd Panzer Division without fuel, therefore it was necessary to clear out this road.

The Corps, knowing about the obstruction of the roads, did not believe that the 9th Panzer Division would arrive so soon. Therefore, the Panzer Lehr Division was given orders not to continue past Ciergnon, but to clear the approach route of the 2nd Panzer Division at Humain and Buissonville from the enemy. The left flank unit (5th Para Division) lost more and more terrain, and it was possible that the enemy on 25 December would re-establish from the south the contact with Bastogne. The advance parts of the 15th Panzer Grenadier Division which had arrived were put under the command of 26th Volksgrenadier Division which was given orders to make an attack against the town on 25 December in order to take it definitively.

Christmas Eve was rather melancholy for the Corps. Its members knew that the decisive moment for success or failure of the offensive had come. If the approach route for the 2nd Panzer Division could be cleared and the 9th Panzer Division arrived in time in order to be brought up behind the 2nd Panzer Division in the morning of the 25 December, an enemy attack against the long flank of the 2nd Panzer Division could be faced with less apprehension.

The reconnaissance detachment at and near Conneux announced that the noise of approaching tanks was heard in the north. Armoured infantry on foot was committed for the attack against the bridge at Dinant. In the late evening the reconnaissance detachment announced that Foy-Notre-Dame was lost and that the detachment was attacked near Conneux by strong enemy armoured forces. The weather had become clear. The enemy air activity already had started on 24 December. On 25 December very strong air activity had to be expected.

For the commanding general, who had been Commander of the 2nd Panzer Division, the situation took the same turn as at Avranches. At that time the division was isolated and far in advance before the front and would probably be destroyed unless our Air Force screened the spearhead. But nobody reckoned any longer with its support.

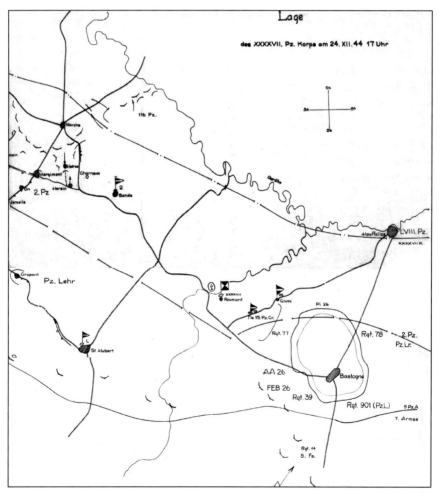

Situation map drawn from information provided by Gen. Pz. Heinrich Von Lüttwitz – 24 December.

All these considerations were reported to the Army, and the suggestion was made to withdraw the advance detachment of the 2nd Panzer Division at least to the area of Buissonville and to commit this division again after the arrival of the 9th Panzer Division. But no authorisation was given. At 2100 hours the Commander of the 9th Panzer Division arrived. He hoped that the advanced parts of his division would arrive on 25 December at 1000 hours in the area around Bande. The bulk of the division would not arrive before 26 December.

METZ: On 24 December the situation caused the senior artillery commander to acquaint the chief and commander-in-chief of the Army with the necessity of bringing up the artillery and smoke shell mortars, which were still left at the line of departure, to commit them before Bastogne.

Considering the existing fuel scarcity which already seriously handicapped the supply of ammunition, he was forced to propose that this idea be discarded for the present in order to supply the artillery already committed and smoke shell mortars with the fuel already at hand. The Chief and Commander-in-Chief agreed to this.

On the 24th the Commander of the 26th Volksgrenadier Division was ordered to capture Bastogne on 25 December. For this purpose, the arriving elements of the approaching 15th Armoured Infantry Division were put at his disposal. For the carrying out of this attack he only had at his command his own division and the reinforced armoured infantry regiment of the Armoured Training Division, both of which were greatly weakened by losses and, since 21 December, encircled Bastogne in a thickly spread line and under great strain.

The senior artillery commander was appointed as artillery adviser and adjutant. In the afternoon of 24 December, he and his entire staff moved to Gives, the new division command post 9½km northeast of Bastogne; this separation, from the standpoint of distance, made personal cooperation with the A.O.K. more difficult. However, it was unavoidable.

An accidental wire-connection (field wire), the particulars of which have escaped my memory, made possible a better telephone-connection with the corps artillery commander of the XXXXVII Armoured Corps. This was important, as at first in this way the corps in Ardennes standing Moerser-battery could take part in the battles around Bastogne.

The assignment of the senior artillery commander to the 26th Volksgrenadier Division was conditioned by not only the artillery strength, but because of the extensive territory which the task entailed.

On 24 December at 1230 hours, a surprise flight of planes approached from the south, whereupon air landings took place and supplies to relieve encircled Bastogne were thrown down. During the next three days, this was repeated every noon with timetable-like precision. Because of air landings in the afternoon of 24 December and thereupon developing minor fighting at the south front, movements of the forces slated for the new attack which came from the southern front were delayed for about three hours.

MANTEUFEL: By 24 December, I realised that the attack was not going as we had hoped; on that day I spoke with Genobst Jodl and asked for authorisation to change to the 'smaller' solution, which called for a sharp swing to the north, with our left flank along the Meuse River.

WAGENER: The weather had cleared up and enabled the enemy for the first time to employ its Air Force in attacks of larger scale. Delays in bringing up of reserves, and supplies, as well as difficulties in our own attacks for LVIII and XXXXVII Panzer Corps resulted. Our own fighter aircraft did not appear. The LVIII Panzer Corps as well as its neighbours failed to make any further progress.

The most advanced elements of the 15th Panzer Grenadier Division arrived in the area of Bastogne, and were assigned to the 26th Volksgrenadier Division by XLVII Corps.

The general situation on the evening of 24 December was as follows: The right wing and centre of the Sixth Panzer Army, had not succeeded in making any real start. The left wing had finally succeeded in its development – although only after St Vith had finally been taken – in the northern strips of the Fifth Army Sector and had crossed the Sale sector in a westerly direction. By this it managed to join up with the LVIII Panzer Corps. The deep northern flank of the Fifth Panzer Army had been secured by this. It seemed very doubtful, however, whether the Sixth Panzer Army would make any further progress.

The LVIII Panzer Corps, with a bold thrust and long forced marches, had pushed through the difficult and wooded regions north of Houffalize, and was at this time standing opposite strong enemy forces on the northern edge of this wooded zone.

The XLVII Panzer Corps was close to the Maas near Dinant; it was obliged, however, to fight off enemy attacks from the north. Bastogne had been encircled by one division.

The *Heeresgruppe* clung to its previous decision, namely, to push up to the Maas on either side of Namur. It likewise weighed the possibility of turning in with its left wing, poised on the sector to the north, with the Fifth and Sixth Panzer Armies, on the eastern bank. This was in order to fulfil the concept of the small–term solution, a push into the rear of the Ninth American Army.

Contrary to the army's view, the *Heeresgruppe* insisted on Bastogne being taken at the same time. Despite the bringing up of new forces, both these possibilities seemed impossible to us as the Army had already been thrown on the defensive almost everywhere. The initiative seemed to have passed to the enemy. We would not admit it at this time, but the events which occurred on 24 December showed that the push of the Fifth Panzer Army toward the Maas had been brought to a dead stop. Its northern wing was no longer secured and its southern flank was menaced.

The second operational phase, the push to the Maas, was also seemingly uncompleted despite all efforts of the troops and their commands.

US FORCES: Colonel Kohls talked to VIII Corps again at 0830 hours the next morning (December 24) and said he wanted additional quantities of ammunition for the 75mm pack howitzer and also of 105mm M3 shell.

He asked VIII Corps to investigate the possibility of using gliders in the further resupply. All the early resupply missions had been done by parachute. As they came in the Germans put up a terrific amount of flak. The troops saw a number of C-47s shot down, but these losses had not made other planes take evasive action. Colonel Harper said of the pilots who flew these missions: 'Their courage was tremendous, and I believe that their example did a great deal to encourage my infantry.'

While Kohls was talking, the first resupply planes of the day appeared over the drop zone and more bundles continued to rain down on the field until 1530 hours. About 100 tons of *matériel* were parachuted out of 160 planes during that second day of resupply. Even so, the division's stocking was not by any means full as Christmas Eve drew on (24th). The shortages weighed more on Colonel Kohls than what had been accomplished. Only 445 gallons of gasoline were on hand. The 26,406 K-rations that had been received were only enough to supply the defenders of Bastogne for a little more than a single day.

The troops were instructed, for a second time, to forage for any food supplies in their areas and to report them to G-4 so that they could be distributed where they were needed most. This had been done from the beginning and a large part of the subsistence of the defence had come from the ruined stores of Bastogne or from the stocks of the farming community. From an abandoned Corps bakery had come flour, lard, salt and a small quantity of coffee. Colonel Kohls got these things out to the troops and during the first days of the siege the favourite menu item along the firing line was flapjacks. The coffee, however, was saved for the hospital.

The farmers had fairly good supplies of potatoes, poultry and cattle. These were taken over on requisition, to be paid for later by the United States. In an abandoned Corps warehouse were found another 450 pounds of coffee, 600 pounds of sugar and a large amount of Ovaltine. These things were all hoarded for the wounded. Prowling about Bastogne, the Civil Affairs Officer, Captain Robert S. Smith, found a large store of margarine, jam and flour in a civilian warehouse. This assured flapjacks for several more days. What was equally important, he found 2,000 burlap bags among the groceries and the bags were rushed out to the infantrymen in the foxholes to wrap around their feet where they lacked arctic overshoes. By Christmas Eve these supplementary stores were pretty well exhausted. Christmas was a K-ration day – for the men who had K-rations.

Soon after dawn of 24 December Colonel Harper went down to look at his lines. He sent a patrol to the hill where Lieutenant Morrison had been and found it was still in enemy hands. His own men still held most of Marvie though the Germans were in some houses in the south of the village. Five men had been killed and seven wounded in the fighting there and 1½ platoons had been wiped out on the hill. There were no further developments in the situation during the morning.

At 0900 hours a patrol from Colonel O'Hara's force went to the old roadblock position and found that the enemy had withdrawn except for two Germans who were sitting fully exposed on a nearby pile of beets. They shot the two beet-sitters and this drew machine-gun fire on themselves, so they pulled back.

At 1340 hours six P-47s bombed Marvie, dropping six 500-pound bombs among the American positions. Then they came in over the housetops and strafed the streets with calibre .50 fire. Colonel Harper was walking through the streets when the first bomb fell. Even as he jumped for a foxhole he saw that there were two cerise-coloured panels clearly showing where the front of the position was. He thought he saw one of the bombs hit among a patrol that was working through the south of the village toward Hill 500 and he sent two runners after the patrol to see if any damage had been done. Then he walked in the same direction. A German wearing a dirty snow suit dodged out of one house and into another so that he could get into a position from which he could fire on the patrol. Harper fired his M1 at the house in order to warn the patrol. The patrol, which seemed OK from the bombing, went to work on the house too, but on receiving rifle fire from the south of the village, they came on back.

During their brief reconnaissance they had seen a German tank completely camouflaged as a haystack except that the Germans had made the error of leaving the gun muzzle sticking out of the hay. Colonel Harper went to the one Sherman tank remaining in the village and gave the gunner the target – just beyond the last houses.

He continued on to the tanks of Team O'Hara along the Wiltz road and told them to start pounding the tank and the houses in the lower part of Marvie which concealed the German infantry. With their first fire the Shermans got direct hits on the tank and blew the hay away. They kept on blasting it and the crews thought they knocked it out. Major Galbreaith (2nd Battalion Exec, 327th) said, however, that he saw the tank get away under its own power.

At 1645 hours the P-47 planes returned again and attacked Marvie with bombs and bullets. At 1945 Bastogne was bombed and strafed by several enemy planes. At 1800 hours, 24 December, Colonel Harper was told that he was in command of the perimeter all the way from Marvie to northwest of Hemroulle.

Colonel Harper said to General Higgins, 'Look at it! This is half of the division's perimeter.' General Higgins replied, 'It's all yours. Do what you can with it. There isn't any other solution.'

Higgins reasoned that it was a fairly safe gamble. He had studied the map carefully and had gleaned all that he could from first-hand study of the country just outside the Bastogne perimeter. The landscape to the south was heavily wooded and therefore not suitable for armour. He considered that the only place where the enemy was likely to strike Harper's sector in force was at the Wiltz road. But the opening there was a pretty narrow corridor and he felt that Harper had enough strength across the Wiltz road to deal with any fresh threat at that point. What concerned General Higgins most was the position in the northwest sector, a gently rolling hill country, with no natural obstacles and very little tree growth. Thus far it had been the quietest portion of the perimeter, but that fact did not lessen Higgins' apprehension; he felt sure that if a real tank strike was coming, this would be the point of danger.

He remarked to General McAuliffe that they could expect to be entertained out there on Christmas Day. 'The Germans are a sentimental people,' he said, 'and they are probably thinking about giving a present to Hitler.'

Christmas Eve was quiet. The commanders and staffs took official notice of the occasion. To all of the command posts within Bastogne went a G-2 reminder from the 101st's chief joker, Colonel Danahy. It was a sitrep overlay in red, white and green, the red outlining the enemy positions completely encircling the town and the green showing only in the words 'Merry Christmas' across the position held by the defenders.

General McAuliffe also rose to the occasion with an inspired communiqué in which he told his men about the German demand for surrender and his answer to them. The rest of his Christmas message read as follows:

'What's merry about all this, you ask? We're fighting – it's cold, we aren't home. All true, but what has the proud Eagle Division accomplished with its worthy comrades of the 10th Armoured Division, the 705th Tank Destroyer Battalion and all the rest? Just this: We have stopped cold everything that has been thrown at us from the north, east, south and west. We have identifications from four German panzer divisions, two German infantry divisions and one German parachute division. These units, spearheading the last desperate German lunge, were heading straight west for key points when the Eagle Division was hurriedly ordered to stem the advance.

How effectively this was done will be written in history; not alone in our division's glorious history, but in world history. The Germans actually did surround us, their radios blared our doom. Allied troops are counterattacking in force. We continue to hold Bastogne. By holding Bastogne we assure the success of the Allied armies. We know that our division commander, General Taylor, will say: "Well done!" We are giving our country and our loved ones at home a worthy Christmas present and being privileged to take part in this gallant feat of arms are truly making for ourselves a merry Christmas.'

Privately, on the phone that night to General Middleton, McAuliffe expressed his true feeling about Christmas in these words: 'The finest Christmas present the 101st could get would be a relief tomorrow.'

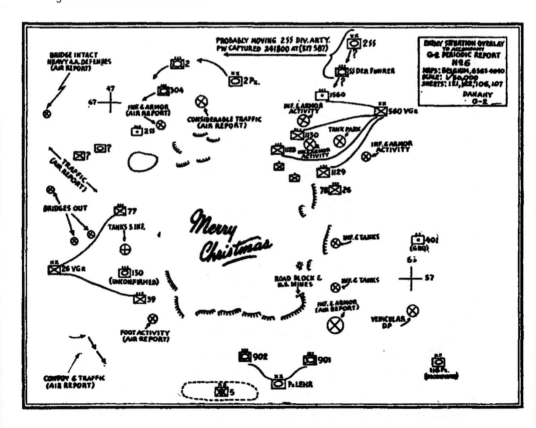

But General McAuliffe's greeting to his troops proved to be in every part a prophetic utterance, though the quiet of Christmas Eve did not last for long. That night the town was bombed twice. During the first raid, in the late evening, a bomb landed on the hospital of the 20th Armoured Infantry Battalion near the intersection of the main roads from Arlon and Neufchâteau. It caved in the roof, burying twenty patients and killing a Belgian woman who was serving as a nurse. Another bomb landed on the headquarters of Combat Command B, doing heavy damage and knocking down the Christmas tree in the message centre. The men set up the tree again, and in an elaborate ceremony, one of the sergeants pinned the Purple Heart on a mangled doll.

Except for those bombings Christmas Eve passed without unusual pressure from the enemy. The journal entries of the different regiments all use the word 'quiet' in describing the period. But that is a word that simply does not record the tumult in the thoughts and emotions of the men of Bastogne. Such was their reaction to Christmas and to the memories surrounding it, that for the first time all around the perimeter men felt fearful. It seemed to them that the end was at hand. That night many of them shook hands with their comrades. They said to one another that it would probably be their last night together. Many of the commanders saw this happening, though they knew it had little relation to the still strong tactical situation.

Chapter 9

25 December: Christmas Day Crisis

In the 502nd Parachute Infantry the officers heard Christmas Eve Mass in the tenth-century chapel of the beautiful Rolle Château which they were using for a command post. It was a happy occasion, well attended by the neighbouring Belgians who had rounded out the regimental messes with contributions of flour and sides of beef from their own stores.

The regimental officers turned in about 0130 hours on Christmas morning. At 0245 hours there was an intense shelling of the forward area by the German artillery. Lieutenant Colonel Patrick J. Cassidy, the 502nd's executive officer, called Captain Wallace A. Swanson of Company A who reported that his front had suddenly become active. But he added that the situation was obscure; he could not figure out yet what the Germans intended.

At 0330 hours Colonel Cassidy called Captain Swanson again. Swanson said that the enemy was on top of him. While they were talking, the line went out. Colonel Cassidy awakened Colonel Chappuis, the regimental commander. Then all lines went out. Chappuis called his 1st Battalion by radio and told them to get ready to move, adding that the commander, Major John D. Hanlon, was to come to Rolle as quickly as possible. By radio Chappuis heard from Swanson that Germans in large numbers were in Champs and that his men were locked in a hand-to-hand and house-to-house fight with them. Major Hanlon reported at the command post and was told by Colonel Chappuis to move Company B to the Champs road just west of Rolle and then get forward into Champs and help Captain Swanson's Company A.

While Swanson was becoming engaged, other German forces had filtered through the woods to the east of Champs on the 2nd Battalion's left flank. After reporting this to regiment, Lieutenant Colonel Thomas H. Sutliffe, the 2nd Battalion commander, shifted part of his force left against this threat. Colonel Chappuis supported his move by instructing Major Hanlon to send one platoon of Company B to the right to join hands with Company E.

Hanlon called in at 0545 hours and said the Germans were still fighting in Champs. He did not want to put the rest of his battalion into the village until it became light because the darkness and confusion were so bad that it was almost impossible to distinguish friend from enemy. Colonel Chappuis told him to hold steady.

As Chappuis and Cassidy estimated the situation at 502nd Headquarters, Company B was already backing up Company A and would still be effective if Champs were lost, whereas it might lose its reserve value if it pushed on into the village and the Germans came around it. So they waited. They knew that somewhere a real blow was coming but they could not figure where. So far the German pressure had jarred them only at the right and centre of the 502nd and was coming at them from the north. They looked anxiously to the west where their sector joined that of the 327th Glider Infantry. Their command post was under heavy artillery fire and was no longer in either telephone or radio communication with Headquarters, 101st Division.

Just as the first light of Christmas morning broke, the S-2 of the 1st Battalion, First Lieutenant Samuel B. Nickels, Jr., came at a dead run into the château where the Headquarters, 502nd, was. 'There are seven enemy tanks and lots of infantry coming over the hill on your left,' he said. He had first sighted them moving along parallel to the ridge southwest of Hemroulle. They were striking toward the ground where the 502nd and 327th joined hands.

The Rolle Château was emptied almost before Lieutenant Nickels had finished speaking. Cooks, clerks, radio men and the chaplains collected under Captain James

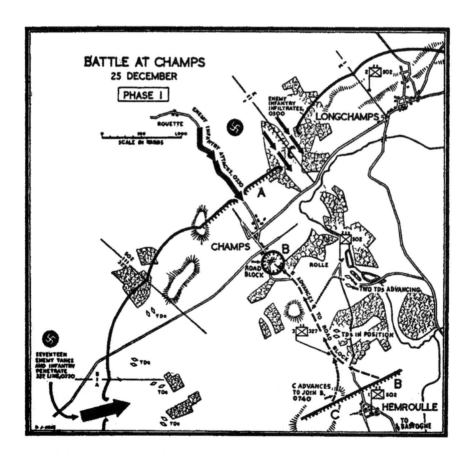

C. Stone, the 502nd headquarters commandant, and rushed west to the next hill. From the château gate at Rolle, the road dips down through a deep swale then rises onto the ridge where it joins the main road into Hemroulle, about 2 miles northwest of Bastogne. The road line is on high ground all the way until just before it reaches Hemroulle where it drops down again to the village.

Captain Stone's scratch headquarters force ran across the swale and took up firing positions close to the road and facing west. Within a few minutes they were joined by the men of the regiment's wounded who were able to walk. Major Douglas T. Davidson, the regimental surgeon of the 502nd, had run to the chateau stable that was serving as a temporary hospital, rallied his patients, handed them rifles and then led them out against the tanks.

They could see the tanks coming on toward them now. From the archway of Rolle Château it was about 600 yards to the first line of German armour. Colonels Chappuis and Cassidy and the radio operator looked westward from the archway and could see just the outline of the enemy movement in the dim light. They were now the only men at the headquarters.

Colonel Cassidy called Major Hanlon and told him to leave Company B where it was, but to get the company ready to protect its own rear and then try to get Company C faced to the west to meet the German tanks as they came on.

The 327th Glider Infantry was already engaged. At 0500 hours Colonel Harper had heard by phone from Company A of his 3rd Battalion that 18 enemy tanks were formed for attack just east of Mande-Saint-Étienne. At 0710 hours the German armour supported by infantry of the 77th Grenadier Regiment smashed through the positions held by Companies A and B. In coming through the companies, the tanks fired all their guns and the German infantrymen riding the tanks blazed away with their rifles. The spearpoint of the German armour had already broken clear through to the battalion command post.

At the 327th regimental headquarters Colonel Harper heard by telephone of the breakthrough, and on the heels of that message came word from Lieutenant Colonel Cooper that his 463nd Parachute Field Artillery Battalion already had the German tanks under fire. At 0715 hours Colonel Allen, the 3rd Battalion (327th) commander, called and said that the tanks were right on him.

Harper asked, 'How close? 'Right here!' answered Allen. 'They are firing point-blank at me from 150 yards range. My units are still in position but I've got to run.' But Colonel Allen's battalion had not been wholly taken by surprise.

'Tanks are coming toward you!' Captain Preston E. Towns, commanding Company C, had telephoned to Allen. 'Where?' Allen had asked.

'If you look out your window now,' said Captain Towns, 'you'll be looking right down the muzzle of an 88.'

MANTEUFEL: On the night of 24/25 December I had a telephone conversation with Genobst Jodl, and although I pointed out that the main effort for the attack was now in the sector of Fifth Panzer Army, neither the OKW reserves nor the available divisions of Sixth Panzer Army were brought up to the Army. All these reserves would have arrived in time, if fuel had been available – a fact with which I was not acquainted. They would have arrived in time to encircle Bastogne and capture it, and to push with the left wing in the direction of Liège – as I had suggested – and would not have crossed the Meuse.

When stronger enemy forces pressed from the direction of Huy past the line Marche–Hotton–Ciney and attacked 116 Panzer Division and later 2nd Panzer Division, I recognised that we were beginning to lose the initiative. We had actually lost it when the enemy launched an attack from Bastogne and to the west, against the Saint-Hubert–Tillet line.

The winter weather could not decisively influence the operation. The troops which had fought in the East were accustomed to ice and snow. The difficulties inherent to the movement of armoured forces and the concealed emplacement of the artillery, anti-aircraft searchlights, etc, were overcome through large-scale traffic direction measures taken by the various units.

The early enemy defence of Bastogne reduced the speed of the attack and finally had a decisive influence on the operation because the enemy was able to use the good roads which led to Bastogne to reinforce the troops occupying the town. Therefore, this pocket of resistance endangered the south flank of the Army. These difficulties increased, because the advance of Seventh Army was stopped sooner than had been expected.

The 5th FS Division reported that it was on the line Hompré–Sibret–Vaux-lez-Rosières and was well advanced towards Neufchâteau. This report was quite exaggerated, as I saw myself when I visited the division on the same day. Nevertheless, I managed to move Panzer Lehr, unperceived, past Hompré, Morhet, Remagen and Saint-Hubert, towards Rochefort. I participated in this operation. My serious concern about the south flank of the Army was transmitted to General Jodl by the Chief of Staff. During the night of 24/25 December, I had a telephone conversation with him about the situation.

Afterwards, when the supply vehicles of Panzer Lehr Division received fire from the enemy posted at Bastogne, they were rerouted past Amberloup to Saint-Hubert. Neither OKW nor I had considered a thrust to the south. I believed that such an operation would have been impossible because: stronger enemy forces already had attacked Seventh Army; Bastogne was still defended by the enemy; the terrain was unfavourable for the panzer divisions, which had already lost some of their combat strength. They would have had to be reinforced by infantry divisions for such a venture.

The German Mk IV and Mk V tanks proved their ability in the difficult terrain, especially the Mk IVs which were not too heavy and were very manoeuvrable. The fire power and accuracy of fire of this tank was excellent, but its armour was too light for modern anti-tank weapons. The total amount of tank losses in the army due to enemy fire from air and ground was – as far as I remember – not higher than 35 tanks. However, we lost a great number from lack of fuel or because the disabled tanks could not be recovered.

The Volksgrenadier divisions were of varying quality. Some were good divisions and others were below average. Most of them were insufficiently trained for coordinated action; had no combat-experienced non-commissioned officers; had not had sufficient time nor ammunition for training in firing of weapons and were not conditioned to marching and fighting to the degree that modern warfare demands, unless they had trained in a quiet front-line sector as 26th Volksgrenadier Division was. This division proved its ability during the breakthrough and attack. Its equipment was generally good and modern, its morale excellent.

A great number of vehicles had to be left behind because of the shortage of fuel. Afterwards, the situation grew more and more critical because, in spite of promises, the replacements were insufficient in number and quality; therefore, the fighting strength of the divisions was continually reduced. The rearguard, formed from armoured vehicles of the panzer or panzer grenadier divisions, covered the withdrawal of the infantry to the resistance line planned for the next day.

KOKOTT: Towards midnight of 24/25 December, several German planes appeared over Bastogne and dropped some bombs. It became clear that this bombing venture was to be the promised air support for the entire attack!

A very strong and concentrated fire barrage from all calibres hit the enemy like a blow at the moment of the attack, destroyed his known pockets of resistance and sealed off in depth. With tremendous force the Grenadiers and Panzer Grenadiers drove towards the enemy and fought their way forward from pocket to pocket. After having recovered from the initial shock, the enemy forces got hold of themselves and along the entire front there began a wild, furious struggle.

Grenadier Regiment 27 had entered the village of Champs and elements fought their way forwards between Champs and Longchamps. A furious battle developed inside Champs. Several enemy counter thrusts – supported by powerful artillery, mortar and tank fire – forced the elements of Grenadier Regiment 27 out of Champs. To the northwest thereof, the German elements were holding, but not repelled the enemy thrusts.

The Grenadier Regiment started another attack on Champs. Tremendous enemy fire was directed at the areas around Champs. Reconnaissance Battalion 26, adjoining to the right, was pushing forward on both sides of the highway to the west in battle.

The enemy put up a desperate defence, carried out counter-thrust upon counter-thrust, again and again brought tanks or destroyers into the battle and consigned quantities of ammunition as had not previously been experienced there. Nevertheless, the German units, supported by the very strongest of fire, were advancing and made their way deeper and deeper into the enemy defence belts.

BAYERLEIN: 25 December
0900 hours. Humain taken by the 902.

GENMAJ OTTO REMER – Führer Begleit Brigade: I received orders from the Corps Commander to move immediately to the area of Bastogne. I tried to change this order because I didn't want to break up an attack during the day. Such a manoeuvre is an extremely dangerous one and could result in disastrous consequences. However, the Corps Commander ordered me to move immediately, regardless of my present situation, and I was obliged to discontinue my attack at once. At this time, I withdrew from the line and started toward Bastogne. Tanks of the 116th Panzer Division, which had been pinched off in the Marenne area, were left stranded by my withdrawal.

I moved my brigade to La Roche and from there to Champlon, and then toward Bastogne. Our gasoline supply was very low and were obliged to tow many vehicles which were out of gas. My orders at this time were to attack south of Bastogne to establish the ring around the town.

KOKOTT: The forces and assault detachments around Bastogne (except for the northern sector) started attacking in the moon-lightened morning. Before the attack some of the assault detachments had already crept as close to the enemy as possible or infiltrated their front line already. A preparatory artillery bombardment began with full purpose. A very strong and intense bombardment fire of all calibres was hitting the enemy in the first minute of the attack, which destroyed their resistance pockets and cut off their rear. The infantrymen and armoured infantry were fighting from resistance pocket to resistance pocket with great momentum.

After the enemy recovered from his first shock, tenacious fighting began. The Grenadier-Regiment 77 had infiltrated the village of Champs around 6pm and parts of the regiment fought their way forward between Champs and Longchamps. The path Champs–Longchamps was crossed. In Champs fierce fighting developed. Numerous enemy counterattacks – supported by artillery, mortars and tanks – pushed back the parts of the Grenadier-Regiment 77 beyond the limits of Champs.

In the northwest of Champs our troops resisted and fought off the attacks. The Grenadier-Regiment 77 started to attack Champs once again. Fierce enemy fire hit the area. Heaviest fire from our side prepared the assault of Regiment 77. While attacks and counter attacks alternated in the Champs area, the 15th Panzer Grenadier Division, under a devastating barrage, cut in deeply into the enemy east of Fond de Laval and the front line was split between 8pm and 9pm. During this period the armoured parts of the Grenadier Division – supported by a rolling artillery barrage – drove through the breach.

The *Aufklärungsabteilung* 26 (reconnaissance troops) aligned to the right side pushed forward along the big *Weststrasse* (West road) in fierce fights. The enemy fought in desperate resistance and launched counterattack after counterattack, called on more tanks and destroyers in the fight and used ammunition in an amount we had not experienced before. Nevertheless, our own troops, supported heavily by artillery, made their way forward and pushed deeper and deeper into the enemy line.

After 9am enemy fighter planes were flying unopposed in the skies above and intervened with bombs and armament in the heavy fighting on the ground. The Grenadier Regiment 77 had attacked Champs a second time and pushed forward with other detachments in a southerly direction. Fusilier Regiment 39 pressed forward along the railway and the road to Neufchâteau as ordered despite fanatical resistance. Panzer Grenadier Regiment 901 advanced to the road Bastogne–Bras with assault detachments from the south-east. Here, like at Grenadier Regiment 78, enemy resistance and firing was heavy. With clear goals in mind the assault detachments advanced and gained ground.

Around 10am the battle seemed to reach its climax and success seemed so close. Grenadier Regiment 77 reported: 'Heavy fighting around Champs. To the south infiltration into the woods located to the west of Rolle. Heaviest enemy resistance.'

15th Panzer-Grenadier-Division: 'The tank attack is gaining ground despite heavy resistance and reaches the road Champs–Hemroulle. Hemroulle and the wooded areas in the north are enemy occupied. Our losses are high.'

Aufklärungsabteilung 26: 'Enemy counterattacks were beaten off. *Aufklärungsabteilung* 26 continues attack towards Isle-la-Hesse.

Fusilier-Regiment 39: 'Attack direction Isle-Le-Pré–Halte continues slowly despite heavy enemy resistance and high losses.'

Panzer-Grenadier-Regiment 901: 'Own shock troops approach – west of Marvie – the road Bastogne–Marvie. Strong enemy resistance, high own losses, last reserves were drawn in.'

Grenadier-Regiment 78: 'Own shock troops attacking on both sides of the railway line Bastogne–Bourcy are closing in on the exit of the woods (1400m) to the northeast of Luzery. Strong enemy firing. Both our own and enemy artillery and mortar fire were extremely fierce. Our own concentrated artillery raids were laid down in an area north of Hemroulle and Isla-la-Hesse. The enemy firing however concentrated in a devastating manner in the area Champs-Grande Fagne. Givry, Frenet, Flamisoul lay under a hail of fire of enemy artillery and were attacked like Salle, Givrouelle and Gives continuously with bombs and armament from enemy fighter planes. The battle continued without a pause. We were under the impression that the enemy resistance should collapse any time soon.

KOKOTT: The regiments had drawn their reserves into battle, stripped down their staff and had runners, typists and other personnel thrown into the firing line. The 14th (tank destroyer) Company was fighting on the front as an infantry regiment already, the heavy guns were manned only with the absolute minimum staff that was needed, everyone else fought in the front line.

The 15th Panzer Grenadier Division also deployed its reserves. Now that everything was at stake, the 26th Division had its reserves deployed to the front, to benefit from the imminent success of the 15th Panzer Grenadier Division and to nourish the attack. Around 11am an observation post from the southwest sector reported: 'Own tanks moving from the West approach the western outskirts of Bastogne.'

A query from the division with the 15th Panzer Grenadier Division informed us that they were not aware of that. It was only reported, that

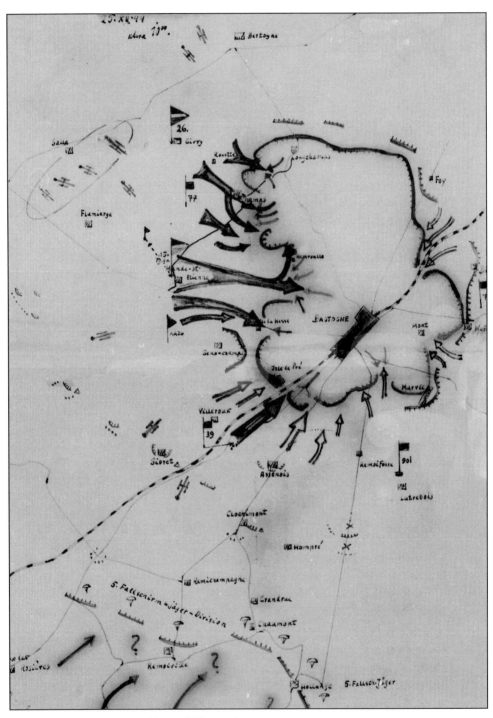

Kokott situation map 10am – 25 December.

'there was no communication link to the forwarding tank troops since an undefined period of time'. It seemed to be evident since the last report that parts of the tank force were fighting a fierce battle with heavy losses around Hemroulle and along the road Hemroulle–Champs. The commander of the tank troops would intend to breakthrough to Bastogne south of Hemroulle. At this point in time, the forward groups of the 15th Panzer Grenadier Division were fighting off heavy enemy attacks in the forests 1000m to the southwest of Hemroulle. The *Aufklärungsabteilung* 26 were putting up a grim fight in front of the village of Isle-la-Hesse, but as it seemed not without success. The Grenadier Regiment 77 reported that the fighting in Champs has become hopeless due to the losses and not being able to draw in new reserves. The regiment asked to give up Champs, so that it would then be possible to hold on to the ridge to the northwest of Champs and attack (through Grande Fagne) with all strength under more beneficial circumstances. The division approved this request.

The aim was not Champs, it was Bastogne. Around afternoon – when it was all in – the artillery had shortages already but was still putting down a flexible and concise barrage on the main areas of battle (forest to the northeast of Grande-Fagne, Hemroulle, and the little forest to the north), but the situation noticeably turned to the worse. The 15th Panzer Grenadier Division reported that it had no more combat-ready tanks left. The armoured department around Champs was worn out and had been annihilated and there was no sign whatsoever from the commando that broke through in the direction Bastogne. Heavy enemy counterattacks including tanks pushed back what was left of the Panzer Grenadier Divisions. The few remaining groups were clinging with all their might to a path which leads along Grande-Fagne to the west direction Senonchamps. All forces were drawn in, no reserves.

The Grenadier-Regiment 77 was involved in heavy seesaw fighting that was raging in the area between Hemroulle and Champs. The losses were not bearable any more.

All forces, including the reserves, were deployed in this area to benefit from the initial success. The Regiment, despite heavy losses, fought tenaciously between Hemroulle and Champs. The shot-down formations lay under heavy enemy fire coming from the forest to the north of Hemroulle. Despite all losses the grenadiers tried to climb the slope to Hemroulle – either on their own initiatives or following their officers and comrades. The storm troops were either smashed in a barrier of fire from enemy machine guns, anti-tank, tank guns and automatic rifle fire or were not able anymore

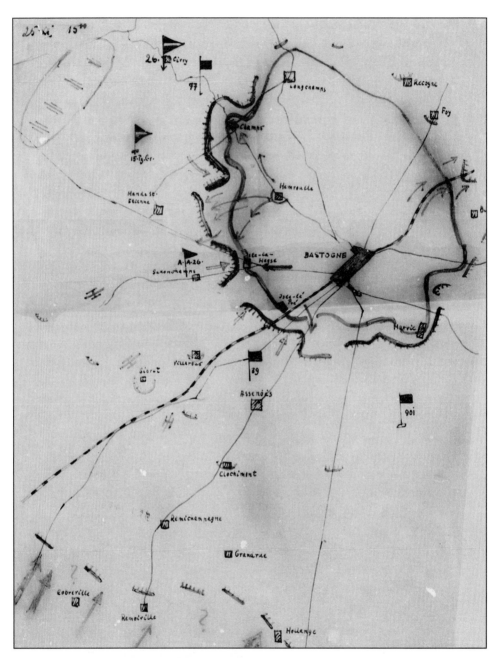

Kokott situation map – 25 December 1500hrs.

to exploit or extend a successful breakthrough. The artillery support and support with heavy infantry weapons, the fighting spirit, fighting techniques and the death-defying bravery could not be topped. But the forces deployed were too weak and got weaker by the hour. They could not succeed against a defender that was tough, tenacious and a skilfully nested enemy. The situation remained the same for the *Aufklärungsabteilung* around Isle-la-Hesse. In a constant urge to attack, the reconnaissance unit tried to move forward and was fighting with the last man.

KOKOTT: The Fusilier Regiment 39 was located in front of Isle-le-Pré, a bastion of enemy defence. Well directed, strongest fire lay in the enemy. Desperately, the remains of the battalions of fusiliers repeatedly attacked the village, trying to encircle it. But again and again the attack waves broke up in the wild defensive fire (above all also from tank cannons), which hit them, despite visible losses. The Panzer Grenadier Regiment 901 reported that 'a shock troop (the size of a company of about 20 to 30 men) had made it to the fork at the southeast entrance of Bastogne. Apparently, it would have been cut off and destroyed there. The regiment would not have had enough forces

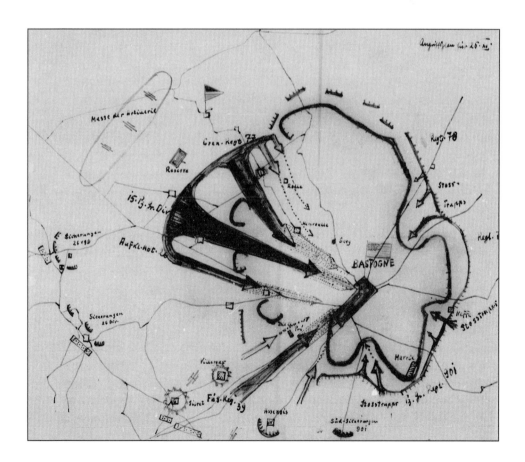

at its disposal to strengthen this shock troop. The small forces that had been pushed into battle were left behind in strong anti-aircraft fire and had been as good as worn out.'

The Grenadier Regiment 76 had to give up a part of the ground gains achieved by the shock troops on both sides of the railway line Bourcy–Bastogne due to enemy pressure, but had been fighting successfully southeast of Mont.

Night of 25 December: I was busy all day with the attack. That night, ObstLt Kaufmann, Commander of 39th Grenadier Regiment, asked to move his command post from Assenois. He said that the situation was most dangerous. I refused his request. When asked about other units of the 4th Armoured threatening his rear, the situation was so bad, however, there was nothing I could do about it. My only hope was to continue with the attack on Bastogne. The 39th Grenadier Regiment had its principal strength in Assenois, Salvacourt, and Sibret. I told Kaufmann to continue facing towards Bastogne, and not to form a front to the south. I warned him, of course, to watch his rear and, when it became worse, to prepare an all-around defence, using all his anti-tank guns.

METZ: Supply of ammunition was no longer known to me; however, it was sufficient for an attack on 25 December which could be expected to be fairly successful. The last days' German attacks had been made simultaneously on the east and south fronts, although artillery was used without success, hereby putting the enemy on guard. Therefore, the commander of the 26th Volksgrenadier Division, contrary to given orders of the Army, which however, had been approved later on, decided not to attack on the east front – where the vegetation and character of the terrain offered too little opportunity for camouflage to cover the approach and the moving into position – but instead from the north west, from the area around Ruette and west over Flamisoul, as well as simultaneously attacking with the regiment of the 15th Armoured Infantry Division from the area south of Flamierge along the main road to Bastogne-south.

The night attack around 0300 hours brought no results and the repeated attacks during the day only slight gains in terrain. At the cost of great losses and expense of ammunition – the latter being especially important in view of the supply difficulties – only a slight contraction of the line of encirclement had been accomplished. At the same time increasing enemy pressure became noticeable in the south near Assenois.

Causes for the failure of this decisive day of attack were:

1. The forces of our own infantry were too weak in number and strength for the allotted task to skilfully exploit the width and depth of the well-adapted, camouflaged, craggy and hilly terrain with riflemen, machine guns and anti-tank guns. Losses and the strain of former battles, as well as exertions form marching had weakened these brave forces too much.
2. The supporting artillery was numerically too weak; the battle area too wide to overcome simultaneously-appearing enemy resistance and the effects of their weapons.

On the morning of 25 December, in order to reinforce the attacking 26th Volksgrenadier Division after their arrival, the following artillery: the Staff of A.R. 33 and III (Heavy)/A.R. 33 (2 heavy F.H. Batteries) were subordinated to the A.R. 26, and committed in the area Béthoment–Gives. The II Battalion was subordinated to the commander of A.R. 33.

Upon his request, the senior artillery commander received the approval for moving up the remaining artillery units II. (Light F.H.)/V.A.K. 766 and its commitment at the centre of attack of the 26th Volksgrenadier Division. Fuel was allotted for this purpose.

During the next few days the battalion arrived battery by battery. Commitment was in the area (as far as I can remember) Gives–Foy.

Although in this situation heavy batteries with great range could have been brought up to reinforce the small artillery forces with its limited mobility, which was due to the fuel shortage, the fuel situation was mainly responsible for the choice of the light Battalion II/766. The fuel which could be placed at the disposal of the senior artillery commander was sufficient to move at a speedier rate more light than heavy guns to the front line. The supply of the light guns could steadily move a greater number of rounds of ammunition, the ammunition that was already stored at the front could be better distributed and moved to the respective centre of activity because of the new existing uniformity of calibre of almost all batteries.

The moving forward of the ammunition distributing point of the army, which moreover had been successfully stored by the O.Qu. [*Ober Quartiermeister*], ameliorated the supply of ammunition on the Bastogne front. It was, however, too far in the rear for the remaining army front on the western edge of the Ardennes. An old German ammunition dump situated near Marche, of which the ammunition was still usable, brought real relief. In the beginning, notwithstanding the proximity of the enemy, it could still be utilised.

As far as ammunition was concerned, during the days after Christmas in the fighting on the Bastogne encirclement front, it became no longer a question of available stocks of ammunition, but of its transport into the firing positions, because the available transportation in the area was too slight and no aid could be given from elsewhere, regardless of the utilisation from the beginning of all train vehicles. In this connection there also existed a tense transport situation to the Ardennes front; the increasing firing activity made it here essentially a question of ammunition for the heavy batteries.

At this time things were particularly bad in regard to the supply of signal equipment for the artillery of the 26th Volksgrenadier Division. Since 16 December the combat losses had become so heavy that it affected the dispatching of observers and mobility in the transfer of observation post and V.B. As the operation of the division's signal battalion could only with difficulty satisfy the necessary demands, which was equally due to the lack of equipment, the artillery of the division could only be supported after a few days with the help of the general of the artillery of the groups of armies, when it was possible to bring up the signal equipment, especially telephone cable.

LÜTTWITZ: XLVII Panzer Corps: Our Christmas was made happy by the number of K-rations which were dropped over Bastogne, because a large amount of them fell into the area of my chateau. On Christmas Day, I was able to issue two K-rations to every member of my staff and to each of the Belgian children.

ZERBEL: 25 December: 2nd Panzer Division: The clearest winter weather and strongest air activity opened this day. The division continued to be in a critical situation. During the day Chavanne was lost. Enemy tanks temporarily penetrated into Harsin. In order to reach Hargimont the road past Grune had to be utilised. The III battery of the Panzer Artillery had been surprised when refilling their gasoline tanks and most of it was destroyed.

9th Panzer Division: The advanced parts of the division reached at 1500 hours the line Roy–Charneux–Hèdrée and attacked Marloie.

Panzer Lehr Division: The division took Humain and Havrenne. The attack against Buissonville failed. In the evening Humain and Havrenne were captured by the enemy.

<u>26th Volksgrenadier Division</u>: The division takes Flamisoul, Uette and temporarily penetrates into Champs. Moreover, Senonchamps is captured and the division advanced to the road crossing and to a point situated at 300m from Isle-le-Pré. An attack on Marvie is repulsed.

The situation of the Corps at the beginning of the night is as follows: The situation had developed as expected. The Corps did not reckon any longer with an advance of the right neighbour. The approaching parts of the 9th Panzer Division were needed for the backing up of the deep right flank. The situation at Clochimont and Assenois had become more critical. If the enemy succeeded in breaking through the encirclement of Bastogne and the bringing up of new forces, a rapid enemy thrust on Houffalize was possible and the situation of the Corps would become very critical. When learning that neither the Sixth Panzer Army had advanced, the Corps knew that the offensive had come to an end. The 2nd Panzer Division could only be saved from being destroyed by a rapid withdrawal to Marche–Rochefort. The Commander-in-Chief and the Chief of the Army had arrived at 1300 hours at the Corps. They showed understanding for the apprehensions of the Corps, but obviously were not authorised to decide the withdrawal of the 2nd Panzer Division. The Corps ordered the division to maintain by all means the contact with the advance detachment.

The 9th Panzer Division was to thrust forward past Humain on Buissonville with the next arriving parts. The 2nd Panzer Division was given orders to advance past Rochefort-Ciergnon on Custinne, in order to reinforce the advance detachment.

The Corps saw the chief danger in the possibility of an enemy breakthrough past Bastogne on Houffalize. The Corps requested from the Army the bringing up of further troops, in order to reinforce the front of encirclement around Bastogne.

The 26th Volksgrenadier Division with the attached units had attacked Bastogne and succeeded – with high losses – to reduce the extent of the encirclement and to eliminate some important enemy strongpoints. But the divisions had not managed to take Bastogne. The enemy had received much reinforcement and, since 22 December, was supplied by air, so the available forces were not strong enough for the definitive mopping-up of Bastogne.

WAGENER: The clear weather continued to enable the enemy Air Force to attack incessantly. But the decision was abandoned before fulfilment; there was no longer any possibility of the Fifth Panzer Army reaching the Maas. The LVIII Panzer Corps was not able again to get moving despite the success of the Führer Begleit Brigade in attacks south of Hotton. The enemy opposite us went over to the attack against our troops who were already much weakened.

The untiring 26th Volksgrenadier Division attacked the area around Bastogne on 25 December. The situation south of the city had become more acute, portions of the Corps had to be committed there to support the 5th Paratroop Division. In the event the enemy should succeed in making further advances against the right wing of the Seventh Army, for the purpose of breaking the siege of Bastogne, then the XLVII Panzer Corps' rear would really be exposed to a serious threat. An enemy push from the south and north toward Houffalize could only lead to the total destruction of the attacking wedge of the Fifth Panzer Army.

The Army then, although with a heavy heart, decided to withdraw the Führer Begleit Brigade from its successful attacks near Hotton, and to assign it to the XLVII Panzer Corps for support in the region of Bastogne. This was the first measure taken by the Army which had actually nothing more to do with the plan of reaching the Maas, on the contrary, it was taken for the sole purpose of getting things straight in the area of Bastogne. With this the thought of further offensive had been abandoned.

US FORCES: Christmas Day was just breaking. Colonel Allen stayed at his 3rd Battalion, 327th, command post only long enough to look out of his window, and prove what Towns had told him, and to call Colonel Harper and tell him he was getting out. Then he ran as fast as he could go and the German tanker fired at him as he sprinted toward the woods. He could see the muzzle blasts over his shoulder in the semi-darkness. But all of the shots were leading him. The Germans were giving him credit for more speed than his legs possessed.

Two members of Allen's staff followed him. As they all came out of the other end of the woods, men of Colonel Chappuis' 502nd Parachute Infantry along the ridge road saw them and promptly pinned them down with heavy rifle fire. The three then crawled back to the woods, circled south through a little valley and returned to Hemroulle. As they came out of the woods the second time, they were fired on by artillerymen of Colonel Cooper's 463rd Parachute Field Artillery Battalion who had formed a skirmish line in case the enemy broke through the infantry. But Colonel Allen was getting tired of all this and he waved his handkerchief vigorously until finally the gunners lowered their rifles and let the party come in.

Colonel Harper, on getting the phone call made by Allen just before Allen had to dash from his headquarters, realized that there was now no control over the 3rd Battalion, 327th. So he sent his own S-3, Major Jones, with his radio to Colonel

Cooper's artillery command post and Jones got there just as Allen did, and he got through at once to the companies with the radio.

In the meantime, the forward line had held, partly because of the quick thinking of Captain McDonald of Company B. He had heard Colonel Allen's urgent report to Colonel Harper over his own telephone and he at once called Companies A and C by radio. 'The battalion commander has had to get out,' he said to them. 'I can see you from where I am. Your best bet is to stay where you are. Hold tight to your positions and fight back at them.'

That was what they did. The main body of the German armour rolled straight through Company A's lines – 18 white-camouflaged tanks moving in column. The men of Company A, 327th (1st Lieutenant Howard G. Bowles was the acting commanding officer), stayed in their foxholes and took it, replying with their rifles and whatever

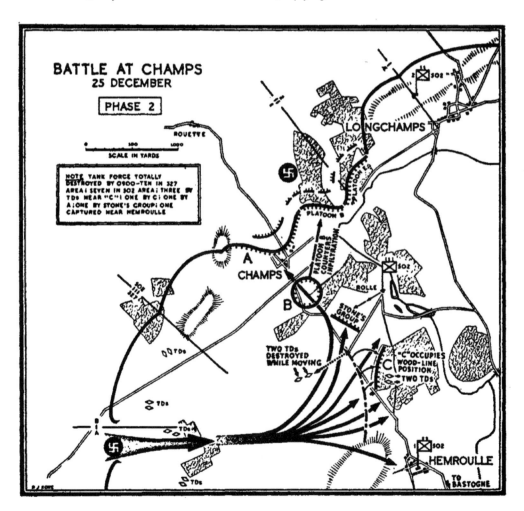

other weapons were at hand. After the tide of German steel had passed over and through them, 4 men of the company were dead and 5 lay wounded. But the 68 survivors were up and fighting, and in the next round of the battle they captured 92 German prisoners.

Having crashed through Colonel Harper's 327th front, the German armour split as it came on toward the ridge and half of it swung north toward Rolle where Lieutenant Nickels saw it and warned Colonel Chappuis, commander of the 502nd Parachute Infantry, in time for him to make his last-minute preparation.

Companies B and C, 502nd, were even then in column of twos moving up the road toward Champs. Thus far Colonel Templeton's 705th Tank Destroyer Battalion had played only a minor part in the defence of the sector, but their best moments were approaching. Two of the tank destroyers had been of some assistance to Captain Swanson (Company A, 502nd) in his fight for Champs. They were already in position there when the German attack got under way, one destroyer in the centre of Champs and another slightly to the west of it, so placed that it could cover the road to the southwest and the ridge to the north and northwest. Upon setting up, the tank destroyer crews manned four machine guns on the ground around their centrally located guns. This position held when the German infantry closed on Champs and the tank destroyer force even spared a few of its men to go forward and help the paratroopers root the enemy out of the houses.

The heavy guns were used for close-up interdiction fire to keep the enemy from moving any deeper into the village. In this work, the 37mm guns, firing canister, were especially effective. Captain Swanson got one of the tank destroyers, under Sergeant Lawrence Valletta, to go forward and blast a house where about thirty Germans had taken cover. Sergeant Valletta moved right in next to the building, trained his big gun on the doors and windows and blew the place apart. He then shelled two more houses and returned to his original position. Just about dawn, he made a second sortie of the same kind.

To the south of Champs where the crisis of the Christmas action was swiftly maturing, the tank destroyers got away to a bad start, but then staged a swift recovery. Two of them from Company B, 705th Battalion, had been in the 327th Glider Infantry area and were out along the road which runs from Rolley toward Grande-Fagne, a mile to the southwest (this put them to the southward of Company C, 502nd Parachute Infantry), when the German attack came over the hill. The crews had at first put their tank destroyers into concealment behind a haystack and from there had engaged the enemy armour at a distance, knocking out two or three tanks. Yet as the power of the German armour became more obvious, they decided to withdraw. That was how it happened that they were moving back toward Rolley and were directly in line with the German tank fire when Company C of the 502nd Parachute Infantry faced toward the enemy.

Both tank destroyers were knocked out almost instantly. The men of Company C saw them reel and stop from the enemy fire and realized that the loss of the tank destroyers had helped spare them the worst part of the blow. The encounter had had one other powerful effect – two tank destroyers from Company C, 705th, were waiting in the woods behind Colonel Chappuis' 502nd infantrymen. The German armour, confident that it was now in full command of the field, came on boldly against the infantry line. Colonel Cassidy (executive of the 502nd) had sent a runner sprinting toward the woods to alert the two concealed tank destroyers. The runner had been told to run from the guns on to Captain George R. Cody's Company C, 502nd, position and tell him that the tank destroyers would be backing him up. But he didn't get there in time.

The guns of the seven Mark IVs were already firing into Company C. About 15 to 20 German infantrymen were riding on the outside of each tank, some firing their rifles. But the ground fog was bad and their fire was erratic. Captain Cody turned his men about and told them to fall back to the edge of the forest. Without any part of its line breaking into a general dash for the rear, Company C fell back to the shelter of the trees and there took up positions and opened fire on the tanks with machine guns, bazookas and rifles. Despite the surprise of the German assault, this movement was carried out with little loss and no disorder.

Then swiftly, there was a complete turning of the situation as Company C's first volleys from its new position took toll of the German infantry clinging to the tanks. Dead and wounded pitched from the vehicles into the snow. As if with the purpose of saving their infantry, the tanks veered left toward Champs and the position held by Company B, 502nd.

Until this moment the two tank destroyers in the woods behind Company C had not fired a round. But as the tank line pivoted and began to move northward along the top of the ridge, the flank of the German armour became completely exposed and the two tank destroyers went into action. So did Company B, which was now firing at the enemy front. Three of the Mark IVs were hit and knocked out by the tank destroyer fire before they completed their turning movement. One was stopped by a bazooka round from Company C. A fifth tank was hit and stopped by a rocket from Captain Stone's scratch group from Headquarters, 502nd. The infantry riding on the tanks were cut to pieces by bullet fire. As Company C's part of the battle ended there were 67 German dead and 35 prisoners, many of them wounded, in the area around the ruined tanks.

One tank did break through Company B and charged on into Champs. Company A, 502nd, fired bazookas at it and it was also shelled by a 57mm gun which had taken position in the village. The tank was hit by both types of fire, but which weapon made the kill is uncertain.

Captain James J. Hatch, S-3 of the 502nd, had gone forward to reconnoitre Company A's situation and was in the Company A command post at the time. He heard the fight going on outside, grabbed his pistol and opened the door. He was looking straight into the mouth of the tank's 75mm gun at a range of 15 yards. Hatch closed the door and said to the others, 'This is no place for my pistol.'

The seventh tank in the German group – it was later determined that this was the same tank that had knocked out the two tank destroyers – was captured intact at Hemroulle. By 0900 hours, 25 December, the action was cleared up around Rolley. Headquarters of the 502nd Parachute Infantry had called 101st Division Headquarters and asked about the situation of 327th Glider Infantry over on its left. Colonel Kinnard (101st Airborne Division G-3) reported that the 327th's lines were generally intact and the situation there well in hand.

In the 327th's sector there had been four tank destroyers behind Captain McDonald's Company B and four behind Lieutenant Bowles' Company A. Captain Towns' Company C was unsupported by tank destroyers, but Colonel Harper had sent him two Sherman tanks on hearing that the German attack was coming.

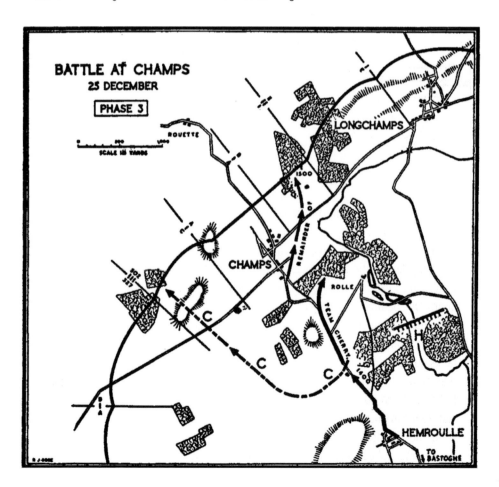

These guns, the bazooka fire of the 327th Glider Infantry outfits and the barrage fire of Colonel Cooper's 463rd Parachute Field Artillery Battalion had dealt in detail with that part of the German armour that tried to ride on through toward Hemroulle after breaking Harper's front. The German tanks were fired at from so many directions and with such a mixture of fire that it was not possible to see or say how each tank met its doom. One battery from the 463rd stopped two tanks at a range of 600 yards and then some men ran out from the battery position and captured the crews. Eighteen German tanks had been seen on that part of the 327th Glider Infantry's front that morning; 18 tanks had driven on through the infantry, but not one got away. When the fighting died at last there were 18 disabled German tanks, many of them with fire-blackened hulls, scattered out through the American positions along the ridges running from Hemroulle to Champs.

In the 502nd Parachute Infantry area, the wire maintenance men had kept on working right through the fire fight and by 0900 hours the lines were again in solid. None of the German infantry had managed an escape. The few survivors, upon recoiling, were rounded up by the members of Colonel Allen's overrun 3rd Battalion, 327th. The German tankers died inside their tanks.

Although Company C, 502nd, had been compelled to engage without artillery support because of the closeness of the action, its losses were negligible. It was put in position along the high ground west of the scene of the skirmish. At about the same time the Company C fight ended, Company A, 502nd, was getting Champs under control and was doing the last of its rat hunting through the village houses. Company B was put over to the east of Company A to fill out the line as far as the 3rd Battalion. In getting to this position, Company B, 502nd, took heavy losses from enemy artillery while moving across the high ground north of Champs, but by 1500 hours the position was complete.

Company A counted 98 Germans killed and 79 enlisted men and 2 officers captured in the Champs action.

About 0800 hours on Christmas Day, 101st Division moved Force Cherry out through Hemroulle to a position on the high ground along the edge of the woods to the south of the 502nd Parachute Infantry. Colonel Cherry stayed there until after dark to cover the restoration of the 1st Battalion, 327th, position. He then pulled back to Hemroulle. A German field order captured during the morning fight showed that the German tank and infantry mission that came to grief along the ridge south and west of Rolley had been attempted by the 115th Panzergrenadier Regiment of the 15th Panzergrenadier Division. Two battalions of the 77th Panzergrenadier Regiment, supported by the division artillery of the 26th Volksgrenadier Division, had implemented the assault against Champs and to the south which preceded the Panzer advance.

Christmas Day closed with Colonel Chappuis and Colonel Cassidy of the 502nd sitting down to a table spread with a can of sardines and a box of crackers. General McAuliffe, disappointed that no relief force had come, called General Middleton and said, 'We have been let down.'

KOKOTT: In the early afternoon of the 25 December, it was clear to the division command – due to personal combat impressions and incoming reports – that the first major attack had failed. The attack had failed due to the inadequate means of the attacker. The personnel and *matériel* strength were, despite all aggregation, despite all massing, despite all limitation of territory, too small right from the outset. With the 15th Panzer-Grenadier Division, the 26th Division had deployed all the concentrated power at its disposal. It could not give more than they had. It wasn't enough!

If ever, since the enclosure of Bastogne, then on this day the battle stood at razor's edge. The enemy had visibly suffered heavy losses; he was without doubt heavily hit in his fighting power. His tanks were shot-up, his units splintered, torn, beaten, he had lost weapons, equipment and prisoners of war. But he still possessed so much strength – moral, personnel and *matériel* – that he was perhaps able at the last minute to offer the bled-out attacker a 'hold'. In the afternoon the division, aware of the situation and in order to limit losses without any gains, ordered the stop of further fights and the partial withdrawal of advance combat groups to more favourable terrain.

The Grenadier Regiment 76 and the remaining parts of the 15th Panzer Grenadier Division were affected. Reconnaissance Division 26 and Fusilier Regiment 39 held the gained positions. The enemy reacted with very strong and effective fire attacks. An after-push behind declining German forces did not take place. Only much later did the enemy test the waters with infantry forces under tank protection and occupied some of the abandoned positions without a fight.

Against the front of the *Aufklärungsabteilung* 26 near Isle-la-Hesse and in the Isle-le-Pré area, the enemy initially launched counterattacks until these also subsided at dusk and only heavy, rolling fire raids fell on the German positions around Bastogne. The information received from the 5th Fallschirmjäger Division, and the occasional status reports of the situation by the higher command posts, did not give a clear picture of the development of the situation in the back of the 26th Division. Only so much was certain – that the 5th Fallschirmjäger Division stood along the whole front line between the road Bastogne–Neufchâteau and the major southern road in the defensive fight against enemies attacking from southwest. By the afternoon, however, the troops had fended off all enemy attacks in a general line: road fork 2km north of Nîves–Remoiville–Hollange.

The division was planning to hit Bastogne again in the evening hours. From the protruding front arch at Isle-la-Hesse a combat group consisting of combined parts of the Grenadier Regiment 77 and parts of the Reconnaissance Division 26, together with about ten fighter tanks, was supposed to attack northeast towards Hemroulle, pierce the woods north of Isle-la-Hesse and then proceed south of Savy on Bastogne.

After passing through the woods north of Isle-la-Hesse, all forces standing between Grande-Fange and Großer Weststraße were to move up in a wedge formation, while guarding to the north and bypassing Hemroulle to the east (of Bastogne). It was a desperate attempt to turn the fate of the day once again, using the last of our strength and strain. It failed. In the provisioning of troops during darkness, the assembled parts of the Grenadier Regiment 76 were smashed to such an extent by a heavy fire raid – which could be described as unusually effective even during the war – that of the remains of a battalion, for example, only about 30-40 men could attack with their battalion commander. The rest had fallen, were wounded or scattered.

Nevertheless, at the commanded time – around 2000 hours – the tank destroyers of Reconnaissance Division 26 with accompanying infantry, followed by the Grenadier Regiment 78, attacked under a dense curtain of fire of their own artillery and heavy infantry weapons. On both sides of the dirt road leading from Isle-la-Hesse to Hemroulle, penetrating in partially fierce attacks, they fought their way up close to some 1000m in front of Hemroulle. There, after overcoming fanatical enemy resistance again, they encountered an enemy PAK defence, where in the darkness the already hardly-usable Hetzer Tank Destroyers were inferior. More than half of the Hetzer Tank Destroyers were shot up at close quarters (including the company commander with his car).

Encountering heavy enemy fire, the decimated remnants of the last combat group retreated under the protection of dense fog to their starting positions. (That night and the following night, all but two of the Hetzer Tank Destroyers shot up were towed back to their own lines by towing vehicles under the protection of voluntary security troops. Despite several attempts it was not possible to reach and rescue the company commander's car). The division reported to the corps late in the evening that, after all means had been exhausted, the largescale attack had failed despite the outstanding bravery and operational readiness of all the attacking units and their leaders, and that a continuation of the attacks on Bastogne by the now burnt-out division was no longer to be accounted for and carried out.

The forces remaining in the division were so weakened that it was questionable whether they could have withstood an energetic thrust from the enemy at all. The corps took note of this report, initially refrained from further attacks and managed to maintain its position. At the same time, the Corps informed the division about the precarious situation in its back. There the 5th Fallschirmjäger Division had not been able to hold their ground against the enemy attacks from the southwest. Chaumont had fallen into enemy hands and the enemy pressure continued in an undiminished strength. The Corps, like the division, was reasonably concerned about the further development. It was known that the 5th Fallschirmjäger Division would do everything in its power to stop the enemy in front of Bastogne. It was hoped that it would last until the Führer Begleit Brigade (a newly assembled, but particularly well-equipped combat unit) arrived in the combat area. The arrival of this unit was expected in the evening of the 26th or during 27 December.

Although the Grenadiers of both the Sixth SS Panzerarmee and the Fifth Panzerarmee at that time left no doubt that the Ardennes offensive plan had failed, the commanders of the Wehrmacht did not draw any radical and generous conclusions and decisions. Instead of a large-scale operation, the army command now put up a bloody, dubious and loss-making fight for an ultimately insignificant, small town, as should prove to be the case in the future. The division received orders from the Corps to maintain the Bastogne enclosure on the grounds it had gained on 26 December and to prevent any outbreak or unification attacks by the defenders of Bastogne with the advancing forces.

It was highlighted that Seventh Army had taken all measures to defeat another enemy attack on Bastogne over the current front line of the 5th Paratroopers. The division passed this order on to its regiments. To arm itself as much as possible against the enemy pressure expected from the south and southwest, the Panzergrenadier Regiment 39 was ordered to prepare itself on both sides of the Great North-South Road and on both sides of the road and railway line to Neufchâteau. To achieve this, the section of Regiment 901 was narrowed. The Grenadier Regiment 78 was extended to the south via the road Bastogne–Bra to Marvie (exclusively), replacing parts of the Regiment 901.

The Fusilier Regiment 39 could only be reinforced by the existing field guards from the Hubermont and Brul–Lavaselle area. The main thrust of the opponent was expected, if the 5th paratroopers did not stop it, on both sides of large north-south road and along railway and road Neufchâteau. The 15th Panzergrenadier Brigade was responsibly assigned the section Great West Road (inclusive) to woodlands 800m west of Grande Fagne for defence. On the right, then until the Bastogne–Senonchamps road, Reconnaissance Department 26 stood, on the left, hard west from Grande-Fagne to Longchamps the Grenadier Regiment 79.

With a certain concern, the division looked forward to 26 December. The 25th had been an incredibly hard day of fighting. It had not brought – despite the employment of all means, despite exploitation of all possibilities and despite a self-sacrificial courage of all units deployed in the attack and fight – the success desired.

What the troops and their leadership achieved on this day can only be properly evaluated by those who have witnessed the struggle. It would be a deliberate, malicious distortion of the truth if anyone wanted to blame the failure on the troops' behaviour. It was the pure misjudgment of the relative strength of power by the high command. It was the lack of the promised air support. It was an enemy assessment that had nothing to do with reality, all together factors which had a decisive effect on the daily events, which could not be balanced out by combat experience, hardness and self-sacrifice of the troops. The troops had devoted themselves with all their will and heart to achieving the goal.

Their leaders had always inspired and pushed forward the troops by example. In the smallest units, the companies and battalions were rushing forward again and again on their own, defending themselves, going forward without a break, without rest, without food, exhausted to death, bleeding to death, but with an iron will to achieve victory. All day long, they were attacking and counterattacking the enemy. Who could not resist a deep impression who has seen the troops during the day and the survivors on the evening of the 25th? The day of attack had brought heaviest losses. The 15th Panzergrenadier Division was practically annihilated. The 26th Division counted more than 800 dead, wounded and missing. The Grenadier Regiment 77 had barely 300 men left in the front line. One battalion counted about 80 men the other maybe 200 men.

The *Aufklärungsabteilung* 26, like the Fusilier Regiment 39, had been melted down to remnants of its former strength. The company strength consisted at best of 20-25 men in the front line. Baggage, staff and rear echelons were largely combed out; 200 men were left at the *Feldersatzbataillon*, which had also assigned personnel to the Panzer Grenadier Regiment 901 as well as to the Fusilier Regiment 30 and the Grenadier Regiment 77.

The losses of the old, experienced non-commissioned officers and persons, the high losses of officers and trained specialist personnel in artillery and on heavy infantry weapons were high. A not inconsiderable number of heavy weapons had been destroyed by enemy fire and could not be replaced. Due to the lack of ammunition, some of the heavy mortars were pulled out of the front line and collected in a division depot. The operating crews as well as the 14th *Panzerzerstörer-Kompanien* went as assault riflemen into the firing line.

On 25 December the division was reduced to ashes. Of course, the opponent was also hit hard by his losses. Beside considerable losses of weapons, tanks and prisoners of war they must have suffered strong bloody losses by the agglomerated German fire, the bitterly led storm attacks and close fights. As you could sense from their behaviour displayed during the occasional German abandonment of positions, they also seemed to be exhausted and at the end of their strength. However, it may be emphasized at this point: it had long been a certainty for the attacking German troops that they were facing an elite unit of the American army. This fighting day of 25 December 1944 had only underlined this knowledge. The same fighting spirit, the same readiness for action, hardness and determination characterized the defender as well as the attacker. As equal opponents, friend and foe fought through this day.

Chapter 10

26–27 December: Breaking the Bastogne Encirclement

During the night from 25 to 26 December, the German surrounding forces carried out minor regroupings and position improvements. The units were organized, small shock troops were formed, lost connections were restored, ammunition supplies were replenished.

Between Remoifosse (on the Great-South Road) and Sibret, as well as in the area around Clochimont, the minefields were reinforced. Where necessary, the PAK positions were improved. From Sainlez via Grandrue–Remichampagne in the direction of Morhet, the 5th Paratrooper Division blocked the front line to the south. Tank destroyers and mobile blocking troops of the 5th Paratrooper Division equipped with mines were allocated over to the assembly lines of the formation there.

On the 26th the artillery fights around Bastogne came alive early. Heavy shelling lay on each other's positions and an enduring, demoralizing destructive fire struck on bases and identified resistance nests. At Champs, in front of Hemroulle, and at Isle-la-Hesse the enemy tanks fired rapidly at everything that was moving. After 9am the fighter planes appeared as usually scheduled. The fire swelled. Swarms of fighter planes dive bombed with guns blazing down on the villages behind the front line as well as on artillery positions. Again, large groups of supply planes flew into Bastogne from the west.

During the morning, the *Aufklärungsabteilung* 26 thought to recognize hostile movements at Isle-la-Hesse. They requested a concentrated firing in this area, which was then quickly taken out. Under the impression of the impact of this firing raid, the commander of the *Aufklärungsabteilung* decided individually to attack yesterday's target with his force and, supported by some tank destroyers, in a daring momentum, infiltrated Isle-la-Hesse eastward up to the street fork. Prisoners were taken, weapons captured or destroyed. With relatively few own losses a nice success was achieved by daring and surprise. However, neither the *Aufklärungsabteilung* nor the division was able to benefit from the situation due to lack of forces. After beating off several enemy counter-tank attacks, the *Aufklärungsabteilung* later gave up the crossroads and retreated a few hundred metres back into the bushes west of the farmsteads Isle-la-Hesse and held this position against enemy attacks.

During the morning the division received several disturbing messages from the Fusilier Regiment 39 about the tense situation at the 5th Paratrooper Division covering their back. Exact information, however, was not available. The reports from the corps indicated hard fighting and strong enemy pressure on the 5th Fallschirmjäger Division. The general assumption was, that the enemy would be kept away from the surrounding front line. Around noon, in the area of the Regiment 39 in front of Isle-le-Pré more intensive battles developed. Tank formations were detected in Isle-le-Pré and various small-scale advances were made. Regiment 39 claimed that Sibret and Assenois received artillery fire from the south. A query with the Corps confirmed that the 5th Paratrooper Division 'had been fighting around Remichampagne against advancing enemy tanks for some time. However, measures to seal off the enemy attacks have been taken.'

The division issued alarm orders to all guarding troops in the southern section via regiments 39 and 901. The artillery and infantry battles at the Bastogne Enclosure Ring, the enemy cross-fire on paths and villages, the attacks of fighter planes – all this went on and on without interruption. The faces and weapons of the weakened battalions of regiments 901, 39, 77, parts of *Aufklärungsabteilung* 26 and the remnants of the 15th Panzer Grenadier Division were directed at Bastogne and the artillery and anti-aircraft guns were firing at Bastogne. Except for the guarding troops securing the southern sector, no man, no gun, no weapon, no officer could be spared at the siege. Everyone who stood there and fought had to rely on his comrade covering his back.

For everyone, commanders and officers and privates in the firing line, those hours were quite stressful. The frequent disconnection of communication links contributed to increased sorrows and anxiety. Despite the many rumours, alarms and exaggerations that came in from the southern section in the afternoon, one did not give up hope (at least on the division level) that the southern front would hold out until nightfall. During this period there was generally nothing to fear, one could then plan ahead and – in this case – take precautions. In addition, the Führer Begleit Kompanie was to arrive on December 27.

Of course, these were all just hopes. And these soon proved to be deceptive. Around 1500 hours the security guards of the 26th Division reported via Fusilier Regiment 39 'that parts of the 5th Paratrooper Division – pressed hard by the enemy – had returned to Sibret and via Hompré and that enemy tanks were attacking Clochimont'.

Shortly afterwards the connection to the Fusilier Regiment 39 broke off. The division asked the Corps what was known about the combat situation of the 5th Paratrooper Division. The Corps only knew about the battles at Remichampagne and was surprised to hear that the front at Clochimont was apparently torn open. Sometime later, Panzer Grenadier Regiment 901 and an artillery detachment reported that the enemy had broken into the weak front line at Clochimont. Parts of the 5th Paratroopers had returned to the east and held the western edges of L'Ardosière and Bois du Vicaire (east of Salvacourt–Hompré). The enemy advances with tanks from the line Salvacourt–Clochimont on both sides of the path Clochimont–Assenois to Assenois. Parts of the Panzergrenadier Regiment 901 were in fighting at the southwest front line.

Almost at the same time reports came in from Sibret 'that a lot of retreating paratroopers were stopped there and then deployed for defence of the village. Sibret was not yet attacked but came under fire from artillery and fighter planes. The batteries standing between Sibret and Clochimont had changed their position to the west (over the railway line), a PAK defence securing the east of Sibret was in battle with the enemy who was attacking Assenois. At Clochimont and between Clochimont–Assenois several enemy tanks and armoured vehicles had been knocked out.'

The last impressions left the division with no doubts that the brave Fusilier Regiment 39 must have run into the most severe difficulties in the Assenois area. Fighting with their faces turned towards Bastogne, it had become an almost untenable situation for the troops. Between 1600 and 1700 hours the Fusilier Regiment radioed: 'enemy tanks in the back. Fighting in Assenois'. At around 1600 the division had ordered the 15th Panzergrenadier Division to bring up some newly arrived or repaired tanks (or armoured vehicles) to the Regiment 39. This group – consisting of some four to six vehicles with mounted infantrymen and pioneers – was to leave as soon as the fighter plane activity died down (that was around 1600 – 1630 hours).

Even before this small, last reinforcing group had marched off, the commander of the Fusilier Regiment 39 called on the telephone to his command post in the forest northwest of Assenois. He reported:

> 'Around 5pm, while his regiment was fighting at Isle-la-Hasse and on the northern edge of the Bois d'Hazy, Assenois had been attacked with tanks from Clochimont. The weak defence line, together with people

from the baggage, scattered paratroopers and the 39 Regiment staff, had taken up the fight. Supported by artillery, the first attack was beaten off. The enemy had again attacked using fog, phosphorous and strong firing support. They had entered the village and some enemy detachments passed to the east of the village. Bitter street fighting had taken place in Assenois. Several enemy tanks and armoured personnel carriers (about 6) had been knocked out by mines, anti-tank weapons and PAK. Some of the crews had been wounded and taken prisoner. Despite a desperate and costly resistance, the rest of the enemy tank force had fought its way through Assenois. Some 10 to 12 tanks had broken through in a group – blasting out of all their barrels – in a wild ride over and through the German encirclement from Assenois to Bastogne. Even if it was only a small group of tanks – the enemy had succeeded in uniting with the garrison in Bastogne.'

MANTEUFEL: On 26 December Jodl called me with a message from Hitler and authorised us to swing to the north as I had suggested. He also promised to employ the OKW reserves, but we discovered they had no fuel with which to move. Thus, only weak forces of the 9th Panzer Division were able to join Lüttwitz's XLVII Panzer Corps, which was furthest to the west.

I had the hope that we might get additional fuel and renew the attack to the north. I decided to reduce Bastogne, which assumed added importance when it became apparent that we were going to fight east of the Meuse River. I had brought Remer's Brigade south to Bastogne on 26 December in an attempt to head off the American forces which were relieving the town. However, he arrived too late and was unable to prevent the relief.

LÜTTWITZ XLVII Pz Corps: On 26 December when CC 'R' 4th Armoured Division (US) broke through 5th FS at Assenois, it had penetrated to the last line of that division. The next enemy troops were those of 26th Volksgrenadier Division, but these were facing Bastogne. The attack caught this German unit literally from the rear and was so swift that 26th Volksgrenadier Division was unable to stop it.

The attack of 4th Armoured Division forced a gap in the German circle around Bastogne. Immediately upon the breakthrough, Gen. von Lüttwitz ordered Führer Begleit Brigade to move from Herbaimont on 27 December, enter Sibret from the west, and on 28 December to launch a strong attack which would close the circle again, but Führer Begleit Brigade, under the command of Obst Remer, always had gasoline trouble. By the night of 27/28

December it has gone only as far as Chenogne. By that time, the Americans had taken Sibret and the gap had now become too wide to close.

GENERALMAJOR (WAFFEN-SS) FRITZ KRAEMER: About 26 or 27 December we received orders to send I SS Panzer Corps to the south to attack Bastogne. I realised the importance of Bastogne early in the attack. I think one of the great mistakes of the offensive was not to take the town earlier, when the opportunity presented itself. On 20 December the Commander of 2nd Panzer Division wanted to take the town, but he was ordered to move west toward Dinant. That was a great mistake.

US FORCES: On the morning of 26 December, the German forces renewed their pressure against the western side of the Bastogne perimeter, but they did not press their attack in real strength and the American lines held solid. Around the other parts of the defending circle, the day was relatively quiet though both sides intensified their air activity.

The intervention of the air directly hastened the hour when the enemy encirclement of Bastogne was broken through by the arrival of the armoured column from the south. Since 0600 hours on December 22, the three Combat Commands of the 4th Armoured Division had been fighting their way steadily toward Bastogne by three separate routes from their assembly areas north of Arlon. They had met intense resistance all the way along the line and had taken heavy losses in men and tanks.

By 1500 hours on December 26, Combat Command Reserve of the 4th had arrived at the high ground overlooking Clochimont and was preparing to attack toward the village of Sibret. This put the command about 4 miles to the southwest of Bastogne with their local objective about a mile to their own northwest.

As the attack was about to get under way, the men saw and heard what seemed to be 'hundreds' of C-47 planes coming directly over them and bound for Bastogne. The spectacle encouraged Lieutenant Colonel Creighton W. Abrams, Jr., commanding the 37th Tank Battalion, and Lieutenant Colonel George L. Jaques, commanding the 53rd Armoured Infantry Battalion, to make a break for Bastogne, disregarding their original mission. They believed that Sibret was strongly held. Colonel Abrams' force had been cut down to 20 medium tanks and Colonel Jaques' force was short 230 men. They figured that it might cost less to ignore Sibret and attack straight toward Bastogne.

KOKOTT: When 4th Armoured Division (US) broke into Assenois in the afternoon, Kaufmann called me. He said there were 12 enemy tanks in the village. The tanks were through Assenois and going to Bastogne.

I knew it was all over. (I gave Kaufmann the order) just to block the road. The corridor was still very small, the width of the road itself, and I hoped that with roadblocks and barriers, we could close the ring around Bastogne. It was a difficult task, however because 39th Grenadier Regiment had been scattered on both sides of the road by 4th Armoured Division (US) tanks, which were firing in all directions. Now it was difficult for 39th Grenadier Regiment to fight back without firing at each other. We tried to get reinforcements there, but the troops of 26th Volksgrenadier Division were so tired from their fighting that they couldn't make the effort.

The Führer Begleit Brigade was ordered by Corps to move to Sibret to close the circle, but it didn't get there in time. When it arrived 4th Armoured Division (US) had already taken Sibret.

US FORCES: At 1520 hours, 26 December Colonel Abrams ordered his S-3, Captain William A. Dwight, to take a light team composed of tanks and infantry, break northeast to the village of Assenois and keep moving until he reached the Bastogne lines. The artillery with Combat Command Reserve, 4th Armoured Division – three battalions of 105mm and one battery of 155mm howitzers – was directed to stand ready to place a concentration on Assenois as the team moved up to it. Such was the plan.

In the execution of it, the commander of the leading tank called for artillery support as soon as he came within sight of the village. The guns poured ten rounds apiece against the target, concentrating their fire against the woods north of town and into an area in the southern edge of town where the enemy was supposed to be strongly fixed with anti-tank guns. Combat Command Reserve's shells were still dropping on Assenois when the first tanks moved in among the houses.

There were some infantry losses from our own fire. In the smoke and confusion, the infantry company of Captain Dwight's team dismounted and engaged the enemy in a fight for the village. But five tanks and one infantry half-track stuck to the letter of their assignment and kept moving toward Bastogne. Three of the tanks had forged several hundred yards to the fore and the enemy strewed Teller mines between them and the rest of the tank force as they were pulling out of Assenois. The halftrack hit a mine and was destroyed. Captain Dwight jumped down from his tank to clear the other mines away, so that he could get forward with his two tanks. Meanwhile, the three lead tanks kept going and at 1650 hours 1st Lieutenant Charles P. Boggess, commanding officer of Company C, 37th Tank Battalion, drove the first vehicle from the 4th Armoured Division to within the lines of the 326th Airborne Engineer Battalion, 101st Division, of the Bastogne forces.

This was the beginning. The German encirclement was now finally broken, though some days would pass before the American lines to the south were again firm and

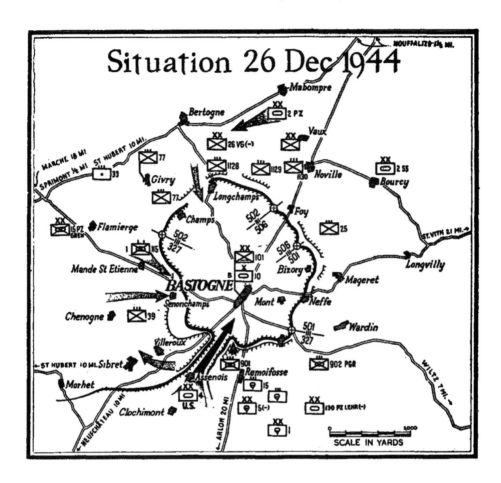

several weeks of fighting would ensue before the siege of Bastogne was finally lifted. Captain Dwight, having followed Lieutenant Boggess on into Bastogne, radioed Colonel Abrams to come up with the rest of the breakthrough team. With them came Major General Maxwell D. Taylor, commander of the 101st Division, who had flown back from the United States to join his division. General Taylor had arrived in time to lead his men through their bitterest days of fighting on the Bastogne ground, the days yet to come...

Captain Dwight then continued on to report to General McAuliffe and arrange for the convoys to enter the town that night. Assenois was cleared by 2000 hours, 26 December, with the capture of 428 prisoners. Before morning, the woods on both sides of the road running north from Assenois were cleared sufficiently to assure relatively free use of this line of communication.

Much hard fighting still remained for the other two combat commands of 4th Armoured Division before they, too, closed to within the Bastogne perimeter. By their drive north, they had opened an avenue to the south which would ensure that the victory won by the Bastogne defenders could be fully exploited by the United States Army and the forces of its Allies.

BAYERLEIN: 26 December. Defensive fighting on the entire divisional front and on the flank near Telling, Hatrival, Moircy and Remagen.

METZ: 26 December became of decisive importance in the Bastogne situation, even for the entire army. After further air landings in the afternoon (this time on a very small scale) and the throwing down of supplies, enemy tanks (American 4th Armoured Division) succeeded at 1600 hours to break through the line of encirclement in the south after a short battle and to advance from Assenois towards Bastogne. An order was given at once to reform the circle.

The moving up of artillery of the encirclement front to that spot – either before enemy pressure from the south made itself felt, or immediately after the breakthrough of the encircling line in the south – was impossible because of continued enemy pressure on the west and north fronts of Bastogne. Only on the night of 26/27 December artillery arrived for the battle at a point of the breakthrough with the commander-escort brigade, which had an artillery battalion of two light F.H. and one heavy F.H. Battery at its disposal. The efforts of this brigade and the extent of artillery support given by the artillery of the 26th Volksgrenadier Division brought no results.

ZERBEL: December 26: 2nd Panzer Division:
The advance detachment reported that it was attacked at by 45 enemy tanks. Other parts of the division reached the bend of the road at 1km northwest of Sanzienne. An Army order at 1530 hours authorised the immediate withdrawal of the advance detachment of the 2nd Panzer Division to the bridgehead of Rochefort. The order was transmitted immediately by radio to the division.

9th Panzer Division: The division attacked Humain and captured this place. A further attack on Buissonville was repulsed. Other parts of the division relieved the Panzer Lehr Division at the bridgehead of Rochefort.

Panzer Lehr Division: The parts which were relieved at the Rochefort bridgehead are needed for the reinforcement of the line Han-sur-Lesse–Remagen.

<u>26th Volksgrenadier Division</u>: Enemy tanks pass through Assenois and penetrate into Bastogne.

At the beginning of the night the situation of the Corps was as follows:

At 1600 hours the enemy had succeeded in breaking through to Bastogne past Clochimont–Assenois. It had to be expected that the enemy would immediately enlarge this narrow passage. The Corps had no forces available to eliminate this danger. At noon the Army announced that the Führer Begleit Brigade would be brought up. This brigade was to attack on the 27 December from Sibret against Hombré and close again the front of encirclement around Bastogne. But the Corps did not believe that the brigade could reach Sibret by the morning of 27 December. After the option of the Corps, a further thrust in the direction of the Meuse was no longer possible, neither at the present time nor later. It had to be reckoned with heavy *matériel* losses of the 2nd Panzer Division at Coustinne. Also, the long left flank which was screened by the Panzer Lehr Division was threatened by the enemy. An enemy attack was made near Moircy.

KOKOTT: The rear cover of the Bastogne encirclement ring was split in the southwest. Officer reconnaissance troops found out in the evening hours of the 26th that not a single man of the 5th Paratroopers stood between Salvacourt and Sibret anymore.

The Fusilier Regiment 39 had immediately closed the breakthrough spot behind the first small group of enemy tanks that slipped through, but it was obvious to them that they could not resist in the long run enemy pressure coming from both north and south around Assenois. The division was no longer able to help with its own resources. It had long since done more than one could demand. Now, not by any stretch of the imagination, were there more forces to be made available that could have been used to reinforce the Assenois sector, let alone to attack the enemy who was pouring in through the corridor to Bastogne. Moreover, one had to expect that the enemy in Bastogne after the unification – now encouraged and strengthened – would try on their own initiative to thrust in the direction of the approaching tank forces to widen the corridor and to break the encirclement in the south. It was probably only a matter of time then when the enemy would make a large-scale push to the north and northeast from Bastogne.

On the German side the shortage of forces was everywhere. In the north there was almost nothing, in the northeast a single regiment (Grenadier 78) guarded the front line in a wide arc from Recogne up to the road Bastogne–Bra.

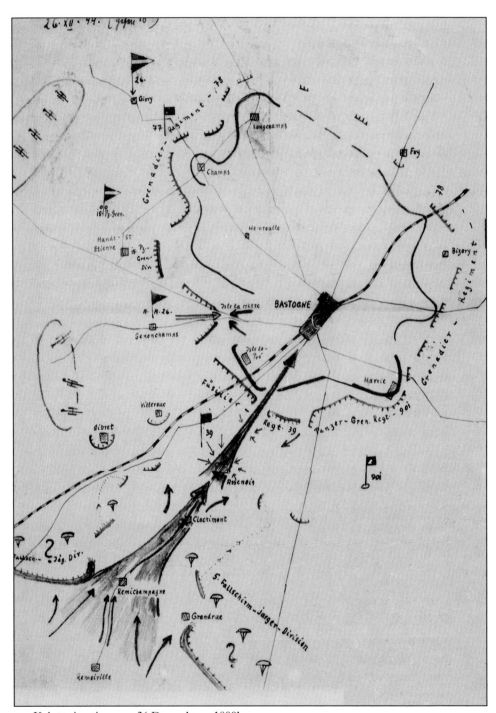

Kokott situation map 26 December – 1800hrs.

In the south stood the hard-stricken regiments 901 and 39, fighting in two directions. In the west (except for the *Aufklärungsabteilung* 26) were the remnants of the 15th Panzergrenadier Division and the Regiment 77, which were annihilated during the attack of the 25th except for a few scattered groups. That was all for the time being.

The 26th Division, which had been under constant attack and in the hardest battles for eleven days, was hardly strong enough to successfully defend a powerful enemy attack. From nowhere in the front line could even a single man with a weapon be recruited, to perhaps enforce one single spot. The bow was overdrawn. On the evening of the 26th the division reported the situation to the Corps including the resulting suspected consequences. The Corps couldn't help either. They had nothing at their disposal. The situation with the 2nd Panzer Division and the Panzer Lehr Division – far away from Bastogne – had worsened. The offensive thrust of the Sixth SS Panzerarmee – formed for political reasons only – had failed completely. The corps ordered for the 27 December to hold the current positions around Bastogne. A succession of enemy forces and an expansion of the Assenois corridor should be prevented until the Führer Begleit Brigade arrives during the 27th. It was intended to use the Führer Begleit Brigade to repulse the 4th American tank division, which was attacking from the south. More reinforcements are on their way to 'finally clean up' the situation in Bastogne.

Eventually the Army and the Corps would have given different orders and acted differently if they had the power to do so. But Field Marshal Model was in command! And he gave orders following the instructions of the man who had centralized the highest political and military power in himself!

On the 26th with the breakthrough of the 4th American Tank Division to the 101st American Airborne Division, the first part of the Battle of Bastogne ended. It was one of the toughest and most bitter battles of this Second World War. Soldiers of the finest quality had faced each other. They fought without hatred, strong and powerful, loyal in their duty, all for their country, believing that their cause was right!

SCHRAMM: It did not surprise the Army in the least when it learned that American Armoured Divisions had succeeded on 26 December in breaking through the defensive front of 5 A/B Division and the encircling ring of 26th Volksgrenadier Division (Fifth Panzer Army) to establish contact with the troops in Bastogne. All attempts to restore the position by closing the front again behind the enemy forces which had stormed through were wrecked by the *matériel* superiority and greater fire power of the Americans.

It was now painfully clear to Seventh Army that the offensive had failed. Daily the decision and order of the Supreme Command for the withdrawal to the West Wall was awaited. But instead of this, the order it did receive was that the ring around the enemy forces was to be closed again by energetic attacks from both sides and that Bastogne was to be retaken at all costs! For such a project it would first be necessary to bring up reserves for Fifth Panzer Army.

BAYERLEIN: On 27 December discussions were made with General von Lüttwitz at the division CP in Saint-Hubert. The attack towards the north over the Meuse was not continued. It was a matter of keeping what had been attained and attacking Bastogne with all forces and taking it. For this purpose, strong elements of Sepp Dietrich's Army were committed. The 901 Panzer Grenadier Regiment of the Panzer Lehr Division (reinforced by more tanks and an artillery battalion) had to remain near Bastogne and participate in the attack. Defensive fighting on the whole front. British forces appear for the first time near Tellin.

ZERBEL: 2nd Panzer Division:
At 0100 hours the division reached the bridgehead at Rochefort. A great part of its *matériel* had to be left behind. The parts of the division which had made the withdrawal were extracted from the outpost line, in order to have a short rest. The other parts continued to hold the bridgehead of Rochefort.

9th Panzer Division: The position of the division in the line: Charneuse–Hargimont–St Remi-Abbey was attacked during the whole day. The enemy air activity was again very strong.

Panzer-Lehr Division: At different points the enemy tried to establish contact with the front of the division but was repulsed everywhere.

26th Volksgrenadier Division: Sibret is lost.

Führer Begleitet Brigade: In the morning of the 27 December the Führer Begleit Brigade had arrived at Bois-de-Hebraimont. As Sibret was lost during the night, an advance during daytime out of the forest towards the south was impossible.

At the beginning of the night the situation of the Corps was as follows: The most important problem for the Corps was to close again the encirclement at

Sibret by making attacks. The situation of the other fronts at that moment was less worrying.

REMER: On 27 December 44, we moved south of Champlin on the main road toward Bastogne with the intention of attacking and taking the town of Sibret. Before we could arrive at Sibret, however, the town was occupied by American forces. Consequently, my plans were changed and instead we built up a flak line north of Sibret in case the American tanks attempted to move north. At this time, our tanks and armoured cars were on both sides of the Marche–Bastogne road in Bois-de-Hebraimont, where they were forced to take shelter because of the American Air Force.

METZ: During 27 December the opponent even succeeded to widen the gap by the capture of Sibret. There was a growing danger that the gap in the ring around Bastogne would widen still further until it would finally split open and the opponent would break through advancing from Bastogne towards Houffalize. It endangered the entire army situation.

During these days the main point of gravity of the army was concentrated at Bastogne, even if enemy pressure increased at the Ardennes front line and the enemy artillery fire became intensified. It became now very important to prevent a further widening of the gap by the enemy near Sibret and in general to re-establish the encirclement of the city and to eliminate the danger which threatened the Ardennes front from the flank and the rear area from Bastogne and its surrounding area.

For this reason on the 27 or 28 of December the A.O.K. moved its command post – which had already been advanced to Larouche on 25 December – further to the rear to Montleban, 8km northwest of Houffalize. The now commencing battles and the immediate counter measures taken by the German command changed so rapidly and were so eventful, that it is impossible for me to give a satisfactory description from memory.

For a firm unified command against Bastogne, Corps Headquarters of XXXXVII. Armoured Corps, which till now had retained responsibility for the Bastogne front, was released from the Ardennes and solely charged with command before Bastogne. The command post of the Corps was Engreux, 13km north of Bastogne.

The artillery command before Bastogne was consequently taken over by the artillery commander of the XXXVII. Armoured Corps, Corps Artillery Commander 447. Numerous new, but not combat-fresh, troops, (except 167th Volksgrenadier Division that had been released from other battle fronts and was moved up in greatest haste) were committed in the last days of December and early days of January in order to restore the situation before Bastogne.

At this time enemy artillery started also to fire with gradually increasing frequency and power at traffic roads and traffic networks further in the rear. Against daily increasing enemy pressure on all fronts around Bastogne and in the Ardennes, one had to be satisfied from now on to hold one's position.

KOKOTT: On 27 December the second phase of the battle for Bastogne begins – on the part of the military/political leadership there were several attempts (mostly with inadequate means and forces) to get at least a modest political prestigious gain from the 'Battle of the Bulge'. What a high waste of power and trust was used for this small-minded thinking. In which form and according to which principles, points of view and considerations this battle was handled.

KRAEMER: Around the end of the year, 12th SS Panzer Division was also ordered to the Bastogne area, and at that time we went completely on the defensive.

BAYERLEIN: 28-29 December. Defensive fighting. Main point near Remagen and Moircy where CC of 902 was committed. (901 all the time still held back near Bastogne.)

US FORCES: The relief of Bastogne signalled the defeat of the German Army in the Ardennes offensive. But it had cost the 4th Armoured Division a price comparable to that exacted from the defenders of Bastogne themselves. In the seven days during which its forces were moving to the relief of Bastogne the division lost about 1,000 men. Its total medium tank strength at the end of the period was equal to the full tank strength of a single battalion.

As for what this victory – won by the defenders of Bastogne and confirmed by the force that relieved them – availed the Allied cause, and as to how it influenced the emergency of December 1944, there is an official estimate from the command of 12th Army Group.

The US After Action Report for December 1944 stated:

'Preoccupation with the key position of Bastogne dominated enemy strategy to such an extent that it cost them the advantage of the initiative. The German

High Command evidently considered further extension to the west or north as both logistically and strategically unsound without possession of Bastogne, as that town overlooks the main roads and concentration areas of the spearheads. By the end of the month, the all-out effort in the north had become temporarily defensive; in the west there was a limited withdrawal, and the array of German forces around Bastogne clearly exposed the enemy's anxiety over that position. Until the Bastogne situation is resolved one way or the other no change in strategy can be expected.'

How well those words were sustained by the further passage of events is now history.

Chapter 11

German Commanders Assess
the Reasons for Failure

Author: The following are the thoughts and comments of the same combat leaders with regard to the whole mission in retrospect. It is pretty obvious that they considered the entire offensive to have been a catastrophic failure and a huge loss of life – and that the continuance of the Bastogne part of the offensive became about prestige rather than objectives.

The lack of proper equipment and clothing for their men and the predicted lack of fuel added to the problems that they had to deal with on a daily basis. It is worth noting that officers at the very start of this book – during the preparation stages – were frightened to speak out for fear of being called defeatist.

It is unlikely that these men would have been so forthright right after the battle for the same reasons... but with the capitulation of the Reich they could speak freely about the errors made by their superiors.

WAGENER: The battle for Bastogne, which covered the next few weeks, was to become a costly consequence of our unsuccessful offensive. Bastogne was to be taken at any cost, according to the original operation plan of the highest authorities. The Fifth Panzer Army had not considered this impossible, figuring that it would have to be taken from the front. The Army thought it of decisive importance, to be brought to a stop by nothing whatsoever on the eastern bank of the Maas, and to push forward with all its might towards its principal goal – the Maas.

After the losses of the past days, this became of double importance. Bastogne was no longer to be the sole aim of the attack, but the Maas, and the Maas only!

Bastogne had never been the supposition of the operational aim anyway and the fact that the enemy had maintained his hold on the city was not the sole reason that the offensive had failed. Now, after the offensive had failed, Bastogne became the centre of very hard battles, for the Fifth Panzer Army, which employed all available power against it. The Army was continually supported by the bringing up of new divisions which were committed, one after the other in the area of Bastogne.

The Army could not understand these measures. Since 18 December it had pleaded for more forces in order to enable it to push toward the Maas with more force. Now that the offensive had been a failure, and the attack toward the Maas was abandoned, it was the Army's opinion that Bastogne could be of no vital importance. The attempt to take this city could be nothing other than a question of prestige. Nothing of decisive importance could be achieved. The operational failure of the offensive was not made less painful by the fact that it appeared that logical thinking was being abandoned, making believe that we were still free to move as we liked by attacking Bastogne in this manner. The troops may have thought the same thing and perhaps that was also the reason that the repeated attacks, which were launched with an adequate number of troops, gained nothing.

The first attacks against the city were made by the XLVII Panzer Corps on 19 and 20 December. The 26th Volksgrenadier Division had been attacking in the Bastogne sector up to 25 December and, in spite of heavy losses, had tightened its encirclement. It had failed to take Bastogne. The enemy was so well emplaced and was supported so efficiently by his Air Force that our own weak units were not sufficient to carry the strongpoint. Actually, the Army had never expected this anyway.

In addition to the 15th and 3rd Panzer Divisions the Führer Begleit Brigade, Army's 12th SS Panzer Division, was now committed in the Bastogne sector. The army CP was transferred to Laroche, as planned.

The situation of the LVIII Panzer Corps remained unchanged. After asking permission of the *Heeresgruppe*, the withdrawal of the sorely pressed 2nd Panzer Division to Rochefort was granted. The XLVII Panzer Corps now stood on the line south of Marche–Rochefort–Saint-Hubert–Bastogne. The Panzer Lehr Division reported the first attacks by the enemy against its front on the south, near Moircy. The expected development of affairs near Bastogne started about 1600 hours, enemy tanks succeeded in penetrating the city by way of Assenois. The encirclement had thus been broken.

The *Heeresgruppe* consequently sent more forces to Bastogne – 1st SS Panzer Division, headquarters XXXIX Panzer Corps, Führer Grenadier Brigade, HQ 1st SS Panzer Corps, 9th SS Panzer Division and later the 340th Volksgrenadier Division. The 5th Paratroop Division on the right wing of the Seventh Army was also subordinated to the Fifth Army, which at the same time caused a change in the Army borders. Gradually nine large forces and two corps headquarters had surrounded the city of Bastogne, with which the hole in the siege was to be again closed, so that Bastogne itself could be taken. In other words, this was a real massing of forces, which had seemed impossible while the actual offensive towards the Maas was still going. The units, however, were all brought up to full strength and most of them consisted of mixed combat groups. Army headquarters shifted back to Montleban.

The further course of events from 27 December to 8 January.

The times of arrival of reinforcements for the Army:

The 15th Panzer Division on 24 December.
The 12 SS Panzer Division on 25 December.
The Führer Grenadier Brigade on 27 December.
The 1st SS Panzer Division on 27 December.
HQ of the 1st SS Panzer Corps 27 December.
The 9th SS Panzer Division on 3 January.
The 340th Volksgrenadier Division on 6 January.

The general situation did not change during the next few days, except defensive battles in which the LVIII and XLVII Panzer Corps were engaged, as well as fruitless attacks by the Führer Begleit Brigade, the 12th SS and 1st SS Panzer Divisions aimed at a new encirclement of the city. The enemy had captured Sibret there and had been able to gain more successes south of the city. The arrival of our new units, however, gradually strengthened our own front more and more around Bastogne so that the enemy was prevented from making more gains, both from the south as well as from the city itself.

It was the plan of the Army to attack westward from the region of Lutrebois with a combat group under XXXIX Panzer Corps and with another under XXXXVII Panzer Corps to attack south-east from Chenogne for the purpose of closing the ring around Bastogne again near Assenois. The XXXIX Panzer Corps was temporarily assigned to the XLVII Panzer Corps for this purpose. The attack was to start on 30 December.

WAGENER: It is not possible to give from memory a more detailed account of the events which occurred during the next few days. The LVIII Panzer Corps maintained its position adjoining the Sixth Panzer Army. The western front of the XLVII Panzer Corps was gradually pulled back, voluntarily however, the southern front of the Corps was being pressed backwards more and more by the enemy attacks which were steadily increasing in strength.

The XXXIX Panzer Corps soon had to be withdrawn and sent back to the *Heeresgruppe* B, where a new offensive was being planned against enemy sectors which were exposed. The attack on 30 December to close the Group south of Bastogne was a failure. Another attack was launched a few days later and likewise failed. The same was the case with attacks starting on 1 January of the 9th and 12th SS Panzer Divisions, under the command of the 1st SS Corps. These were launched against Bastogne from the north, and after at first achieving minor gains, broke down under enemy fire and came to a standstill. In Bastogne the enemy became more active, encouraged by our failures. They succeeded in hard fighting on the south to widen his breach in our envelopment, which was finally reduced to a semicircle about the northern half of the city.

An order was issued on 8 January, for a general retreat to the line of La Roche–Bastogne, shifting the boundary line of the Sixth Panzer Army simultaneously, to the line Marche–La Roche–Houffalize–Prüm. This operational phase also ended as a failure. Bastogne had not been taken. The results that the conquest of Bastogne at this time, might have had, could not be overlooked by the Army. Probably nothing more than a short respite would have been gained. Doubtless large enemy forces would have been tied down thereby. Our own losses around Bastogne were considerable.

The retreat back to the point of departure was from 9 to 20 January. Even before Christmas our own forces on the left wing of the Seventh Army had to be withdrawn to the West Wall and the whole army front had to be drawn back behind Wiltz and Sauer following reverses on the right flank. After this from early January, enemy attacks of ever-increasing intensity gained ground against the defensive front of Sixth Panzer Army, on the western and southern front of XXXVII Panzer Corps and in the Bastogne sector. When it became apparent that Bastogne could not be taken, despite our mass of forces around it, the German command decided on 7 January to withdraw the entire front back to the point of departure, with the aim of pinning down even more the enemy elements which had been tied down all the while, and by setting up a coherent front, to prevent the enemy from breaking through anywhere.

Even though the fruitless attacks against Bastogne had cost us very heavy losses, nevertheless the decision to retreat came at a time when it could be carried out undisturbed by the enemy. The retreat movements were executed under difficult terrain and weather conditions which again resulted in serous losses in weapons, motor vehicles, and equipment, so that all the divisions in the West Wall were committed as weak combat groups. Nevertheless, the German command controlled the speed of withdrawal up to the last minute. It would also be possible that all the SS formations would be withdrawn according to plan.

SCHRAMM: The next few days brought with them a further worsening of conditions in the breakthrough area. The counterattack made against Bastogne led to no success of great proportion; on the contrary the enemy succeeded in so broadening the original pipe-like entrance to the road crossing that our chance of once again closing it off finally disappeared. The front thus originating in the south and southwest of Bastogne was exposed to strong attacks and had to be withdrawn more and more. Consequently, the situation on the south front was not only unsatisfactory, but gave rise now to serious concern.

At the same time the enemy attacked from the north and the northwest; attaining slow but steady successes against Sixth Panzer Army, so that the situation at the point of the attack wedge was untenable in the long run. A new Führer directive released on 8 January, drew the conclusions: it approved the withdrawal of the front to the line.

Estimates of losses Army Group B:

102 Assault guns
77 Mark IV Tanks
132 Mark V Tanks
13 Mark VI Tanks

324 – total assault guns and tanks

METZ: At the beginning of January the development of the total situation around Bastogne in the Ardennes, in the adjacent armies to the right and left, on the remaining German fronts and especially of the entire German supply situation, were the main reasons for the decision to abandon the attacking and the withdrawal to an essentially shorter front line.

Furthermore, the encirclement, or rather the presently existing envelopment of Bastogne, had to be given up and the elements holding the western edge of the Ardennes had to be gradually withdrawn and were moved to the area north of Bastogne. Beginning with 8 January 1945, withdrawal from the Ardennes front took place by sectors. As far as I remember, the withdrawal from the Bastogne front brought no extraordinary tactical difficulties. Nevertheless, due to the shortening of the front, necessary marching and evacuation movement were at some places very much impeded because of icy roads and long, deep snowdrifts. Weather difficulties arose, similar to those we experienced at the Russian theatre of war. The number of worn-out vehicles that had to be finally discarded increased considerably.

The approach, concentration, moving into position and the battles to break through the enemy position took place in the central mountain area.

There resulted a considerably increased expenditure of physical strength of man and horse, of fuel for all motorised vehicles and great technical wear and tear of all driven weapons and vehicles. The horses that had for many years been underfed, lacked the necessary strength for such expectations and in the first days of the attack and still within range of their own front many a horse perished.

Even the number of highways, although in the West Wall rear area, was not sufficient for troop movements on a large scale; these highways were often narrow, angular and steeply descending village streets instead of detouring roads. Two-way traffic was impossible and there was a lack of personnel equipped with mobile signalling devices.

These terrain difficulties were very much increased by the weather he had hoped to use to his advantage. Ice and snow were on the roads, against which nothing could be done because civilian personnel or manpower from the troops was lacking, and there also existed no snow fences and snow clearing equipment. During the night of 24/25 December, it became severely cold and a few days later it started to snow heavily. During the assembly period it alternatively snowed and rained. On the first and second day of the attack there was fog and driving rain and the ground was consequently soft. The weather greatly harmed the physical and moral strength of the forces. Drenched by the rain and wet ground while marching and fighting, lying at night out in the open and exposed to all sorts of weather (the wind and the cold of the night), the forces sought cover and protection from the enemy. An orderly supply of food did not always succeed in reaching them.

During Christmas night a heavy frost set in; then came a period of intense cold with heavy snowfall, which moreover made the visibility of targets easier for the enemy. Camouflaging suits were not always available. Therefore, terrain and weather injured the strength of the forces enormously. At times an increase in sick calls was unavoidable, even though the forces conscientiously and with iron will tried to overcome all these mishaps and difficulties. The rapidly increasing breakdown of weapons and vehicles towards the end of the Ardennes operation is, next to the influences of weather and terrain, to be attributed to the wear and tear of many years of war in the most widely differing theatres of operation.

The failure to capture Bastogne: The two-days fighting in the unexpectedly deep main defensive area of the American position before the West Wall cost the XXXXVII Armoured Corps precious time, which was taken advantage of by the enemy to push the 101st Airborne Division forwards to Bastogne (this became known on 20 December by prisoners of war of this division). Again, the fighting around Bastogne (near Noville and on the south front) cost the Corps time and strength, which caused it to reach the area eastward of the Maas late and not strong enough for a push forward; moreover, it was held up because of the non-arrival of fuel and consequently delayed arrival of the 9th Armoured Division.

The part of the Luftwaffe: The operation of the Allied Air Force had a decisive effect. Supported by an apparently excellently working weather service, which enabled it to attack after reconnaissance of the weather situation in the shortest possible time, also involving the most restricted area, it had been smashing up the railroads leading to the front and villages located in the rear areas. Even far in the rear many a traffic jam and heavy damage to the supply situation resulted. In the front area the Allied Air Force caused the greatest hardship and damage to the supply and the entire traffic. Finally, with excellent flying weather beginning with 21 December, these services were practically entirely paralysed.

Our own supply-situation: After the end of the preparations for the attack, assurance of a steady supply was given to us. In my opinion the deciding factor in the failure of supply was the Allied Air Force, which dominated and disrupted railroads and roads deep into Germany, destroying great quantities of supplies while being transported in depots and in production centres.

The speed of the American countermeasures: I do not believe that such quick American reaction had been anticipated. It was indicated by the speed in moving the 101st Airborne Division to Bastogne and in the quick, combat-ready assembly of so many divisions opposite the western edge of the Ardennes. The speed of the countermeasures of the American Army is probably due to a well-organised radio-network with highly developed command-radio traffic and primarily to the motor.

Next to the Air Force the motor is the factor which contributed to the victory by the American Army. With the help of the motor, the forces could quickly reach the enemy, especially the infantry which was fast, strong in numbers and fighting strength and physically fresh; moreover, the infantry could be moved quickly and combat-ready covering great distances.

The main cause of the failure of the offensive: Reviewing the course of events and the effect of the aggravating and hampering factors, one comes to the conclusion that on the German side a great undertaking had been attempted with insufficient means as to the personnel and *matériel*, and that moreover the completeness and thoroughness of the preparatory plans had been located in the highest places.

SCHRAMM: Enemy losses, as well as our own, in the period of 16 to 31 December 1944.

1. From 16–31 December Army Group B lost –

assault guns	102
Mark IV	77
Mark V	132
Mark VI	13
total assault guns and tanks	**324**

2. Losses in enemy aircraft in the *Bodenplatte* Operation of 1 Jan 1945 are presented in the text above, also

3. Enemy losses, as well as our own, in the period 16 December 44 to 25 January 45.

Enemy
Dead and wounded (estimated):
about 100,000
Prisoners: 26,430

126,430

Our Own
Dead: 12,652
Wounded: 38,600
Missing: 30,582

81,834 (according to another account: 98,024)

4. Enemy casualties in tanks etc:

	Loot	Destroyed
Tanks & assault guns	91	1,242
Armoured Rcn cars	65	220
Guns, AT, AA	193	225
Airplanes & gliders	22	125

The enemy's losses mean loss in combat effectiveness of at least ten divisions, reinforced by army troops.

Lüttwitz XLVII Pz Corps: The fact that Bastogne could not be captured, was one of the main reasons for the failure of the offensive. Had we succeeded in taking Bastogne, which would have been possible on 18 December, the 2nd Panzer Division and the Panzer Lehr Division would have reached the Maas at the latest on 22 December, maybe even would have crossed it. In that case it would have been possible to bring up immediately the 9th Panzer

Division and the 2nd and 15th Panzer Grenadier Division, and to reinforce the spearheads or to protect part of the left flank of the army. In this case the attack of Patton's army would not have been launched against Bastogne, but northwest of the Maas.

However, with clear weather prevailing since 24 December, the enemy Air Force would have stopped in any case any further movement, and from that day, in spite of the rapid capture of Bastogne, the operation could no more have been a success. Against such an air superiority it would never have been possible, even with the double the amount of divisions and the bravest troops to accomplish this mission.

Generalmajor Rudolph Freiherr von Gersdorff – 7th Army: The Ardennes offensive was Hitler's last effort to obtain a decisive decision in directing the war's course. Had his intentions been successful in cutting decisively the Anglo-American invasion armies apart he believed himself able to bring the Russian general offensive to a standstill by quickly re-shuffling strong units from the west to east, and thus win more valuable time for further developments. Hitler hoped the time eventually had come when political differences among the Allied Western Powers were now weakened by offensive action. Further, he hoped to gain enough time to bring out his 'wonder weapons', atomic energy, V-weapons, and increased submarine warfare; he hoped to employ them simultaneously with the utmost effect.

Hitler set his whole hope on this one card and gambled everything he had. Germany's very last reserves, which could be scraped together, were used for this act. Therefore, a failure of Hitler's plan had to result in an unavoidable catastrophe for the whole German war effort and in all theatres of operations.

If the German High Command had realised the failure of the Ardennes offensive before Christmas, they would have at that time ordered a quick withdrawal to the West Wall and would have undertaken large scale reorganisations; then, there might have been a possibility in obtaining an effective resistance for the defence of Germany's frontiers in the east and west. But their stubborn holding to offensive intentions and the grinding down of the strength of the units during the battle for Bastogne, left German units bleeding mortally, more and more. Then the heavy losses of personnel and *matériel* made itself felt, especially that resulting from the ever-increasing Allied airforces and shortage of fuel.

This added to the fact that when German units crossed the German frontier Germany was nothing more than a heap of ruins. Divisions could be identified as being only small or weak combat groups.

von Rundstedt: The loss of Bastogne was of the greatest importance. Bastogne should have been reached by Fifth Panzer Army on the first day of the offensive. This Army, however, bypassed Bastogne on the north and south several days later with many divisions. Bastogne should have been occupied by the divisions of the second wave (11th Panzer Division and 17th SS Panzer Grenadier Division), but these, OKW did not send.

While the Allies continually reinforced their troops, supplied them, and closed in Bastogne from the air, our own Luftwaffe was unable to cooperate with the urgently requested bombardment of Bastogne.

St Vith was captured 24 hours later than anticipated in the plan of the offensive. This delay influenced operations, especially as it resulted in Fifth Panzer Army's left wing becoming more exposed than before. The Sixth Panzer Army, unlike Fifth Panzer Army, was never up to full strength, and was unable to advance to its points of attack. This, therefore, hampered other corps which were held up on the roads of communication.

The Allied counter movements were made more quickly than expected by OKW, with the reasons being the high mobility of the enemy forces (which had abundant fuel at their disposal), the excellent road, and their absolute domination of the air.

Reasons for the failure of the Ardennes Offensive in order of priority
A. The failure to take St Vith in time, before the construction of a strong line of defence by the Allies on the north flank of the breach point.
B. The good flying weather on and about 24 December which enabled the Allies to fully exploit their superiority in the air.
C. The failure to take Bastogne.
D. The failure to capture large Allied stocks of fuel and war *matériel*.
E. The ability of the Allied High Command to rush reinforcements to threatened positions.

Generalmajor (Waffen-SS) Fritz Kraemer:

Reasons for the failure of the attack
The length of the war had reduced the standard of our individual soldier and our leadership. Terrain difficulties were encountered which, in conjunction with the poor state of driver training, led to difficulties; often, mistakes of the drivers delayed entire columns for hours.

Generalmajor Otto Ernst Remer – Führer Begleit Brigade: During the entire Ardennes Offensive, our tanks destroyed an estimated 178 American tanks. We lost 17-18 tanks and assault guns through enemy fire and an additional 18-19 tanks and assault guns through mechanical and technical difficulties. Our personnel losses during the campaign ran at approximately 2,000 men, and, at the end of the operation, we had only the strength of a regiment.

Deitrich: Casualties for the whole operation: I lost 37,000 men killed, wounded and frozen, and from 350-400 tanks. The whole attack was a big mistake. To use those two armies at that time of the year was the biggest mistake they made in the war.

I am one of the oldest tank men in the Army and having been in tanks in 1916-17. If I had been asked, I would have been against that terrain with swampy territory and few roads. The Ardennes was the worst terrain imaginable for a thousand tanks. Only four to five of them could fight at one time because there was no place to deploy. A big tank attack in this terrain is impossible. In the Ardennes, we could develop nothing.

Jodl: Of course, if we had not sent all these divisions for the offensive, but instead, had waited for you to attack, we could have kept them at home and on 12 January 45 used them to meet the Russian offensive. Had the offensive not been made in the west, naturally, the Russians would not have advanced so rapidly.

Three of the four newly-formed divisions were sent to the East, at the urgent plea of Genobst Guderian. In the East we had shorter interior lines than in the west, and communication zone units could be moved more easily to the Eastern Front. We felt, however, that a large-scale victory in the East was now impossible.

Italy offered more hope for an offensive, but the railroad connections were much worse than in the west. Allied aerial reconnaissance would have eliminated any chance for surprise, because planes would have observed the long marches. The west was the only place in Europe where we had a chance of success.

Manteuffel: After 25 December 44, superiority of the Allied Air Force made movement on the battlefield impossible. We had no means of anti-aircraft defence to speak of. In my opinion, the failure of the operation was due to the following reasons:

Incorrect commitment of Sixth Panzer Army, which had unqualified commanders, and whose units did not fight with the same sorority as the other units of the army. Fifth Panzer Army attacked on a wide front with three corps and six divisions committed to the assault wave. These units formed assault companies which were specially trained and equipped.

The completely insufficient fuel supply was another reason for the attack's failure. Based on experiences gained in the Russian winter campaign, I had requested enough fuel for 500km normally, which, because of the terrain of the Ardennes and the additional difficulties of the weather, would have been sufficient for 250kms only. However, the Army received only enough fuel for 150kms.

From the very beginning, the number of reserves and replacements was insufficient. Sixth Panzer Army received two divisions; Fifth Panzer and Seventh Armies received three divisions less than was planned.

Schramm: Genfldm Keitel was the man who was responsible for the quantities of POL (petrol and oil), which were made available to Army Group for the offensive, as well as for its procurement, transportation and storage. As C-of-S of OKW he had always been responsible for the distribution of POL.

The calculations, which had been made in connection with the first draft, showed an estimated consumption of approximately 17,000 cubic metres, the C-of-S of OKW was able to simultaneously report that, in spite of the intervening further deterioration of the POL production, it would be possible to raise the OKW reserves to the desired level by the time the attack was to start. It had occasionally been mentioned during the discussions of this problem that the capture of enemy POL stocks was to be expected; this factor had been of considerable importance during the campaign in the West and in Africa. But this uncertain factor was not being considered for the evaluations.

It was attempted to cut down the daily consumption of the entire Western Front to 500 cubic metres in order to increase the OKW reserves. But this proved to be impossible because the extension of the damage to the railroad network necessitated an increase in the consumption of POL.

Genfldm Keitel received some very urgent requests to release POL stocks because the prevailing shortage was expected to have the most serious consequences. The C-of-S of OKW granted these requests only very slowly, and then only for the smallest possible quantities which amounted to only a few thousand cubic metres. Thus, it was after all possible to accumulate the 17000 cubic metres which had been promised in the beginning.

The problem, which overshadowed the offensive even before its start, was therefore not really the shortage of POL, but the timely delivery from the dumps of the units.

Bayerlein: I did not rely on captured fuel – but did hope to get some, especially in Bastogne, Saint-Hubert and Rochefort. Booty during the whole offensive was so small as to be near vanishing point. We only captured a few trucks of fuel and got some fuel by draining the tanks of captured or damaged or destroyed tanks and trucks. e.g, near Longvilly, (east of Bastogne).

Other booty:
A. Near Mageret and Longvilly. 14 armoured cars, 23 Sherman tanks, 15 SP guns, 30 jeeps, 25 trucks (all undamaged).
B. Near Gerimont and Tillet (east of Saint-Hubert) 53 trucks and 15 jeeps (all undamaged).
C. In Rochefort 15 jeeps, 18 trucks (all undamaged).
D. North of Saint-Hubert: American and German ammunition, especially 105mm, in great quantities. This ammunition was used near Saint-Hubert and Rochefort and in view of the difficult supply situation was a great help.
E. In all the division captured undamaged and put to use some 120 jeeps and more than 150 trucks.

Looking back at the battle for Bastogne during the days 19-21 December. The forces of the three divisions employed at Bastogne were scattered instead of being used combined for the attack on Bastogne, together with the combined parts of the 47 Panzer Corps. After the so–called 'bold stroke' (the capture by surprise) had failed, because the German forces arrived late, e.g. after considerable US forces were concentrated there, a combined attack would have been more important and certainly would have been successful. Especially it was a big mistake, that on 21 December the 2nd Panzer Division was not employed for the attack on Bastogne via Foy, where there was hardly any enemy.

Another big mistake was the scattered commitment of Panzer Lehr before Bastogne, after the division had been uselessly employed and scattered, in the first days of the offensive. Another mistake was to keep during the 20 and 21 December, the mobile forces of Panzer Lehr in the stable front before Bastogne (Neffe, Marvie, Remoifosse) and to have the movable, slower parts of 26th Volksgrenadier Division march for the all–embracing attack into the area west of Bastogne. All this worked together, so that a full-scale attack on Bastogne was never able to be carried out.

Reasons for the failure of the offensive

A) Improper engagement of forces: The left (enveloping) wing should have been stronger than the right. The strength of the enemy was on the right (Aachen and further south) and there he had mobile reserves ready for counter blows. One should have been strongest where the enemy was weak. Also, the German command withheld reserves which could have been committed during the battle at points where progress was being made.

B) Insufficient forces for a far-reaching operation (Meuse and then Antwerp). The forces did not suffice even for an advance to the Meuse.

C) Not sufficient forces to protect the long southern flank (Western flank). The worst division in the Army Group, the Fifth Parachute Division was committed for this.

D) Commitment of worn out and badly equipped divisions.

E) Slipshod preparation, especially in supplies, which were insufficient and based in part on the hope of booty.

F) Poor approach march and jumping-off group. The difficult roads were an unfavourable circumstance for the combat troops and for the supply echelons. In good flying weather, the narrow passes were catastrophic for the supply of the troops in the Eifel and North Luxembourg. Hence, few tanks could be committed and the attacks and defence could not be supported with sufficient ammunition.

G) The artillery preparation of the first attack was wasted over the Our since the troops were too far away and could not exploit the advantage. Hence delays occurred through resistance on the road St Vith–Diekirck and from Clerf sector. The result of these delays was that we did not get to Bastogne in time to take it by a sudden coup.

H) Bastogne. It was one of the greatest mistakes at Bastogne that, on failure of the coup it was not immediately captured by a concentrated attack of all our forces. If this had been done it would certainly have fallen.

Leaving this key point to the enemy resulted in a too narrow base for the attack on the Maas. Bastogne absorbed and later tied down so many troops that the offensive could not be continued. If Bastogne were relieved the enemy would have a base for an attack to cut off the front part of the German salient.

I was sceptical from the beginning and felt that this offensive, with its advanced aims could not succeed. I am not being wise after the event but confided this view of mine at the time to my chief of staff and other trusted persons, but not to my subordinate commanders since I did not want to deflate their aggressive spirit. I tried to persuade myself that the attack would succeed, so as to give my orders and measures the necessary force although I was really convinced that the offensive would fail. I considered the offensive as the last gasp of the collapsing Wehrmacht and the supreme command before its end, which I had foreseen as early as December 1942 after the US landing in North Africa. So if at any time at all this offensive could be undertaken this was it.

As far as the intrinsic form of the offensive itself was concerned it was clear to me on 25 December that it was over, after the Sixth SS Panzer Army, in spite of its excellent equipment, was making no more gains. The attacks of the 116th and 9th Panzer Divisions fell wasted, the bulk of the 2nd Panzer Division was surrounded and annihilated. Finally, my own attacks failed at Buissonville and Humain. Bastogne not being captured, the strong threat to the German southern flank by the American Third Army became apparent.

Actually, already on 25 December it was clear we should have to retreat, as no further German forces came up. After the attack on Bastogne again failed and the junction of the garrison with the American Third Army was affected, then the base line for the Fifth and Sixth German Armies was too small and the corridor to the units fighting much farther west too narrow. The danger of being cut off was only a question of time. To hold this salient any longer would have been madness. Then think of the effect of the enemy Air Force on the narrow corridor and the endangering of the supply lines on the few narrow roads. Every day that the troops waited and continued to hold the salient meant further losses in men and *matériel* which were disproportionate to the operational significance of the bulge for the German command.

This value lay in the tying up of strong enemy forces and preventing their making an attack on other points on the Western Front (OKW later gave me this motive as the real sense and object of the Ardennes offensive as if they had never really meant to reach Antwerp – but only to tie down enemy forces and prevent attacks in the Saar and near Aachen).

The first surprise for the Germans was the prompt occupation and strong defence of Bastogne and the brave determination of the US 101st Airborne. Also important was the quick movement of armoured forces in the area east of Bastogne for an aggressive defensive against the German attack.

The second surprise was the rapid turning of the American Third Army against the German southern flank. Already on 21 December the situation on each flank was such that the roads for an advance near Moircy and Remichampagne towards Saint-Hubert could be utilised only under fire of enemy tanks or armoured cars. It was already one of the main issues in the preparatory discussions and the rehearsal of the attack, whether Bastogne must definitely be captured at all or not, whether by a coup, or, if this did not succeed, by a full-dress attack. (They settled in favour of the coup).

When the coup failed on 17/18 December, the question was renewed, whether it must be systematically attacked or whether we could march ahead past it and merely keep watch on it. My view was then – attack with a concentration of all available forces of the XLVII Corps. We did not do this, however, the separate attacks were ordered. One part of the troops were to attack and another part push on toward the West. Through this decision no adequate attack was made. Then we tried to do it by appealing to the garrison to capitulate, the text being composed by Manteuffel and Lüttwitz.

Finally, half of the Panzer Lehr was withdrawn from Bastogne and the fortress was to be taken by the already much weakened 26th Volksgrenadier Division. All the partial attacks failed. Hence, valuable time was lost, Bastogne was continually reinforced, and the relieving forces (American Third Army) came close and closer.

The quick capture of Bastogne was especially important for the following reasons:

1) The excellent road hub was indispensable for the offensive on the Meuse. Without Bastogne there was no good road, useable in winter), and that road was also seldom useable as a result of the continual air raids and destruction).
2) Bastogne was always a thorn in the flesh of the German troops. The corridor towards the West was too narrow without Bastogne and the base for the continuation of the attack towards the west was too narrow.
3) Bastogne constituted a continual threat to the German attack. Strong forces had therefore to be left there as a screen and therefore were missed by the forces attacking toward the Meuse.
4) Should it be impossible to absorb the flank thrust of the American Third Army from the south, Bastogne, after it had been re-united with the Third Army, formed the best springboard for the American counter-offensive to cut off the German salient or to cut off the German troops towards the West.

5) Bastogne was a particularly indispensable point for German supplies, as a traffic hub and staging point, after most of Houffalize fell. A glance at the map is sufficient for someone with no military training to realise that Bastogne was vital for the offensive. The German command did not realise this or did not act according to that idea.

I do not know to what extent Belgian or Luxembourg civilians were used to get intelligence. During the offensive a Belgian gave me very good and clear – even expert information in Mageret (east of Bastogne) as to the movements and composition of a combat command of the American 9th Armoured Division.

Chapter 12

The US Bastogne Forces

Here is a brief resumé of each of the participants from the US side. The list was prepared for the US Army by Colonel S.L.A. Marshall for *BASTOGNE – The First Eight Days.*

Units, Commanders, Staff Members and members of units mentioned in this narrative.

101st AIRBORNE DIVISION
Commanding General: Major General Maxwell D. Taylor
Acting Division Commander during the first phase of Bastogne operations:
Brigadier General Anthony C. McAuliffe
Assistant Division Commander: Brigadier General Gerald J. Higgins
A. C. of S., G-1, and Acting Chief of Staff: Lt. Col. Ned D. Moore
A. C. of S., G-2: Lt. Col. Paul A. Danahy
A. C. of S., G-3: Lt. Col. H.W.O. Kinnard
A. C. of S., GA Lt. Col. Carl W. Kohls
Surgeon: Lt. Col. David Gold
Civil Affairs Officer: Captain Robert S. Smith
Aide to the Commanding General: Lt. Frederic D. Starrett
Division Artillery Commander: Col. Thomas L. Sherburne, Jr.

501ST PARACHUTE INFANTRY REGIMENT
Commanding Officer: Lt. Col. Julian J. Ewell
S-4: Major William H. Butler

1st Battalion (Companies A, B, C and HQ.)
Commanding Officer: Major Raymond V. Bottomly, Jr.

2nd Battalion (Companies D, E, F and HQ.)
Commanding Officer: Major Sammie N. Homan

3rd Battalion (Companies G, H, I and HQ.)
Commanding Officer: Lt. Col. George A Griswold

Members of this regiment who figure in the narrative:
Company A: Capt. Stanfield A. Stach; Lt. James C. Murphy; Lt. Joseph B.
  Schweiker; Sgt. Lyle B. Chamberlain; Pfc. William C. Michel
Company D: Cpl. Frank Lasik; Pvt. Manzi

502D PARACHUTE INFANTRY REGIMENT
Commanding Officer: Lt. Col. Steve A. Chappuis
Executive: Lt. Col. Patrick J. Cassidy
S-3: Capt. James J. Hatch
Surgeon: Major Douglas T. Davidson
Commander, HQ. Co.: Capt. James C. Stone

1st Battalion (Companies A, B, C and HQ.)
Commanding Officer: Major John D. Hanlon
S-2: Lt. Samuel B. Nickels, Jr.
Company A Capt. Wallace A. Swanson
Company C: Capt. George R. Cody.

2nd Battalion (Companies D, E, F and HQ.)
Commanding Officer: Lt. Col. Thomas H. Sudiffe

3rd Battalion (Companies G, H, I and HQ.)
Commanding Officer: Lt. Col. John P. Stopka

506TH PARACHUTE INFANTRY REGIMENT
Commanding Officer: Col. Robert F. Sink
S-4: Capt. Salve H. Matheson

1st Battalion (Companies A, B, C and HQ.)
Commanding Officer: Lt. Col. James L. LaPrade
Commanding Officer (after Col. LaPrade was killed in action): Major Robert
  F. Harwick
Commanding Officer (after Major Harwick was wounded in action): Lt.
  Col. Robert L. Strayer

2nd Battalion (Companies D, E, F and HQ.)
Commanding Officer: Lt. Col. Robert L. Strayer
Commanding Officer (after Col. Strayer took over 1st Battalion): Major
  Lloyd E. Patch

3rd BATTALION (Companies G, H, I and HQ.)
Commanding Officer: Major Gus M. Heilman

327TH GLIDER INFANTRY REGIMENT
Commanding Officer: Col. Joseph H. Harper
Executive: Lt. Col. Thomas J. Rouzie

1st Battalion (Companies A, B, C and HQ.)
Commanding Officer: Lt. Col. Hartford F. Salee

2nd Battalion (Companies E, F, G and HQ.)
Commanding Officer: Lt. Col. Roy L. Inman
Executive (and Commanding Officer, following the wounding of Col.
    Inman): Major R.B. Galbreaith

3rd Battalion (Companies A, B, C and HQ.)
Carried as the 3d Battalion, 327th Glider Infantry, and considered such by
    the command, this battalion was actually the 1st Battalion, 401st Glider
    Infantry, which accounts for the presence within the one regiment of two
    battalions with A–B–C letter companies. This battalion had served as the
    3d Battalion of the regiment since the Normandy landing.
Commanding Officer: Lt. Col. Ray C. Allen
Members of this regiment who figure in the narrative:
Company F: Capt. James F. Adams; Lt. Leslie E. Smith; Tech. Sgt. Oswald
    Y. Butler; Staff Sgt. Carl E. Dickinson.
Company G: Capt. Hugh Evans; Lt. Stanley A. Morrison
Company A, 3rd Battalion: Lt. Howard G. Bowles
Company B, 3rd Battalion: Capt. Robert J. McDonald; Tech. Sgt. Mike
    Campano
Company C, 3rd Battalion: Capt. Preston E. Towns

321st GLIDER FIELD ARTILLERY BATTALION
Commanding Officer: Lt. Col. Edward L. Carmichael

907th GLIDER FIELD ARTILLERY BATTALION
Commanding Officer: Lt. Col. Clarence F. Nelson

377th PARACHUTE FIELD ARTILLERY BATTALION
Commanding Officer: Lt. Col. Harry W. Elkins

463rd PARACHUTE FIELD ARTILLERY BATTALION
Commanding Officer: Lt. Col. John T. Cooper, Jr.

81st AIRBORNE ANTI-AIRCRAFT BATTALION
Commanding Officer: Lt. Col. X. B. Cox, Jr.

326th AIRBORNE ENGINEER BATTALION
Commanding Officer: Lt. Col. Hugh A. Mozley

426th AIRBORNE QUARTERMASTER COMPANY
Commanding Officer: Capt. George W. Horn

101st AIRBORNE SIGNAL COMPANY
Commanding Officer: Capt. William J. Johnson

801st AIRBORNE ORDNANCE MAINTENANCE COMPANY
Commanding Officer: Capt. John L. Patterson

326th AIRBORNE MEDICAL COMPANY
Commanding Officer: Major William E. Barfield

ATTACHED UNITS:
COMBAT COMMAND B, 10TH ARMORED DIVISION
7015th TANK DESTROYER BATTALION
755th FIELD ARTILLERY BATTALION
COMPANY C, 9th ARMORED ENGINEERS
969th FIELD ARTILLERY BATTALION
COMBAT COMMAND R (37th BATTALION), 4th ARMORED
   DIVISION

COMPOSITION AND COMMAND OF MAJOR ATTACHED UNITS
Combat Command B, 10th Armoured Division. This unit operated independently
in conjunction with the 101st Airborne Division until December 21, when it
was attached to the 101st and came under its command.
Commanding Officer: Col. William L. Roberts
Combat Command B was divided for tactical purposes into four main parts:
the units held directly under the commander, and Teams Cherry, Desobry
and O'Hara. The following units of Combat Command B were directly
under the commander:

HEADQUARTERS AND HEADQUARTERS COMPANY
3rd TANK BATTALION (LESS COMPANY C)
COMPANY C, 21st TANK BATTALION
54th ARMORED INFANTRY BATTALION (LESS COMPANIES A
   AND C)
20th ARMORED INFANTRY BATTALION (LESS COMPANY C)
COMPANY C, 609th TANK DESTROYER BATTALION (less platoons
   with teams)

COMPANY C, 55Th ARMORED ENGINEER BATTALION (less platoons with teams)

420TH ARMORED FIELD ARTILLERY BATTALION Commanding Officer: Lt. Col. Barry D. Browne

BATTERY B, 796th ANTI-AIRCRAFT BATTALION

TROOP D, 90th RECONNAISSANCE (CAVALRY) SQUADRON (less platoons with teams)

Team Cherry

Commanding Officer: Lt. Col. Henry T. Cherry (also commanding officer of 3d Tank Battalion)

3rd TANK BATTALION (LESS COMPANY B AND 2D PLATOON, COMPANY D)

COMPANY A: Lt. Edward P. Hyduke

COMPANY C, 20th ARMORED INFANTRY BATTALION: Capt. Willis F. Ryerson; Lt. Earl B. Gilligan

3rd PLATOON, COMPANY C, 55th ARMORED ENGINEER BATTALION

ONE PLATOON, COMPANY C, 609th TANK DESTROYER BATTALION

2nd PLATOON, TROOP D, 90th RECONNAISSANCE SQUADRON

Team Desobry

Commanding Officer: Major William R. Desobry (also commanding officer, 20th Armored Infantry Battalion). Major Charles L. Hustead took command after Major Desobry was wounded.

20th ARMORED INFANTRY BATTALION ((less companies A and C)

HEADQUARTERS COMPANY: Capt. Gordon Geiger; Lt. Eugene Todd

COMPANY B: Capt. Omar M. Billett

COMPANY B, 3rd TANK BATTALION

ONE PLATOON, COMPANY C, 609th TANK DESTROYER BATTALION

ONE PLATOON, COMPANY D, 3rd TANK BATTALION (LIGHT TANKS)

ONE PLATOON, COMPANY C, 55th ARMORED ENGINEER BATTALION

ONE PLATOON, COMPANY C, 609th TANK DESTROYER BATTALION

ONE PLATOON, TROOP D, 90th RECONNAISSANCE SQUADRON

Team O'Hara

Commanding Officer: Lt. Col. James O'Hara (also commanding officer of 54th Armored Infantry Battalion)

S-2: Capt. Edward A. Carrigo

54th ARMORED INFANTRY BATTALION (less companies A and C)

COMPANY B: Lt. John D. Devereaux

COMPANY C, 21st TANK BATTALION

ONE PLATOON, COMPANY C, 55th ARMORED ENGINEER BATTALION

ONE PLATOON, COMPANY D, 3rd TANK BATTALION (LIGHT TANKS): Lt. Sherwood D. Wishart

ONE PLATOON, TROOP D, 90th RECONNAISSANCE SQUADRON

FORCE CHARLIE 16: Lt. Richard C. Gilliland

705th Tank Destroyer Battalion. This unit operated independently in conjunction with the 101st Airborne Division until December 21 when it was attached to the 101st and came under its command.

Commanding Officer: Lt. Col. Clifford D. Templeton

Headquarters Company (less the battalion trains which were ordered to 'find a haven in the west')

Reconnaissance Company

COMPANY A (less one platoon detached to guard the road junction at Laroche)

COMPANY B: Lt. Robert Andrews; Lt. Frederick Mallon; Sgt. Floyd A. Johnson; Sgt. George N. Schmidt; Sgt. Darrell J. Lindley

COMPANY C

Ninth Air Force (members of liaison group attached to 101st Airborne Division during Bastogne operation): Capt. James E. Parker; Lt. Gorden O. Rothwell; Sgt. Frank B. Hotard.

Chapter 13

The German Commanders

MAJOR HERBERT BÜCHS
A fighter pilot in the Luftwaffe, he was later appointed General Staff Officer at Hitler's headquarters. In July 1944 he was injured by the 'briefcase bomb' assassination attempt on Hitler. He died in Hanover in 1970, aged 88.

GENERALFELDMARSCHALL GERD VON RUNDSTEDT
He was charged with war crimes but did not face trial due to age and poor health. He was released from captivity in 1949 and died in 1953 aged 85.

GENERAL HASSO von MANTEUFFEL
He became a representative of the Free Democratic Party of Germany (FDP) in the Bundestag. In 1968 he lectured at the US Military Academy at West Point on combat in deep snow conditions and also worked as a technical adviser on war films. He died in 1978 aged 81.

GENERALOBERST ALFRED JODL
He was indicted for war crimes and crimes against humanity at the Nuremberg Trials, sentenced to death and executed in Nuremberg in 1946.

MAJOR PERCY ERNST SCHRAMM
An academic and Professor of History at Gottingen University, in 1933 he was invited to teach at Princeton, USA. He was the official historian on the German High Command and wrote several books on the history of the German military. He died in 1970.

GENERAL SIEGFRIED WESTPHAL
He surrendered to the Americans in May 1945 and was a witness at the Nuremberg Trials. He was released in 1947. He wrote *The German Army in the West* which was published in 1952 and died in 1982 aged 80.

GENERALLEUT FRITZ BAYERLEIN
He was a prisoner of war until April 1947 and was one of many generals in Allied captivity who wrote the European battle histories for the U.S. Army Historical Division. He died in 1970.

GENERALLEUTNANT HERMANN PRIESS
In 1946 he was one of 73 defendants at the Malmedy massacre trial held in the Dachau internment camp. Along with Sepp Dietrich, Joachim Peiper and others, he was charged with the murder of over 300 Allied PoWs and 100 Belgian civilians. Sentenced to 20 years imprisonment, he was released in 1984 and died in 1985.

GENERALMAJOR HEINZ KOKOTT
Born in Poland in 1900, he was a German general in the Wehrmacht and a recipient of the Knight's Cross of the Iron Cross. He died in 1976.

COLONEL ALFRED ZERBEL
After being captured by the Americans, he was a prisoner of war until 1948 and then served on the US Army's Operational History Section. He later became commander of the German Army. He retired in 1964 and died in 1987, aged 83.

GENERALMAJOR (WAFFEN-SS) FRITZ KRAEMER
A chief of staff with the 6th Panzer Army, he surrendered to the U.S. Army, along with Dietrich, in May 1945. He was tried in 1946 for his role in the Malmedy Massacre and was sentenced to 10 years imprisonment. He died in 1959.

GENERALOBERST JOSEPH 'SEPP' DEITRICH
He was convicted of war crimes at the Malmedy massacre trial and later in West Germany for his involvement in the 1934 purge. Upon his release from prison, he was active in HIAG, a lobby group established by former high-ranking Waffen-SS personnel. He died in 1966, aged 73.

WALTER STAUDINGER
From October 1944 to May 1945 he was senior commander in the Sixth Panzer Army. He died in 1964.

GENMAJ OTTO REMER

He played a major role in stopping the 20 July plot in 1944 against Hitler. After the war he was charged with inciting racial hatred and imprisoned. Later he was influential in post-war neo-Fascist politics in Germany. He died in 1997, aged 85.

GENERALMAJOR RUDOLF FREIHERR von GERSDORFF

In 1943 he was part of the conspiracy to kill Hitler and one of the few plotters to survive the war. He worked with the US Army Historical Division after the war and later devoted his life to charity. He died in 1980, aged 74.